Courts and the Culture Wars

Courts and the Culture Wars

Edited by
Bradley C. S. Watson

LEXINGTON BOOKS
Lanham • Boulder • New York • Oxford

LEXINGTON BOOKS

Published in the United States of America
by Lexington Books
A Member of the Rowman & Littlefield Publishing Group
4720 Boston Way, Lanham, Maryland 20706

12 Hid's Copse Road
Cumnor Hill, Oxford OX2 9JJ, England

British Library Cataloguing in Publication Information Available

Library of Congress Cataloging-in-Publication Data Available

ISBN: 978-0-7391-0414-9

Library of Congress Control Number: 2002004874

Printed in the United States of America

∞™ The paper used in this publication meets the minimum requirements of American National Standard for Information Sciences—Permanence of Paper for Printed Library Materials, ANSI/NISO Z39.48-1992.

Contents

Acknowledgments

This book is based on lectures delivered at a conference of the same name held at Saint Vincent College from April 19–21, 2001. The conference was sponsored by the Center for Economic and Policy Education, an interdisciplinary public affairs institute of Saint Vincent's Alex G. McKenna School of Business, Economics, and Government. The center combines the resources of the college's political science and economics departments. It was founded in 1991 to sponsor research and educational programs in public policy and sociopolitical thought, seeking to advance knowledge of America's political economy, moral-cultural order, and civic traditions.

We at the center are indebted to many individuals and organizations that made the conference and the book possible. Prime among them is Rosey Doelling, then the center's program coordinator, who handled the daunting logistical tasks associated with staging a major academic conference attended by hundreds. Our current program coordinator, Eva Kunkel, has been helpful in many ways with the preparation of this volume. The student staff of the center also helped in ways too numerous to count. Sandra S. Quinlivan, M.A., indexed the book.

We should also thank Saint Vincent College as a whole for providing a wonderful environment for our biennial Culture and Policy Conferences, as well as other lectures and conferences sponsored by the center—all of which deal with the conditions necessary for a free and decent political, social, economic, and moral order. As the Benedictine Order did so much to preserve and transmit classical learning and thereby lay the foundations for the civilization of the West, so Saint Vincent today maintains an openness to the conversation about ideas that continue to be so central to that civilization. Special mention should be made of the Rt. Rev. Douglas R. Nowicki, O.S.B., the archabbot of Saint Vincent Archabbey and chancellor of the seminary and the college; Mr. James F. Will, president of Saint Vincent College, who began the conference with a welcoming message; Br. Norman W. Hipps, O.S.B., provost of the college; and Dr. Thomas C. Mans, academic dean of the college. We are grateful also to Don Orlando, the college's director of public relations, for his active support of all that we do.

We owe special thanks to the foundations and individuals that supported us. The conference would not have been possible without a generous grant from the Sarah Scaife Foundation. Other support was provided by the Philip M. McKenna Foundation, Inc., the Massey Charitable Trust, B. Kenneth and Marg Simon, the Intercollegiate Studies Institute, Inc., and an anonymous donor.

Lexington Books and its executive editor Serena J. Leigh continue to be a pleasure to work with—something that can hardly be said of all in the field of academic publishing. High standards, swift decision making, and efficient production schedules are virtues that do not so happily coexist at many other publishing houses.

As editor, I would be remiss if I did not express personal gratitude to my colleagues at the center, who offer encouragement as well as aid, consistent cheerfulness as well as professionalism. Dr. Andrew R. Herr, the center's fellow in economics and policy, is always ready with advice or assistance. T. William Boxx, the center's senior fellow, was a sounding board for my ideas on the organization and structure of the conference, and never tired of offering timely help. Dr. Gary M. Quinlivan, the executive director of the center and dean of the McKenna School, possesses all the attributes one could ask for in an administrator—boundless energy in providing for and guiding the infrastructure of the center, a sharp mind, common sense, and a commitment to academic excellence. I should also thank my family—Barbara, Victoria, Charles, and James—who make everything seem worthwhile.

The conference participants met and then exceeded our expectations in every regard, intellectually and socially. I only hope that we met theirs.

Introduction

Courting Disaster: Jurisprudence as Moral Philosophy

Bradley C. S. Watson

As Robert H. Bork wryly notes in chapter 1, the role of courts in the culture wars is often overlooked. We thereby fail to give the legal profession the credit due for significant contributions to our cultural collapse. This volume attempts to make amends for our oversight. It is premised on the recognition that for much of the second half of the twentieth century, America's courts—state and federal—have injected themselves willy nilly into fundamentally moral and political disputes. By agreeing to constitutionalize these disputes, courts have reduced the ability of Americans to engage in traditional, political modes of settling differences over moral and political controversies that excite particular passion. While legal discourse is well suited to choosing decisive winners and losers, political discourse is more conducive to reasonable compromise and accommodation. Judicial engagement in the moral, religious, and cultural realms—including school prayer, abortion, homosexual rights, expressive speech, and many other areas—has led some to suggest the very legitimacy of the American republican regime is at stake.[1] The contributors to this volume join this debate in an effort to describe it implications and limits, and offer suggestions for our future.

In part one of the book, Bork laments the decline of traditional moral standards hastened by Supreme Court decisions. He then goes on to show the manner in which feminism, self-expression, and secularism are not in the process of being vindicated by the Constitution—as some on the cultural left would have it—but are rather in the process of triumphing over it. But in undermining moral certitudes, particularly in the area of religion, courts are undermining law itself, as legal sanctions are increasingly necessary—and feckless—in the face of a burgeoning amorality or, indeed, immorality. In addition, he argues that self-government cannot long stand when democratic and constitutional choices are not respected by the judiciary—the branch of government that so many of the founders (wrongly) believed to be the "least dangerous" to the liberties of the people.

While Bork finds the proximate origins of many of our cultural tribulations in the 1960s, Father Francis Canavan makes the radical claim that the liberal jurisprudence decried by Bork and others has its roots in medieval nominalism.[2] Canavan uses "liberal" not as an epithet, but in a very specific philosophical sense. For Canavan, personal autonomy is central to the Western philosophical enterprise and is a dominant characteristic of contemporary liberalism and the Supreme Court jurisprudence that mirrors it. The centrality of autonomy is in turn derivative from the epistemological and ontological mistakes of medieval nominalism. For William of Ockham and the nominalists, the claim to have any knowledge of universals, categories, relations, or natural laws is hubristic and impious insofar as it implies that God is bound by something outside Himself. Foreshadowing Hume, such knowledge claims are merely creations of the human mind, having nothing to do with things-in-themselves. All of creation is contingent, subject to flux at the whim of the creator.

All we as human beings have access to are the individual, unconnected products of divine creation, whose place in the cosmos is of our own making. Nature is less a revelation of the rational mind than of the unfettered will of God. Modern science becomes free to investigate and impose order as it sees fit on this otherwise unordered cacophony of sense experiences. We cannot violate natural laws when we are their authors. Individual preferences come to be seen as worthy in and of themselves because only they are in any sense authentic or real; choice comes to be seen as more important than right choice. This primacy has political and moral consequences—from the social contract theory of the state to the rejection of natural limits on human choice.

We see the jurisprudential consequences of this liberalism in Harry Blackmun's reasoning in *Roe v. Wade* and *Bowers v. Hardwick*. His is an insistent dogma that explicitly masquerades as jurisprudential modesty, and is all the more immodest for doing so. It is impatient enough not to be bound even by constitutional text or intent, much less the choices of actual citizens expressed through deliberative, republican institutions. Of course, all this moralism is infuriatingly dressed up as some form of constitutional neutrality, a lavish costume ball, which each year is eagerly anticipated by denizens and protégés of elite echo chambers, from the editorial pages of the *New York Times* to the corridors of national law schools. Whoever comes up with the fanciest dress wins, the prize often taking the form of glowing accolades in the *New York Review of Books*.

That things are in fact getting worse, not better, is confirmed by Keith E. Whittington, who points to the fact that in the past decade alone the Supreme

Court struck down some twenty-eight acts of Congress. This historically unprecedented activity amounts to something like a sense of entitlement to rule, even over a coequal branch of government. Not that all of these acts impinged on matters cultural, or that the Court spoke with a single ideological voice. Nevertheless, the present Court has shown stunning boldness in the imposition of its own hardly settled constitutional doctrines on an unwilling Congress and nation. The Court does this even when a minority of its own members write to express vehemently their view that the precedents relied upon are themselves in error.

No apologies required, none offered.

From whence does this enormous power come? Whittington claims the Court has absolved itself of the responsibility—much less does it have the interest—to reflect seriously on this question. The Founders' Constitution was largely oriented toward protecting human liberty through structural mechanisms designed to limit power and its exercise. This structural approach relies little on judicial superintendence. The Constitution itself, and the relationship of its various parts, was to be a bill of rights—no abstract declarations or judicial interpretations would be necessary. As it turned out, however, the Founders also bequeathed us a legalistic approach in the form of enumerations of powers, and the Bill of Rights itself. This legalized constitution created the grounds for the older form of judicial review that no longer exists. It was a judicial review that relied on faithful interpreters (and the belief that faithful interpretation was at least theoretically possible) in all branches of government. In short, people who would argue over, refine, and defend their constitutional interpretations so that, over time, our collective constitutional understandings would become both cemented and enlarged. This class of interpreters has vanished largely because, under the strains of Progressivism and legal realism, its members have come to lose certain epistemological certitudes, and, one could argue (although Whittington doesn't, explicitly), the virility to back them up. Also gone is an older understanding of social and economic "applicable conditions" conducive to a neutral constitutionalism.

We are left with a principled constitutionalism in which modern judicial power tries to root and justify itself. The fullness and sincerity of commitment to liberal democratic principles, rather than the outcomes of structural or legal constraints, come to define what is constitutional. This principled approach finds its exponents in theorists like Ronald Dworkin, who "is markedly more interested in a handful of textual majestic generalities than the structural or legal details of the Constitution." And, one might add, he is certainly clever enough to knit elaborately detailed garments from these barest of threads.

As Whittington notes, the legalized constitution is long since dead, but judicial review haunts us from beyond the grave. It never could ground itself very effectively, and certainly not extravagantly, in constitutional structuralism; it was most at home in the now-defunct legalistic environment. Today, by default, it is left afloat on a sea of competing principles, which are appealed to by constitutional scholars on both the left and right (although it seems the appeal is even greater, and more effective, on the left). The most obvious problem with all this is that the judiciary has no particular authority or expertise when it comes to such nuanced matters of moral and political philosophy. While the legalized tradition could plausibly claim that courts speak in the name of the Constitution, the principled alternative can make no such claim. The basis and fundamental assumptions of judicial review have died with our older understanding of the nature and limits of constitutionalism itself.

Judicial institutions are B-grade actors purporting to play Shakespeare, but they're not even masters enough of their craft to understand why the reviews are so bad. One might think that "continuing, reasonable, and significant disagreement about the substantive content of constitutional principles" would be their cue to leave the stage for others who can claim—if not more talent—then at least a proper sense of the audience. But this happens all too rarely. Instead, Themis struts naked, only dimly aware of the duties she owes mere mortals. Whittington's concern is not with courts frustrating majority will, but rather with the creation of a class of philosopher kings who have the final say on matters of fundamentally contested political principle.

Part two of the book moves from these broad theoretical concerns to particular cultural controversies that beset our times and ourselves. Most fair observers of abortion litigation from *Roe v. Wade*[3] onward will concede that abortion—perhaps more than any other cultural controversy—is to jurisprudence what a gravitational field is to physics: something that bends the path of matter and light itself. Indeed, abortion cases have a way of altering the rules of constitutional interpretation and judicial self-definition in a manner that might be the subject of comedy, were the moral stakes not so high. Abortion rights are nominally based on the alleged constitutional right to privacy in matters sexual, which itself is, in Justice Douglas's immortal words in *Griswold v. Connecticut*,[4] one of the penumbras formed by emanations from the Bill of Rights. One idly wonders how, in a precomputer age, the justices managed to track so rapidly evolving a constitution, emitting as many penumbra-spawning emanations as it did from the Third, Fourth, Fifth, Ninth, or Fourteenth Amendments, depending on which justice's opinion one reads. To this long list, Justice Blackmun in *Roe* added "psychological harm" to the potential mother as one of the great constitutional problems facing the Court.

Of course, all this is little more than jurisprudential legerdemain—having close observers lose track of the cup that conceals the marble almost seems to be the point of the exercise. The Constitution—originally designed to restrain the federal government—is now understood by many to be the vehicle by which the conditions for a relatively unfettered self-expressive individualism are guaranteed. In a more recent abortion case, *Planned Parenthood of Southeastern Pennsylvania v. Casey*,[5] Blackmun, in fact, took time to lament that his imminent retirement would result in the Court's relying on a "stunted conception of individual liberty." As Francis Canavan reminded us, the real inspiration for the Court is not the Constitution, but a way of thinking whose origins lie in another age.

Charles E. Rice makes a similar point when he defines the Enlightenment to be the systematic attempt to build a society "as if God did not exist." The consequence is a "culture of death" traceable to the Enlightenment's secularism, relativism, and individualism. The secularism, rooted in nominalism, recently manifested itself when the Supreme Court upheld, albeit narrowly, the right of the Boy Scouts not to appoint a homosexual scoutmaster, in *Boy Scouts of America v. Dale*.[6] As Rice notes, the dissenters could barely disguise their contempt for religious teaching in general, and Catholic teaching in particular, referring to the ancient roots of the atavistic opinions about homosexuals nourished by sectarian doctrine.

One might plausibly argue that this was a dissent joined by the Court's least thoughtful members, but this misses the point. In the routinely occurring seesaw battles that result in 5-4 or 6-3 outcomes from a bench unchastened by a sense of modesty about its purpose, limits, or the changed circumstances in which it operates, the Court's members become the prime culture warriors in our society. And Rice's argument, like Canavan's, recognizes that the conclusions reached by many of these culture warriors, while clearly not deducible from the Constitution, are not made from whole cloth either. According to Rice, *Roe* would not have been possible if we were not at the end of the Enlightenment, wantonly mixing legal positivism and individualism with our secularism. Exemplified by Hans Kelsen, legal positivism becomes the jurisprudential expression of relativism, premised on the notion that there is no reality that exists independent of human knowledge and, therefore, human construction. This leaves the legislators (often the courts) free to lay down such positive laws as they see fit, without cognizance of moral limits. The Enlightenment's individualism, which today finds expression as a defense of radical autonomy, destroys our sense of the natural relationship and obligations of autonomous individuals to other members of their species. Thus the tools for an insistent and incessant nationwide defense of hedonism are provided by our primary culture warriors.

According to Rice, we are a nation that needs to be born again (in his words, "reconverted") to our ancient faith. The "laws of Nature and Nature's God" express, after all, an understanding of the Enlightenment that is neither secularist nor relativist. And it is individualist only in the sense of securing the freedom of the individual by linking him to the larger order of nature that discloses not only rights but obligations and limits. The jurisprudence in cases such as *Roe* is so patently awful that a judge need not have recourse to natural law in order to overturn it. But Rice's provocative suggestion is that judges should apply the higher law if and when circumstances warrant, as a precursor to a larger effort to overcome the culture of death.

Jeremy Rabkin reminds us of the highest meaning of America's constitutional order by urging us to salvage something from the great junk heap of false dogma stemming from privacy litigation. He challenges us to think logically and clearly about the limitations on government that are required by a free society, and not to shrink from proper judicial enforcement of such limitations simply because we have come to oppose spurious forms of judicial activism. Claiming that the protection of private life from the intrusions of government is one of the Constitution's primary purposes, Rabkin tells us that the notion of privacy can cut more than one way. The *Roe* decision was not in fact grounded in privacy—this was simply a rhetorical ploy; it was, rather, grounded in a belief that equality demands no one, in this case women, ought to be excluded arbitrarily from the full range of pursuits and passions that a liberal society holds open. The doctrine of privacy, attached in *Griswold* to sexual intimacy, has come to be used at will to defend the equality principle. (As have other constitutional doctrines, including free speech.) Privacy could—and should—also be used by courts to limit the scope of state intervention into the affairs of nonstate actors, which could well temper the pursuit of state-sponsored egalitarianism.

Those who pursue an egalitarian vision in court and elsewhere do so with a genuine moral passion and religious moralism; they are not the herd animals they seek to create, but vigorous shepherds leading a sometimes reluctant flock to a utopian field of dreams. Private life could be as effective a slogan for those who seek to stand in the way of this movement to a new republic, as equality is for those who seek to promote it. In *Dale*, the Supreme Court's majority expended energies expounding the Boy Scouts' right to exclude homosexuals on the basis of their First Amendment right to express a point of view that was somehow central to their self-definition. Of course, the unseemly spectacle of state actors determining just which views are central to citizens' self-definition is akin to watching people wearing ski mittens pick fly droppings out of pepper. Why would they want to—and what makes them think it's within their capacity?

As Rabkin says, "all of this wrangling is surely beside the point. The Scouts should have the right to determine their own membership—period." If they do not, they or other private associations might one day be put in the position of having to claim to be something they are not. They would be driven to this position not through fraudulent intent, but merely as a defense mechanism against the dogs of a legal system that can be set loose at the will of their enemies, or those who find reward and pleasure in arguing for a principled constitutionalism. Furthermore, Rabkin asks an important question: why should any organization be able to claim exemption from generally applicable and otherwise valid laws on First Amendment grounds? If the Court entertains such a notion, as it occasionally has, a Pandora's box—minus the consolation of Hope—is opened, from which escape the ills of boundless judicial prying, weighing, and balancing.

It surely makes more sense to concentrate judicial inquiry on a different question: has the government shown that it has interests compelling enough to intrude on the conduct of private individuals or organizations? If not, the courts should step in to prevent such intrusion. Constitutionalism, properly understood, requires this form of judicial activism. The very purpose of the Constitution is to stop government from prosecuting a culture war against private organizations (including churches—the Church of Rome being the target of Bismarck's original *Kulturkampf*). Such activism might have the ancillary benefit of providing the moral and legal clarity to encourage rights-bearing citizens to assert themselves against the leveling tide, in a manner that does not rely on mere populism.

Of course, the nature and limits of the public-private distinction are bound to be the subject of disputation, as Murray Dry makes abundantly clear in his examination of toleration, judicial power, and homosexuality. Like Rabkin, Dry believes there is a relatively broad role for courts in expounding constitutions and constitutionalism and in restraining public actors from infringing on the rights of private citizens and associations. Dry, however, is much more concerned with encouraging judicial definition of the boundaries of the toleration principle—imported into America through Locke, Montesquieu, and Tocqueville—than with grounding and utilizing, judicially and politically, a doctrine of privacy. Thus, unlike Rabkin, he is happy enough with the Court's invocation of the First Amendment as the primary guarantor of rights of association.

Invoking the spirit of John Marshall and Alexander Hamilton, he claims that on the question of homosexuality, state and federal courts have, for the most part, done a reasonable job of expounding a vigorous yet reasonable constitutionalism. With respect to the military and private associations, they have shown an appropriate deference. In the case of other government activities and regulations, they have been "nudging legislatures toward toleration," but not too far and not too fast. For example, in the Vermont Supreme Court's unanimous decision granting homosexual couples the same benefits as would flow to married couples (based on broad language in the Vermont State Constitution), the Court made the state legislature a "partner" with respect to the manner in which benefits would be equalized. And it did not make the mistake of the Hawaii Supreme Court, which was too ambitious in mandating same-sex marriage—only to be overturned by a state constitutional amendment explicitly defining marriage as a relationship between a man and woman.

Dry would encourage courts, and legislatures, to act at a level of high moral and constitutional principle: the use of law to enforce morality must be connected "in some clear way to the fundamental purposes of liberal democracy." Determining whether this nexus exists is, for him, at least partly an empirical question. He claims that homosexuality is given, not chosen; therefore there is little fear that toleration will result in a higher incidence of homosexual behavior (something that his argument can be read to imply is undesirable or at least morally ambiguous).

Of course, a central debate in the culture wars is over the extent to which governmental regulation, or lack thereof, teaches moral lessons. Graham Walker argues that courts have become moral—and moralistic—schoolmasters to the nation, and he is none too sanguine about the long-range consequences of the lessons currently being taught. He argues that religious freedom does not imply or require governmental religious neutrality. As he notes, the conventional wisdom on this matter has been so skewed by judicial misinterpretation and the ideological mendacity of our times as to obscure what should be obvious to anyone reading the Constitution: the document protects religious establishments below the federal level, and even permits noncoercive federal patronage of religion. It is quite possible for any level of government, including the national, to publicize its religious preferences without coercing assent to them. The First and Tenth Amendments taken together can have no other meaning: jurisdictional restrictions on the national government are inexorably suggested, but not substantive restrictions limiting all levels of government equally. Incorporation as applied to religious establishment comes in for withering criticism by Walker as a doctrine that forces states to abide by provisions that are explicitly worded to prevent federal intrusions into state jurisdiction. Such an interpretation, as he notes, is simply unintelligible. (Of course, such procrustean poppycock has not much troubled the high court for several generations.) The fact that one risks "derision or worse" on most American university campuses for suggesting such things does not change either the Constitution's text or its interpretation for the first 160 years of republic's existence.

In addition to the argument based on text and tradition, Walker tellingly claims that neutrality cannot be constitutionally required because it is impossible—a fact evidenced by our quixotic pursuit of it over the past half century. Judicially enforced neutrality in fact amounts to a kind of sectarianism—full of pieties, albeit of a hidden and therefore particularly dangerous sort. In acting to protect citizens—especially the impressionable young, from religious inputs in the public square—the Court has been strangely oblivious to the fact that the impressionable will draw lessons from the absence of God as much as from His presence. Moral relativism is the result insofar as children are induced to regard their deepest beliefs as only private matters. There simply is "no default, neutral position that state authority can assume toward religion." Some of the most intelligent defenders of liberal neutralism now openly acknowledge that our habits of the heart are deeply affected by it. In the process, consent and resistance are mooted because of the very invisibility of the phenomenon. Thus the ground of the defense of religious neutrality has shifted: secularism and a certain conception of "tolerance" are its explicit goal. But with this shift, it becomes obvious that neutrality is in no sense neutral; it is simply the new piety. Walker suggests that "neutralism will appear, in retrospect, as a kind of interregnum, temporarily necessary to dissolve the old pieties until the new ones were ready to receive governmental patronage under the new dispensation."

One is reminded of Marx's vision that despotism would be a temporary stage on the road to true communism, wherein the peoples' beliefs would be so restructured as to allow despotism, and government itself, to disappear. The difference is that Marx was not writing or acting esoterically, as are many of the contemporary neutralists; his was a philosophy of history whose premises and conclusions were writ large for all to see. The fact that some of the neutralists are coming out of the closet seems to be evidence for their confidence that history, finally, is in fact moving in their direction. Americans still have the liberty to escape the secular religiosity of this world turned upside down through—among other things—various private schooling options that are being exercised in record numbers. So, ironically, as Walker notes, we now have a different version of what we have always had—religious liberty without religious neutrality.

Part three of the book deals with two matters that appear on their face to be devoid of substantive content and therefore neutral or at least relatively apolitical vis-a-vis the outcome of cases. However, as John C. Eastman and Edward J. Erler point out, each is a major tool in the culture wars being launched in and by courts of law. Eastman limns the cultural implications of the ancient common law practice of stare decisis, meaning to adhere to decided cases and not unsettle that which is settled. Few judicial doctrines could seem more inherently conservative than this. The problem arises when stare decisis is used from "beyond the grave," as it were, of the legalized constitution to uphold the torrent of cases wrongfully decided since the New Deal. Progressive justices in this century have proved themselves more than willing to overturn precedents, even recent ones, when it suits the new constitutionalism. To the extent that conservative or at least nonactivist judges are more willing to abide by stare decisis, they end up accomplices in the reinforcement of this constitutionalism.

Eastman's analysis of the recent *Dale* case is particularly telling. He claims that this case should have been governed by the unanimous decision of the Court in *Hurley v. Irish-American Gay, Lesbian, and Bisexual Group*,[7] decided only five years earlier. Justice Souter's majority opinion in *Hurley* held that a privately organized parade need not include groups whose message the organizers did not wish to convey at any given time. Only five years later, the Court split 5-4 in *Dale*, with Souter now in the minority, explicitly inviting future challenges to the majority's opinion protecting the Boy Scouts. Justice Stevens' dissent claimed that *Hurley* should not be followed because public perceptions of homosexuality had changed in the (obviously brief) time since *Hurley*. So, with the whipsaw of pubic opinion comes the redefinition of constitutional rights, according to certain members of the Court. One can't help but speculate on why even public opinion has changed so rapidly. Could it be that constitutional rights follow popular acceptance of the latest "groundbreaking" television dramas and sitcoms?

On the abortion matter, the majority in *Casey* reaffirmed what it claimed to be *Roe's* "central holding," thus signaling the Court's intent to disallow incremental corrections of the much criticized case. Thus in the view of the progressive majority, adherence to stare decisis "prevents not just the reversal of incorrect past decisions, but adherence to decisions rendered subsequent to the incorrect precedent that might narrow the ruling that was flawed in the first place."

In such an environment of newly developing precedents, ratcheting the law toward an ever-more progressive constitutionalism, stare decisis becomes something of a revolutionary doctrine. Even Justice Thurgood Marshall—himself one of the justices most likely to overrule established precedent—took the occasion of his retirement to excoriate other members of the Court for their alleged repudiation of stare decisis.

Erler alerts us to the importance of the "independent state grounds" doctrine in California, a state that has long been at the forefront of the cultural revolution still sweeping America. Its state courts—especially its Supreme Court—seek to take that revolution where angels (not to mention federal jurisprudence and mere politics) fear to tread. According to the doctrine, language in state constitutions that is similar to language in the federal Constitution can be interpreted by state courts independently of interpretations of the federal language, provided the state interpretations do not result in lower standards of protection for rights than the federal. In other words, there is a federal floor, but no ceiling. While Erler does not question the doctrine, he does note that it has become, since the 1970s, the back door through which judicial activists insert ever more expansive interpretations of rights into the American polity. Justice William Brennan, exasperated by the Burger Court, became a convert to something he passed off as federalism—the Warren Court's more progressive will could be adequately extended, in his view, only by its enunciation on independent state grounds. His tendentiousness thus reminds us of Justice Marshall's in becoming a latter-day defender of stare decisis.

When it comes to matters cultural, the independent state grounds doctrine becomes a hammer used to destroy not only laws, but well-established social mores that laws embody. Battles over the California Supreme Court's use of the doctrine have become a routine part of the political landscape in that state. Initiatives have been passed to rein in the Court's radical expansion of federal protections for criminal defendants. (Like a fox guarding the hen-house, the Court stepped in to defend itself by declaring the most recent of these amendment initiatives to be unconstitutional.) But the main controversy on which Erler concentrates has to do with a law passed by a Democratic California legislature requiring parental consent before minors may obtain an abortion. The bill was a popular one, and was carefully drafted to comply with the guidelines of the U.S. Supreme Court. In a 1996 case, the California Supreme Court upheld the law by the narrowest of margins, despite a privacy guarantee in the California state constitution. (It is worth noting, as Erler does, that the privacy guarantee in question was added in 1972 to protect privacy of information, not personal autonomy.)

The dissenters would have struck down the law whatever the "deeply rooted social norms" that continued to distinguish adult from minor when it came to autonomy and privacy. Despite the dissenters' vehemence, one might have expected the matter to end there. However, shortly after the decision, two members of the Court's majority retired and the Court promptly agreed to rehear the case. Not much more than a year after the original had been decided, the new majority decision airbrushed the old one away, Stalin-style, with hardly a mention that it had ever existed. (Indeed, a quick search by the editor of this volume has confirmed that the promotional and informational literature of various pro-abortion groups touts the second case—the name of which the Court left untouched—with nary a mention of the first.) The rapidity and seamlessness of the reversal puts to shame even the dissenters' best efforts in *Dale*. It is as if, to borrow the words of George Orwell from *1984*, "Oceana had always been at war with Eurasia." Of course, Orwell's hero, Winston Smith, knows this to be counterfactual nonsense for he can remember the time—in the very near past—when it was not the case. But with reeducation everything is possible.

Let's see if we can follow the bouncing opinions as Erler describes them: "In the new decision, bearing the same name as the old one, Justice Mosk's majority opinion became a dissent, and Justice Kennard's dissent became a concurring opinion and Justice George's dissent became the opinion of the Court." So much for the notion of a constitution being anything other than what judges say it is. The California Constitution, under Chief Justice George's new majority opinion, now equates privacy with personal autonomy. Dissenters in the second case warned of dismissing societal values and substituting the rights of children for the rights of parents, but to no avail. As Erler notes, with due disdain, California is now a land wherein a girl whose age barely enters the double-digit range can get an abortion but not a tattoo. One is reminded of Judge Bork's sound legal advice to youngsters at high school football games: it is safer, constitutionally, to dance nude than to pray.

We hardly do justice to Erler if we neglect to note that his argument goes well beyond judicial practice or procedure. He argues that the reduction of constitutional liberty to autonomy makes gibberish of the notion that a constitution embodies any conception of moral, social, or political order whatsoever. And if it doesn't, why bother? Such a conception of liberty would be radically incompatible with the rationally bounded liberty in which American liberal democracy is grounded.

And this observation brings us nicely to the fourth and final part of the book, which examines the relationship of the judicialized culture wars to liberal democracy itself. This of course is a topic that is at least implicit in each of the book's parts and chapters, but which deserves to be dealt with fully on its own terms. Christopher P. Manfredi and Anthony A. Peacock are more than up to the task. Manfredi shows us what it means to have a liberal-democratic constitutional politics. It surely cannot entail a politically unchecked judicial review, whether it be justified on activist or originalist grounds. Manfredi, relying on his knowledge of the Canadian as well as American constitutional systems, notes in passing what the future might hold for America. The Canadian courts and their hangers-on, including highly successful, taxpayer-funded interest-group litigants with names like Equality for Gays and Lesbians Everywhere, have made Canada a poster-country for judicial activism. The phrase "lunatics running the asylum" was not invented as a metaphor for the relationship of Canadian courts to that country's political and social institutions, but it easily could have been. But unlike its Canadian counterpart, American judicial activism did not spring upon the scene, full-blown, in the late twentieth century.

Manfredi notes that American progressive intellectuals for the most part found the Supreme Court to be antithetical to their desire for political, social, and economic change, from the infamous *Dred Scott* case all the way up to *Brown v. Board of Education* nearly a century later. *Brown* seemed to lay the foundation for a new consensus on the positive role that courts could play from the point of view of progressive politics. However, that consensus began to dissolve less than twenty years later when, in *Roe*, the Court purported to find an absolute right to abortion in the Constitution. In so doing, it resurrected the discredited doctrine of substantive due process, which had once been the bane of progressive thinkers because it had so often been used as a barrier to their favored legislative initiatives. Not anchored in text or constitutional tradition, *Roe* destroyed any possibility that there could be a broad consensus in America on the legitimacy of judicial review. Certainly the Court's own dissenters made this clear in their characterization of the majority's opinion as a show of force, not reason. Even scholars otherwise sympathetic to judicial review have been moved to criticize its reach and reasoning.

Manfredi points to one such scholar in particular: Cass Sunstein, who defends judicial minimalism. According to this understanding of judicial review, judges should avoid overbroadness, either in laying down rules or relying on theories of constitutional interpretation. This minimalism is particularly appropriate in morally complex cases, according to Sunstein, where overreaching can undermine judicial legitimacy. *Roe* is a classic example of a case that decided too much, too quickly, and thereby foreclosed the possibility of a cooperative relationship between courts and democratic institutions. Better than the decision in *Roe* would have been a holding that struck down the impugned Texas statute without also proclaiming a broad constitutional right to abortion.

Indeed, in a case of which Sunstein likely would have approved, the Canadian Supreme Court in 1988 found relatively narrow, technical grounds on which to strike down Canada's federal abortion law.[8] All this sounds, on the surface, rather appealing. However, as Manfredi shows, Sunstein's minimalism seems tailor-made to constrain today's justices—in the name of modesty and minimalism—from striking down the constitutional precedents that Sunstein finds particularly appealing (especially those that arose from *Brown* to *Roe*). Sunstein cleverly argues for a judicial conservatism that could only appeal to liberals. He is able to criticize *Roe* while at the same time arguing that the originalist theory of interpretation that might overthrow it would be hubris masquerading as modesty, thus reminding us of Eastman's warnings on the nature of the one-way ratchet.

Having one's cake and eating it too, while simultaneously affording oneself the opportunity to accuse opponents of playing charades, is a hallmark of sophisticated legal theorizing such as Sunstein's. But such theorizing is not simply too clever by a half, it is also undertaken with a fundamentally political intent. In Manfredi's less judgmental phrasing, we cannot help but notice the "ineffectiveness of a minimalist Court when confronted with an improperly maximalist precedent." Manfredi examines the minimalism that overturned Nebraska's attempt to restrict partial-birth abortions in *Stenberg v. Carhart*,[9] wherein the majority claimed that such a law placed an undue burden on a woman's right to an abortion, contrary to this (very subjective) test enunciated in *Casey*. Ignoring normative concerns in favor of technical ones (and indeterminate technical ones, at that), the Court clearly tried to conceal the moral nature and significance of its decision. Manfredi puts it adroitly: "minimalism functions not as a check on judicial overreaching in a context of normative and empirical uncertainty, but as a guarantee that judicially created pseudo-rights will survive despite widespread recognition that they have no roots in constitutional text."

But will originalism save liberal democracy from such judicial value-positing, through which courts baldly and boldly substitute their judgments for those of legislatures? Not quite. According to Manfredi, the weakness of originalism is not, as activist critics would have it, that it results in moral or political stasis. In fact, deference to legislative judgments leads to just the opposite:

change, growth, creation of statutory rights and privileges, and so forth. The nonoriginalist critics are upset because these changes are neither quick enough nor in the right direction for their tastes. Their moralism is Kantian in its insistence on "right" over utility, expediency, political accommodation, or competing conceptions of the good.

Originalism's weakness, according to Manfredi, lies elsewhere: it is not really original, insofar as it fails to take notice of the nature of liberal democracy itself, which is not grounded in mere majoritarianism. The sooner the people and the other constitutional branches of government recognize the political nature of the judicial enterprise and oppose it with a politics of their own, the better. But the people can do this from the moral high ground, as it were, because such a liberal politics rests on principles that embody something more than mere will, or majoritarianism. Manfredi implicitly suggests that liberal politics has its basis in natural equality and the right of consent that flows from it, and therefore a dignity of its own that judicial politics decidedly does not possess. The founders of American liberal democracy put their faith in structural constraints and checks, not the self-restraint of the judiciary, on which originalism tends to rely. The politics we should oppose to judicial politics must come not just at judicial appointment time, partly because of the unreliability of this approach (it seems no living Constitution appointees become originalists while on the bench, but originalists frequently "grow" in office). In addition, overemphasizing the importance of appointments teaches the lesson that judges really are the ones who have the final say on constitutional interpretation.

Rather, the political community must reassert itself as a legitimate source of constitutional meaning, particularly through the vigorous use of the Article III, Section 2 exceptions clause. The people, in short, must go on a sustained "take back the Constitution" march, reclaiming large swaths of territory from the federal judiciary. The point of such an exercise would not be to assert popular or majoritarian supremacy, but constitutional supremacy. Manfredi notes that the Canadian Constitution contains an analogous clause but, like its American counterpart, it goes unused. There might thus be a general inability on the part of liberal democratic politics and peoples to assert themselves in the face of judicial supremacy. This is perhaps due to a loss of robustness stemming from the soft despotism of the administrative state, which puts into question the sustainability of an effort to take back anything. But if Americans remain passive, the Canadianized future that awaits them is destined to be even less appealing than the present—a dystopia wherein the principled justice of philosopher kings rules the day, yet happiness for most remains elusive.

Anthony A. Peacock takes a different route to teach us a similar lesson: that courts as culture warriors threaten not just some versions of liberal constitutionalism, but liberal constitutionalism itself. The American Founders were well aware that passionate, sectarian factionalism was something that had to be contained. The best means of containing it was through commercial republicanism, reducing politics—in the old, preliberal sense—to political economy. By contrast, the politics of multiculturalism—openly fostered by courts in their interpretation and enforcement of the Voting Rights Act (VRA) of 1965—creates legal categories that ground factional claims to political rule in the preliberal sense. The Fourteenth and Fifteenth Amendments were intended to further the possibilities of a constitutionalism by making race politically irrelevant and individual rights triumphant. But voting rights cases now have to do with far more than fair access to a ballot. Paradoxically, race has once again become very relevant as courts interpret the VRA to require racially gerrymandered districts guaranteed to produce the "right" electoral result. Race as a proxy for ideas, outlooks, and cultural solidarity—illegal in the realms of employment and jury selection—becomes the norm in voting rights law.

A redefinition of one of liberal democracy's axes—equality—is required for such a jurisprudence. We are now told that skin color matters more profoundly than most or all other human characteristics when considering the question of political representation. Proportional representation based on race cuts against the notion that we can and should restrict politics to questions of liberal interest rather than preliberal passion and accidents of birth. Incentives have been created for groups well beyond historically disenfranchised blacks to define themselves as "racial minorities" entitled to special political consideration. An Afghan-style tribalism—which sensible leaders in nonliberal societies try assiduously to escape—has become the new American standard in voting rights cases. The great octopus of the administrative/judicial state entwines even the most fundamentally political of questions: the size, shape, and composition of electoral districts. Voting rights jurisprudence has been in the vanguard of our movement from early progressive and New Deal economic regulation to a postmodern social regulation in which both Republicans and Democrats acquiesce because, at least in the short-term, it serves bipartisan interests. (Democrats have more "guaranteed" districts and more minority faces in the legislative halls; Republicans have more faces in total because of the "bleaching" of what would otherwise be racially diverse districts.)

In addition, as Peacock argues, the Founders' Constitution was meant to serve a complex multiplicity of proximate ends in service of the overriding objective of defanging the most dangerous dogs of faction. This calculus involved not so much specifying a particular theory of democratic representation, but rather who should get to choose this theory. It was certainly not the intention of the Founders that the federal government, much less the federal courts, would do this choosing on behalf of states. Yet this shift of power has been yet another consequence of voting rights jurisprudence, converting some of the most local and political decisions imaginable into federal and "apolitical" decisions, which are incapable of responding to mere interests rather than high and incendiary principle. As Justice Clarence Thomas has noted, the judiciary has imposed a particular theory of representation on the entire nation—a theory that can only heighten racial tensions by creating a system of electoral apartheid.

But what analysis justifies this encouragement of tribalism and yet another form of principled constitutionalism? Can minorities only be represented by minorities? Is this representation really more effective at promoting minority interests when the political fortunes of the party to which minorities tend to belong are hurt? How can we even speak of effective representation when all the normal concerns of partisan politics are washed out of the process? These are questions advocates of race consciousness have failed to answer even as they continue their attack on the formal equality and liberal constitutionalism of the American founding. According to Peacock, American multiculturalists—unlike their European counterparts—are more inclined to link culture to biology, rather than nation, language, and ethnicity. American cultural categories include African American, Asian American, female-American, and so forth, each with (ideally) special group entitlements (even though they represent groups whose members might in fact have little in common with one another). The nature and scope of these entitlements are bound to be the subject of contest, to which there is no end and no answer that stands above the fray of the battlefield. This presents the possibility for passionate factionalism at least equal to, and perhaps in excess of, the ethnic rivalries that have beset European civilization for so many centuries. We cannot hope to be united at the level of interest if we are divided at the level of prerational and pre-national passion.

And so we come full circle. We see the sense in which the contemporary understanding and practice of judicial review undermines the constitutional system it intends to serve. It does this not because of its counter-majoritarianism, but because of its incompatibility with the foundations of a system that is itself counter-majoritarian, while still allowing for government by the people. It operates in a context largely of its own, as opposed to the Constitution's, creation. In so doing, it substitutes judicial for constitutional principles, which according to the Founders were rooted in an understanding of the limits of human nature and constitutionalism itself. In the Founders' modest constitutionalism, justice can be approximated, not achieved, and it can only be approximated through recourse to the principle of consent, stemming from human equality. This principle in normal times requires, practically speaking, working out by humans and the seed of humans, rather than by those self-appointed gods among men whose powers and passions are so much greater.

NOTES

1. See, for example, the spirited arguments and rejoinders, originating in a symposium in the November 1996 issue of the journal *First Things*, reprinted and expanded as a book entitled *The End of Democracy? The Judicial Usurpation of Politics* (Dallas: Spence, 1997).

2. I like to think that the claim, while radical, is eminently sensible, insofar as I have made it myself. I have argued that modern liberalism (and therefore liberal jurisprudence) is partially traceable to nominalism, but is ultimately rooted in the nature of the human soul adumbrated even in *Genesis*. See Bradley C. S. Watson, *Civil Rights and the Paradox of Liberal Democracy* (Lanham, Md.: Lexington Books, 1999).

3. *Roe v. Wade*, 410 U.S. 11 (1973).

4. *Griswold v. Connecticut*, 381 U.S. 479 (1965).

5. *Planned Parenthood of Southeastern Pennsylvania v. Casey*, 505 U.S. 833 (1992).

6. *Boy Scouts of America v. Dale*, 147 L.Ed.2d 554 (2000).

7. *Hurley v. Irish-American Gay, Lesbian, and Bisexual Group of Boston, Inc.*, 515 U.S. 557 (1995).

8. *Morgenthaler et al. v. The Queen*, 1 S.C.R. 30 (1988).

9. *Stenberg v. Carhart*, 530 U.S. 914 (2000).

I

COURTS AND CULTURE: FUNDAMENTAL THEORETICAL ISSUES

1

Courts and the Culture Wars

Robert H. Bork

It is appropriate to begin a discussion of culture wars by noting that they are not infrequent, though they change in nature over time. The one we are engaged in today is not the first we know of. The term culture war was coined by Bismarck to describe the struggle between Catholics and Protestants in Germany. In America, of course, we had our most serious culture war between the proslavery and antislavery forces, which ended in civil war.

Today we are engaged in a different kind of culture war. This one has been likened to a moral and even religious war. Two moral visions are locked in combat and the winner will define what America is to be. One moral vision rests upon the belief that the achievements and traditions of the past are worthwhile and should guide us in today's and tomorrow's challenges. It is not a reactionary vision. Our tradition has always been willing to accept new ideas and to reform itself from within. Nevertheless, it is often called a conservative tradition, although I do not think it is exclusively the province of conservatism. Opposed to this traditionalism is a moral view that is suspicious and even hostile to tradition. It regards the past as characterized by oppression. This moral view is taught in the schools nowadays. It is the moral vision of the student rebels of the 1960s. They talked of the emancipation of the human spirit. But, as we know, people who are zealous emancipators can be very authoritarian toward people who do not want emancipation on the terms offered.

Our current culture war did not commence in the 1960s, but that loathsome decade can be said to have jump-started it. Today men and women who distrust tradition, and especially the traditions of this country, hold positions of power in institutions that shape ideas and culture. The traditionalists, who once defined the dominant culture in this country, are now themselves a counterculture. Irving Kristol brought us the bad news when he said that there is no war in the culture—there used to be, but it is over and the other side won. In one sense he is right. The cultural left has captured almost all of the universities, the print and electronic media, the entertainment industry, the foundations, and much more. They command the heights of our culture. They have more benefits to confer upon the young who are eager to establish careers than do the traditionalists, and that makes the left particularly powerful. Nevertheless the war is not over. There is a growing resistance. The resisters are still in the minority, but it is a minority that is increasingly coherent and active.

The effects of 1960s morality and rebellion are all around us today. Roger Kimball wrote in *The Long March* of the devastating power of the 1960s and the new spirit that swept America in their wake. He claimed that the demands of the radical emancipators of the 1960s have triumphed throughout society.

> That ideology has insinuated itself, disastrously, into the curricula of our schools and colleges; it has significantly altered the texture of sexual relations and family life; it has played havoc with the authority of churches and other repositories of moral wisdom; it has undermined the claims of civic virtue and our national self-understanding; it has degraded the media, the entertainment industry, and popular culture; it has helped to subvert museums and other institutions entrusted with preserving and transmitting high culture. It has even, most poignantly, addled our hearts and innermost assumptions about what counts as the good life: it has perverted our dreams as much as it has prevented us from attaining them.[1]

That catalog of disasters seems to me entirely accurate so far as it goes. But I have one reservation. Kimball fails to mention law and judges. We lawyers all feel diminished because our contribution to cultural collapse has not been recognized. There is an infinite number of lawyer jokes around, but when it comes to serious matters like the decline of Western civilization everybody talks about the media and Hollywood, not a word about law and the degradation it has produced. The role of courts in the culture wars, too, is often overlooked. I will attempt to rectify that injustice to my profession.

Law of course is a central element in Western culture and it deserves to be recognized as a cultural phenomenon more than it has been. I am glad to say that this conference recognizes that fact. Law helps to create and reinforce cultural trends. For half a century the Supreme Court and lower federal courts—and their acolytes in the law schools—have supported the idea that courts are not and should not be governed by the actual Constitution. They invoke the name of the Constitution to justify their results, but those results are to be found nowhere in the Constitution. Lack of reliance on the Constitution is a necessary condition for courts to enact the cultural agenda of the liberal left.

One cannot stick to the actual Constitution to find new rights that were never anticipated or allowed for by the people who wrote the Constitution.

Since about 1950 we have had a Supreme Court that has gone into high gear with activist decisions. This is not to say the Court of today is identical to the Warren Court. The Warren court politicized almost every subject that it came across. It politicized antitrust law, the consequence being that antitrust defendants always lost. It even politicized tax law; taxpayers never defeated the government. And so it went, in field after field. Social and cultural sympathies overrode doctrine and precedent. The current Court is not like that. Today's litigant—on strictly legal matters such as taxes, administrative law, antitrust, and the like—is likely to get a highly intelligent, apolitical response from the Court.

But when a cultural issue arises, the present Court moves left. Justice Scalia described the situation exactly. Scalia has written some of the most vitriolic dissents in the Court's history, and I think justifiably so. He once asked, "What secret knowledge one must wonder is breathed into lawyers when they become justices of this Court. . . . Day by day, case by case, [the Court] is busy designing a Constitution for a country I do not recognize."[2] The Court is removing from democratic control the most important moral, political, and cultural decisions that affect our lives. Since the Court speaks with finality and can override the legislature, the cultural left prizes control of the courts, and especially the Supreme Court, perhaps more than any other institution of government. The cultural left favors judges who will enact its agenda, and indeed most judges seem to agree that they are not bound by the Constitution as it was originally understood. (I have had a Supreme Court justice tell me precisely that.)

The stakes in this war are quite high and this is where, at the risk of being thought to go over the top, I advance a strong proposition for discussion. Some commentators think that what hangs in the balance in our culture war, in which law plays a pivotal role, is nothing less than the civilization of the West. For example, an article by Charles Murray recently appeared in the *Wall Street Journal*. Murray recalled Arnold Toynbee's observation that one of the consistent signs of the degeneration of civilization is that the elites begin to lose their confidence. They no longer set an example for the rest of society and in fact those at the top begin to emulate those at the bottom. Murray remarks particularly on the rejection of obligations of citizenship, which Toynbee called truancy. We saw a good deal of that during the Vietnam War when the obligations of citizenship were evaded on a massive scale. But he also speaks of the vulgarization of manners, arts, and language. In our society we have undergone a process of vulgarization that would have been unthinkable in 1960. To take only a few examples: the consistent use of four letter words on television, motion pictures, and even in pubic discourse; the rise of rudeness and decline of civility; the hooker look in fashion; tattoos and body piercing; the increase in the number of unmarried couples living together; the skyrocketing rate of births by unmarried women.

The interesting thing about this disintegration is that we no longer condemn it in moral terms. We are afraid to use the language of morality to say that something is wrong for we are afraid of being labeled judgmental. Nonjudgmentalism has become a fetish with many Americans, not only those on the left. We have been taught to tolerate almost anything. Some of that instruction comes from the courts.

FEMINISM AND THE CULTURE WARS

Kenneth Minogue points to yet another symptom of our decline as a civilization: the growth of radical feminism, which has caused a massive shift in power in this society. He contrasts radical feminism with liberal feminism. Liberal feminism emerged from the flexibility of the Western tradition. It argued for the admission of women to new professions without dramatically altering the wider relations between the sexes. But radical feminism is different. It is doctrinaire and it demands that all women should live in the one true manner. The radical feminists, of course, speak in terms of justice, which is a very hard rhetoric to counter. They will not define the point at which their objectives will have been met, but whatever the particular circumstances, reality never quite seems to them to measure up to their aspirations.

One of the their objectives is quotas. They will not put it this bluntly, at least in public. But they start from the premise that there are no essential differences between men and women, and the conclusion follows, naturally enough, that women should make up 50 percent of every occupational category. The fact that they do not is invariably linked, in the feminist ideology, to the oppression of women by men. We can say that the character of a civilization is revealed in its understanding of achievement. European civilization responded to achievement wherever it could be found. To replace achievement with entitlements is to destroy our civilization from within and replace it with another. We are no longer what we were, and this is Minogue's point, as it is Murray's. When civilizations begin to die without external violence, the death is not likely attributable to a single cause. Murray assigns blame to the loss of confidence of the elite, who formerly set high standards and now adapt themselves to the standards of the underclass. Minogue sees radical feminism as an agent of deterioration. I believe the two work together, each affecting and strengthening the other.

Radical feminism fairly recently triumphed over the Constitution when the Supreme Court held that Virginia could not support an all-male military school, the Virginia Military Institute (VMI).[3] VMI had been all male for more than 150 years and had coexisted peacefully with the Constitution and the equal protection clause for 128 of those years. Nobody thought it was unconstitutional. It took radical feminism to see that we had been wrong all along and to persuade an easily persuadable, and intimidatable, Court to end America's traditional understanding of the military and the different roles of men and women.

Americans had rejected the equal rights amendment (ERA), which promised equality between men and women even as it recognized that in some spheres equality would be inappropriate. The ERA purported to leave to judges the task of deciding when equality was required and when it was not. The American people, acting through their deliberative institutions, almost ratified the ERA, but had second thoughts. They decided that they did not want judges making these basic cultural decisions about the relationship between men and women. So they rejected the ERA. Nonetheless, the Court has in effect adopted it. It has made and continues to make the crucial cultural decisions about the nature and role of men and women.

Of course, the Court's ruling on matters of sexuality and abortion owe a great deal to radical feminism because the Constitution is silent on these matters. Abortion is one of those matters properly left to the moral sense of the American people. But the Court has taken over that area so that the moral sense of the American people expressed through law is no longer a subject for debate, except in a most marginal way. In doing so, the Court has really made abortion a sacred cause, impinging even on First Amendment principles. In one case, a state passed a law that banned abortion protesters from approaching too close to women when they go into an abortion clinic.[4] The protesters' aim was to advise women of alternatives and dissuade them from having abortions. The Court held that the statute passed constitutional muster. It is quite clear that had that statute applied to people protesting a war or to striking workers, it would have been declared unconstitutional under well-established First Amendment principles. But in the minds of the majority, abortion presents a special case.

Even that decision fades into insignificance compared to the invalidation of a Nebraska statute prohibiting partial-birth abortions.[5] The majority thought that it was a rather poorly drafted statute—and indeed it was. But they also held the statute unconstitutional or invalid because, though it made an exception where the mother's life was in danger, it didn't make an exception where her health might be affected. Yet medical opinion is overwhelmingly to the effect that there is never a case in which it is necessary to do a partial-birth abortion for the sake of a woman's life or health. The Court's decision appears to be a response to the arguments of pro-abortion forces, which are a ruse to preserve a procedure that is indistinguishable from infanticide. The demand for a health exception effectively blocks any effort to end the procedure because any abortionist will find a reason to claim that the mother's "physical, emotional, or mental health" requires the procedure. Indeed, all these decisions are manifestations of the deep changes radical feminism has made in our society by persuading the Court to adopt its agenda.

At the same time, the Court is moving toward the normalization of homosexuality. For example, it overturned a Colorado constitutional amendment that forbade local government from adding homosexuals to the list of groups protected from private discrimination.[6] The Court, in effect, decided that the Colorado voters were moved by nothing but bigotry. There was indeed a culture war going on in Colorado, but the Court was so deeply in the grips of modern antitraditionalism that it could see only bigotry on the other side. The judgment in the case did not bother to mention a prior case in which the Court allowed a state to actually criminalize homosexual behavior.[7] But it has to be said, I think, that it effectively overruled that case. And, indeed, I suppose it is quite likely that in five to ten years we will see the Court following the courts of Hawaii and Vermont in making same-sex marriage a constitutional right.

"FREE SPEECH" AND THE CULTURE WARS

Another major sign of cultural disintegration is the Court's inversion of the First Amendment's guarantee of the freedom of speech. Historically it was understood that this guarantee was really about political speech. (In fact, in the first prosecutions brought against pornographers, their lawyers didn't even think it worthwhile to raise the First Amendment.) But the Court has begun to change that and in the process it is turning the free speech clause inside out.

In a recent Missouri case, the Court deformed the speech clause by upholding severe contribution limits in political campaigns.[8] One result of this is a shift of political power, away from grassroots citizens groups and toward journalists, incumbents, and labor unions. (Although unions may not be able to contribute money under such laws, they can put much manpower on the streets and on telephone lines.) Citizens' groups will find it more difficult to speak during campaigns, and incumbency will be an even more significant advantage than it now is. Journalists will, of course, be able to speak freely and extensively during those same campaigns. And I am quite sure these effects were understood and welcomed by supporters of the decision.

There are many items on the cultural left's agenda that the courts are busy enacting. Decades ago, the Supreme Court opened the door to extreme vulgarity or obscenity with its decision in *Cohen v. California*.[9] The case dealt with a young man who entered a courthouse and refused to remove his jacket, which had printed on it a short word suggesting that that the reader perform a sexual act of anatomical impossibility with the Selective Service System. He was convicted of public obscenity. The Supreme Court struck down the statute and said the young man had a right to do what he did. The reason was particularly instructive. The Court explicitly asked, "How is one to distinguish this from any other offensive word?" One would have thought, by the common sense of the judge and the jury. How is one to distinguish negligence from intentional vehicular killing? Distinctions are of the essence of legal adjudication, yet we are told that we cannot distinguish when a moral question is before us. Indeed, the Court went on to say that one man's vulgarity is another's lyric. One might equally say one man's armed robbery is another man's redistribution of wealth. The message was that there are very few standards of decency that a community is allowed to enforce, and the floodgates were thereby opened to the extreme vulgarization of our society. The Court only talks in such ways when morality is at stake, and its members talk that way because they have serious doubts that citizens are entitled to enforce morality with law.

For some reason that is not immediately obvious, the Court continues to take up the profound constitutional issue of nude dancing. Why they keep taking cases about nude dancing I do not know. They have held that such dancing is entitled to considerable protection as "expressive behavior" (as opposed to, say, the mere act of walking around in public without clothing).[10] We need not linger over the question of what it is the young ladies are expressing.

RELIGION AND THE CULTURE WARS

A dominant characteristic of the intelligentsia worldwide is hostility or indifference to religion. Social scientists have long proclaimed that the elite of most societies are indifferent or hostile to religion. Our own Supreme Court, through the latter half of the twentieth century, has been actively hostile to religion. In this respect, the Court follows the intellectual fads and fashions of the intelligentsia. Judges after all come out of the intellectual class (not a very good word because a lot of people we think of as being in the intellectual class are not good in intellectual matters. I need mention only Barbra Streisand).

But it is clear why judges respond to this class, which is far to the left of the general public. It is because they have been conditioned to respond. Coming from that class, judges look to it for approval. They look in particular to the law schools, the university faculty, and the media. (When a judge comes to Washington and moves from right to left, the *Washington Post* announces that he has "grown.") The movement from right to left is the only movement justices make in Washington. I cannot think of an example in the past fifty years of a justice on the Supreme Court who went from being somewhat liberal to somewhat conservative, but there are many counterexamples.

It is because the elite are hostile to religion that the Supreme Court is—and indeed is so dramatically—hostile, too. There was, for example, a recent case wherein the Court held that high school students must not be allowed to pray before a football game.[11] This is ripe for parody. A prominent Supreme Court advocate remarked that students should dance nude before the game, because nude dancing is preferred to prayer as a form of expression. (Of course even this would not work if the students did the Dance of the Seven Veils, which has Biblical connotations and would therefore likely be considered a forbidden establishment of religion.)

The Supreme Court's hostility to religion is fairly new. For most of our history law and religion lived together quite amicably. It was not until the middle of the last century that the real antagonism toward religion developed. And, I might add, religion did not start the quarrel. The Supreme Court attacked. Occasionally there is a bright moment in this attack. When I was on the Court of Appeals, we heard a case brought by atheists who were challenging the Senate policy of paying chaplains. They did not get off to a very good start because the first thing that happened in the courtroom was the marshal standing up and saying, "God save this Honorable Court." I thought they might slap a writ on us right there. But the argument went on and I finally asked the atheists' lawyers if a court should be involved in this. Had their clients taken their complaint to the leaders of the House of Representatives and the Senate? He said that they had but were told to "go to hell." To this day, I do not know why that bothered him.

In constitutional law, major philosophic shifts often occur through what appears to be a minor tampering with technical doctrine. In the case of religion the doctrine has to do with what lawyers call "standing." Persons who claim an interest in a constitutional issue only as citizens and taxpayers do not have standing to challenge alleged constitutional violations. Individuals cannot present themselves before a court merely for the sake of litigating a matter they find ideologically offensive. In order to have standing they must show the matter in dispute directly affects them, through a loss of property or liberty.

However, in 1968 the Court suddenly created a rule that taxpayers and citizens could sue under the establishment clause of the First Amendment, which states that Congress shall make no law respecting an establishment of religion.[12] People may now sue under the establishment clause even if they are merely citizens and taxpayers who have an aversion to religion. This has unleashed the hounds of the American Civil Liberties Union (ACLU). Now a litigant need only say he finds some religious symbol in the public arena to be personally offensive. That is why we have suits successfully challenging the display of the Ten Commandments on high school walls,[13] and why a Baltimore ordinance was struck down because it prohibited the sale of nonkosher food on the false representation that it is kosher,[14] and why a court said that a principal of a school must stop a teacher from reading a Bible for his own purposes during a silent reading period.[15] The theory was that some of the students might notice that the teacher was reading a Bible and might therefore be influenced toward acceptance of religion. More recently, the Court has held that there cannot be prayer at a middle school commencement.[16] The prayer in question was a short nonsectarian prayer, but the Court said that a young woman and her parents might nevertheless be injured because she might feel pressured to maintain a respectful silence during this period of prayer. If the reader had been reading from *Mein Kampf* or *The Communist Manifesto*, she would have had no standing to litigate: she would have had to sit there and maintain respectful silence.

On no other topic is mere ideological interest sufficient to confer standing. Taxpayers and citizens have no standing to sue over ideological disagreements with respect to any other clause of the Constitution, from Article 1, Section 1 to the Twenty-Seventh Amendment, with only one exception—the establishment clause of the First Amendment. That qualifies as hostility to religion. The only ideology enforceable in a court of law is anti-religious animus.

SELF-GOVERNMENT, CIVILIZATION, AND THE CULTURE WARS

We are losing much more than the right to democratic self-governance, although we are certainly losing that. We are losing also the traditional values that lie at the heart of our civilization. A large majority of Americans still think that religion is the sole or primary source of morality. If religion does not create morality, it does reinforce it and spell it out in detail greater than the average human mind might comprehend in the absence of religion. Even those who are not religious, yet are moral, are arguably living off the moral capital left by prior generations of believers. The prospect therefore exists that, as this capital dwindles, society will gradually become less moral. I have no doubt that our culture has been moving in that direction. This does not prove the moral capital theory, but it does provide some evidence for it. James Q. Wilson has written that, "In the late nineteenth century England and America reacted to the consequences of industrialization, urbanization, immigration, and affluence by asserting an ethos of self-control, whereas in the late twentieth century they reacted to many of the same forces by asserting an ethos of self-expression."[17] In his view, the difference is that religion and allied voluntary associations are the sources of an ethos of self-control, which must work through the process of habituation in the family, the schools, and the workplace. But certain elites in the twentieth century have refused to support that habituation and have leagued to undermine it. As a result we live with the ethos of self-expression rather than self-control. Religion was a vital force in the nineteenth century but declined and became pallid in the twentieth.

The late Christopher Lasch argued that the gradual decay of religion is what accounts for our society's wholesale defection from the standards of personal conduct, civility, industry, and self-constraint once considered essential for democratic self-governance. He argued that the liberal elite, "whose attitude to religion ranges from indifference to active hostility"[18] has succeeded in marginalizing religion from public recognition and debate. That is certainly the case, but the exile of religion could not have been so effective had the Supreme Court not ordered that it be removed from the public square and contemplated only in private.

Justice Potter Stewart once wrote in a dissent that banishing religion from the public school environment effectively teaches children at a very impressionable age that religion is a harmful thing. The lesson is not neutrality, but a counter-religion of secular humanism. I think this is true, and it has consquences. Law—all law from the most mundane regulations to the most profound guarantees of liberty—rests upon morality. And morality to be effective requires reinforcement from religion. In attacking religion, therefore, judges are attacking the foundation and authority of law. It remains an open question how long the rule of law can remain vital if its foundations are seriously weakened. Lord Devlin, a British jurist, said that law depends on a shared social morality. If that disappears and the weight is placed entirely upon law, law probably cannot stand the strain that seems to be coming to pass. We now litigate questions that used to be settled by community approval or disapproval. What has happened in the religion cases is not only wrong historically and constitutionally. It is also highly dangerous.

Invasion by the courts into territory belonging to the people and their elected representatives represents a gradual weakening of democracy. This weakening does not happen in America through the sudden actions of violent men, but slowly, one case at a time. Courts have been systematically taking over areas of private and public life that the Constitution leaves to private behavior, or morality expressed through legislation. Two men put the matter well. Robert Maynard Hutchins wrote that, "the death of democracy is not likely to be an assassination from ambush. It will be a slow extinction from apathy, indifference, and undernourishment."[19] James Madison said in a speech at the Virginia ratifying convention, "I believe there are more instances of the abridgment of the freedom of the people by gradual and silent encroachments of those in power than by violent and sudden usurpation."[20] The framers took care to construct a system of checks and balances between the legislature and the executive, but they did nothing about checking courts because they did not think courts would be a problem. Some of the anti-Federalists did, but not so the Federalists, who systematically overlooked the danger from that branch. In their defense, they had never seen a court like the one we have today anywhere in the world, and had no idea what judicial power could become.

CONCLUSION

What I have been describing is not only the retreat of democracy and disintegration of our civilization's culture, but also the increasing irrelevance of the ideal of the rule of the law, which has become little more than an empty slogan. The reality is that the rule of the law is central to the practice of democracy. The rule assumes that voters will choose those who will enact rules, and judges will apply those rules as intended; that they will not declare them unconstitutional unless the Constitution rather clearly says they are out of bounds. Unless judges are able to contain themselves, to be faithful to the intended meaning of the laws and the Constitution, public debate, elections, and legislative deliberations will become increasingly beside the point. In short, whether or not Murray or Minogue's pessimism is justified, there is one basic feature of Western civilization that is clearly being eroded, and that is democratic government. In illustrating how the Supreme Court has supported the cultural left in attacking this society and its basic traditions, I have mentioned the Court's relationship to the vulgarization of society, to radical feminism, to sexuality, to political speech and pornography, and to religion. These are among the topics of central importance to our civilization. And therefore it is a matter of great concern when the Court begins to undermine our moral views of such matters. And it is particularly troublesome when the Court does so without a shred of support from the Constitution it claims to be interpreting. In so doing, of course, the Court has made itself antithetical to the rule of law.

A long time ago I read a sentence by Walter Bagehot that seems highly relevant to the relationship between courts and our culture today. Bagehot wrote that, "The characteristic danger of great nations like the Romans and the English, which have a long history of continuous creation, is that they may at last fail from not comprehending the great institutions which they have created." That is certainly a danger in America today. We no longer fully understand the proper relation between our courts and our Constitution. I have often found myself giving some of the most pessimistic speeches certain audiences have ever heard, much to the dismay of the people who invited me. But it is not necessary to be entirely pessimistic. Intellectual pessimism can coexist with an optimistic spirit and will. And that is the balance we must strike. The first step is to recognize what is happening to us. With this recognition, along with a spirited resistance, we at least have a chance to revitalize the great institutions that we and other Western nations have created.

NOTES

1. Roger Kimball, *The Long March: How the Cultural Revolution of the 1960s Changed America* (San Francisco: Encounter Books, 2000), 14.
2. *Board of County Commissioners v. Umbehr*, 518 U.S. 668, 711 (1996).
3. *U.S. v. Virginia*, 518 U.S. 515 (1996).
4. *Hill v. Colorado*, 530 U.S. 703 (2000).
5. *Stenberg v. Carhart*, 530 U.S. 914 (2000).
6. *Romer v. Evans*, 517 U.S. 620 (1996).
7. *Bowers v. Hardwick*, 478 U.S. 186 (1986).
8. *Nixon v. Shrink Missouri Government PAC*, 528 U.S. 377 (2000).
9. *Cohen v. California*, 403 U.S. 15 (1971).
10. *Erie v. Pap's A.M.*, 529 U.S. 277 (2000).
11. *Santa Fe Independent School District v. Doe*, 530 U.S. 290 (2000).
12. *Flast v. Cohen*, 392 U.S. 83 (1968).
13. *Stone v. Graham*, 449 U.S. 39 (1980).
14. *Braghout v. Bureau of Kosher Meat and Food Control*, 66 F.3d 1337 (4th Cir. 1995).
15. *Roberts v. Madigan*, 921 F.2d 1047 (10th Cir. 1990).
16. *Lee v. Weisman*, 505 U.S. 577 (1992).
17. James Q. Wilson, *On Character* (Washington, D.C.: The AEI Press, 1995), 28.
18. Christopher Lasch, *The Revolt of the Elites and the Betrayal of Democracy* (New York: W.W. Norton, 1995), 215.
19. Robert Maynard Hutchins, *Great Books, The Foundation of a Liberal Education* (New York: Simon and Schuster, 1954), 23.
20. Jonathan Elliot, *The Debates in the Several State Conventions on the Adoption of the Constitution,* 2nd ed., vol. 3 (Philadelphia: J.B. Lippincot Company, 1907), 87.

2

From Ockham to Blackmun: The Philosophical Roots of Liberal Jurisprudence

Francis Canavan

One of the more famous self-introductions to popular literature is, "Me Tarzan, you Jane." Every word in that sentence is singular, referring to one and only one individual. But once we get beyond that level of discourse, it becomes necessary to use class terms that refer not only to single individuals, but to some common feature in individual persons or things that identifies them as members of a category.

Thus Tarzan could have said, "Me boy, you girl," identifying himself and Jane as members of the two distinct sexes that constitute the broader category of human beings. Or, distinguishing himself from what he was not, he could have said, "Me man, me not ape," marking a distinction between two species of animal. All of these are what are called universal terms—that is, terms that refer to all the members of a given class.

But what do these universal terms tell us about reality? It is a question that has engaged the minds of philosophers at least since the time of the ancient Greeks. The answer is one of enormous significance to political thought, but in the universities of the Middle Ages it became a disputed topic in logic. To put it very briefly, in the thirteenth century, the school of philosophical realism, exemplified preeminently by St. Thomas Aquinas, held that universal terms referred, or could refer to, essences or natures that defined what kind of being something is in objective reality. In the following century, a movement called nominalism arose, preeminently exemplified by William of Ockham (1285–1349), which held that universals are logical terms by which the human mind groups beings that are unified, not by common natures, but by similarities that suffice to admit classing them under common names (hence nominalism, from the Latin *nomen, nominis,* name). For the nominalists the universals were concepts in our minds, and did not refer to real common natures outside the mind.

I should state at once that what I am going to say about Ockham is drawn not from his own writings, but from secondary sources, principally *A History of Philosophy*, volume 3, by Frederick Copleston, S. J.,[1] with assistance from the introduction to *Philosophical Writings* of William of Ockham, by Philotheus Boehner, O.F.M.[2] Both Copleston and Boehner are highly reputable scholars, and Boehner in particular is concerned to defend Ockham, his fellow Franciscan, against sweeping charges that have been made against him. Their interpretation of Ockham is fair-minded and, to say the least, not unfriendly. So I rely on it.

I should also explain that I do not believe that one can draw a straight line from Ockham to Justice Blackmun or to any particular thinker in between them. I mean only that one can see a current in Western political and legal thought that flows from Ockham, whom Copleston calls, "the fountainhead of the terminist or nominalist movement," and whom Boehner describes as, "perhaps the greatest logician of the Middle Ages." Nominalism helps to explain the radical individualism that manifests itself in contemporary American jurisprudence, of which the opinions of the late Justice Harry Blackmun are a startling example.

My view on that point finds support from David A. J. Richards, professor of law at New York University, who believes that his thought had an influence on Justice Blackmun's dissenting opinion in the Georgia sodomy law case, *Bowers v. Hardwick*.[3] Richards says in his book, *Toleration and the Constitution*,[4] that his own political theory comes down through Locke, Rousseau, Kant, and Rawls, and that Locke's conception of politics, "arises from a larger repudiation, rooted in medieval nominalism, of the Platonic and Aristotelian epistemology of the chain of beings," —that is the rising curve from inanimate beings to plants, animals, men, and God. The significance of Richard's statement is that for Locke, as for Ockham, we do not know the common natures of kinds of things, but only the concepts we have formed of them.

In the century following Aquinas, metaphysics (the science of being as being) began to give way to logic. Ockham criticized metaphysics in the name of logic and thereby undermined it because it was not self-evidently true, although he admitted that some metaphysical propositions are probable. For Ockham, intuition of the existent individual thing is primary. Only individual things exist (we never meet Humanity walking down the street, but only individual men and women). The reality that class names stand for is individual things alone.

In Ockham's own words, as quoted by Copleston, "no universal is anything existing outside the soul, but everything which is predicable of many things is of its nature in the mind, whether subjectively or objectively; and no universal belongs to the essence or quiddity of any substance whatever." It follows not only that only individual things exist, but that only individual things are real.

Copleston goes on to say that Ockham's, "main point was always that there is no need to postulate any factor other than the mind and individual things in order to explain the universal. The universal concept arises simply because there are varying degrees of similarity between individual things. . . . There is no nature common to Socrates and Plato, in which they come together or share or agree; but the nature which is Socrates and the nature which is Plato are alike." This likeness is enough to make science possible. Science is knowledge of universal propositions, but the universal terms that the propositions employ stand for individual things, not for universal realities existing outside the mind.

We thus live in a world of our own definitions, by which we group the existent realities that we encounter in experience, and about which we reason in accordance with the rules of logic. This premise, once accepted, leads to both empiricism (the observation of individual facts) and the rationalism of pure logic (of which mathematics is the best example). David Lindley explains: "Newton mathematicized physics to turn the 'tendencies' and 'potentials' of Aristotelian thought into what we now recognize as true science, based on quantitative and precise relations between masses, forces, and motions. Numbers were needed to measure these quantities, so physical laws had to take the form of relationships between numbers—mathematical laws, in other words."[5]

One of Ockham's main principles, says Copleston, is "that when two things are distinct there is no absolutely necessary connection between them." Note the term "absolutely necessary." Ockham conceded necessity only to logically necessary propositons that could not be denied without self-contradiction. His "tendency was always to break through supposedly necessary connections which might seem to limit in some way the divine omnipotence." As Boehner says, Ockham was a great logician, but, "first and foremost a theologian," intent on asserting the total dependence of everything in the universe on God's power against anything that might seem to limit it.

Ockham's concern for God's omnipotence and liberty is closely associated with his "empiricism." He tended to split up the world into absolutes (substances and "absolute accidents," without which a substance could not be itself), which are distinct entities, each totally dependent on God's creative act, but between which there is no necessary connection. The order of the world is logically posterior to the divine choice of individual contingent entities.

As Boehner puts it, "Everything that is real, and different from God, is contingent to the core of its being." It follows that one "must not call any truth necessary unless it can be shown that its denial implies a contradiction"—that is to say, unless it is logically impossible. This premise had a powerful effect on Ockham's philosophy and theology: "the logician is all the time at the elbow of the metaphysician and the theologian, ever reminding them that the requirements of a demonstration are exacting and difficult to fulfill. In a strictly scientific metaphysics Ockham wants only demonstrative conclusions." Boehner remarks that Ockham seems to have been interested in showing how much it is not possible to demonstrate.

Nevertheless, Boehner also calls Ockham, "a realist in his epistemology." But this seems to mean no more than that we really know the individual things that make up the world, because Boehner goes on to say that, "Ockham refuses to admit that in the real world there is anything that corresponds to the universality of a concept; in other words, he does not admit any universal *in re*, common nature, etc.—anything which is not completely individual."

Copleston agrees that for Ockham there is in the world no order constituted by the natures with which God created His creatures, therefore no natural order that is accessible to human reason. The order that exists is simply the result of God's totally free choice, which could have been, and still could be, other than it is, and is known to us only through God's revelation of His will. Natural law would be a limitation of God's power and therefore is to be rejected as a non-Christian idea.

The same tendency is evident in Ockham's treatment of relations. They are not real entities but concepts in the mind. In any given instance there are only the two (or more) existent absolutes, and there is no need to postulate a third entity called a relation. For the only distinction that is independent of the mind is one between separate or separable entities, but a relation is not separable from its foundation and is therefore not a reality. This, again, is a reason for denying a natural order accessible to reason.

Ockham also "shows a tendency to interpret the causal relation as invariable or regular sequence." Copleston admits that "to state without more ado that Ockham reduced causality to regular succession would be incorrect." But he also says, "With him [Ockham] relations and connections in nature were really reduced to the co-existence or successive existence of 'absolutes.'" This would be in harmony with his theological view, in which God has created distinct things, among which the order that we in fact observe is purely contingent and does not depend on any necessary connection between existing things. The connection depends on God's choice, which He could change but ordinarily does not.

Ockham thus drives a wedge between philosophy and theology. It is not that he questions divine revelation or divine creation of the world; on the contrary, he exalts them. But he does question the conclusive force of proofs of the existence of God. The reason is that they depend on the principle of causality, but "only analytic propositions are absolutely certain," and the principle of causality is not an analytic proposition. Ockham was not a skeptic or an agnostic, nor was he a fideist tout court. But his philosophy moved in that direction, held in check by the certitude of faith, which he did not question. His universe was a divinely created one, known, however, by faith, not by rational demonstration.

Ockham did not reject metaphysics—the science of being as being—out of hand. But for him, "being as such is a concept, not a thing." That is to say, the reality to which the term, being, corresponds, "is simply different beings which are simply conceived as existing." Furthermore, being is a univocal term, which is predicated of God and creatures, and of different kinds of creatures, in exactly the same sense. Things either are or they are not; there are no different levels on which being is predicated analogously.

In Ockham's universe there is no natural teleology and no ordination of human nature toward a natural end. In this case, says Copleston, "it would scarcely be possible to analyze the goodness of human acts in terms of a relation to an end which is necessarily desired," because implicit in human nature. The content of moral obligation is furnished by the omnipotent will of God, who is not bound by the natures of His creatures. Man's obligation follows simply from God's will, which is the norm of the obligation.

"The whole created order, including the moral law, is viewed by Ockham as thoroughly contingent, in the sense that not only its existence but also its essence and character depend on the divine creative and omnipotent will. Having got rid of the universal idea of man in the divine mind, Ockham was able to eliminate the idea of a natural law which is in essence immutable." St. Thomas had held that "there are acts which are intrinsically evil and which are forbidden because they are evil; they are not evil simply because they are forbidden." Ockham, to the contrary, held that there are no naturally and intrinsically evil acts; acts are evil because God has forbidden them, and God, whose freedom and power are not limited by His creation, could command the opposite.

Not to make Ockham mean more than he did mean, Copleston points out: "Absolutely speaking, God could command or prohibit any act, provided that a contradiction is not involved. Actually God has established a certain moral law." Thus Ockham can and does speak of the obligation to follow, "right reason." In his own words, he means an act, "which is intrinsically and necessarily virtuous *stante ordinatione divina* (while the divine order stands)." In the same sense he says that, "in the present order (*stante ordinatione quae nunc est*) no act is perfectly virtuous unless it is elicited in conformity with right reason."

Copleston's final comment on Ockham's morality is that it is ambiguous: "He appears to imply that reason can discern something of the present moral order but, if he did mean this, it is difficult to see how this idea can be reconciled with his authoritarian conception of morality. If the moral law is dependent simply on the divine choice, how can its content be known apart from revelation? Very probably he did not clearly realize the difficulties created by his authoritarian conception." But Ockham's conception of morality is rooted in his epistemology, which denies extramental reality to relations and therefore to order.

Boehner defends Ockham against the charge of seeing God's will as arbitrary, explaining that this is, "to overlook Ockham's belief that God not only has a free will but is also infinitely wise and good. But His wisdom is a free wisdom, His goodness a free goodness; He is bound only by the law of contradiction, if this means being bound at all." As for Ockham's well-known statement that by His absolute power, God could command a creature to hate Him or at least not love Him, Boehner explains that, "this possibility is admitted in the purely ontological and logical realm." It would be, "an ethical impossibility," however, because if given such a command, "the creature would be obliged to obey, but it could not obey since in obeying it would love Him." This, says Boehner, would be an antinomy, "the only real antinomy in Ockham's philosophy."

Ockham thus leaves us with a world of individual objects and persons, each with its own individual nature. There are no common natures in extramental reality, no natural teleology, and no natural order. We have only the concepts and names by which we classify them, and these refer only to individual things, which alone are real. As Umberto Eco has one of the characters say in the last line of his nominalist novel, *The Name of the Rose*, *"Stat rosa pristina nomine . . . nomina nuda tenemus"* (the archetypical rose consists in its name, we have nothing but names).

From this starting point certain nominalist assumptions became widely accepted in Western moral, political, and legal thought. It cannot be said that the whole of Western thought is a consequence of Ockham's nominalism, but the modern mind has been heavily influenced by it, particularly in English-speaking countries. A few citations from scholarly works will serve as examples of support for that claim.

In his introduction to Hobbes's *Leviathan*,[6] Michael Oakeshott says:

> Individualism as a gospel has drawn its inspiration from many sources, but as a reasoned theory of society it has its roots in the so-called nominalism of late medieval scholasticism, with its doctrines that the reality of a thing is its individuality, that which makes it *this* thing, and that in both God and man will is precedent to reason. Hobbes inherited this tradition of nominalism, and more than any other writer passed it on to the modern world. His civil philosophy is based, not on any vague belief in the value or the sanctity of the individual man, but on a philosophy for which the world is composed of *individuae substantiae*.

As we saw earlier, David A. J. Richards says that Locke's political theory "arises from a larger repudiation, rooted in medieval nominalism, of the Platonic and Aristotelian epistemology of the chain of beings." Locke himself says in his *Essay Concerning Human Understanding*, "Metaphysical truth . . . is nothing but the real existence of things conformable to the ideas we have annexed to their names. This, though it seems to consist in the very beings of things, yet, when considered a little nearly, will appear to include a tacit proposition, whereby the mind joins a particular thing to the idea it had before settled with a name to it."

Of Jeremy Bentham, Crane Brinton has remarked, "It may seem no small violence to Bentham's memory to describe him in a term drawn from those Middle Ages he so disliked, but he really is the perfect nominalist. The individual, John Doe, is for him the ultimate reality."[7]

For nominalists, every human being has a nature that is peculiar to him. In this we may see a foreshadowing of the present-day argument advanced by homosexuals that they are justified in following their sexual orientation, because it is their nature. More broadly, we come to understand the primacy now so widely accorded to personal autonomy. If there is no common nature to say to him nay, the individual may claim the right to determine his own moral universe based on the individual preferences that are his nature.

From the nominalist idea of the individual there emerged the contract theory of the state, according to which civil society—society organized under government and law—is necessarily contractual and dependent on individual consent. Since it is not possible for men to live together in the war of all against all that Thomas Hobbes described as the natural state of men, they are forced by their fear of violent death to contract with each other to set up a common government. Strong enough to keep peace among them, this government will establish, "the means of peaceable, sociable, and comfortable living," which is the purpose of civil society.

In Hobbes's view civil society is not a response to man's social and political nature as Aquinas and Aristotle had held, but a means to the secure pursuit of private ends. Hobbes is usually described in the textbooks as a proponent of absolute government, preferably an absolute monarchy, and so he was. Some scholars, nonetheless, call him the true founder of liberalism, and there is merit in this claim.

For Hobbes, as for his utilitarian successors, "*Good*, and *evil*, are names that signify our appetites, and aversions," which differ widely among men and societies. In *Leviathan*, Hobbes recognizes "laws of nature," but explains that "they are but conclusions or theorems concerning what conduces to the conservation and defence of themselves."

Hobbe's preference for absolute monarchy should not keep us from recognizing that his central themes are those of our contemporary liberalism. The goal of society is to allow us to enjoy in peace what we now call "the good life." The meaning of good is determined by our appetites and aversions, our quest for pleasure and our flight from pain. In the famous words of David Hume in a *Treatise of Human Nature*, "Reason is, and ought only to be, the slave of the passions, and can never pretend to any other office than to serve and obey them."[8] More recently George F. Will has written,

"The fundamental goal of modern liberalism has been equality, and it has given us government that believes in the moral equality of appetites."[9]

But this egalitarianism does not save us from political absolutism. As George H. Sabine remarked somewhere in his writings, "The absolutely sovereign and omnicompetent state is the logical correlate of a society which consists of atomic individuals." In its drive to guarantee the moral equality of individual appetites, liberalism has given rise to a forest of anti-discrimination laws, bureaucratic ordinances, and court decisions that impose the liberal idea of equality on a growing number of society's nongovernmental institutions.

The Ockhamite principle that relations are mental constructs subject to human choice dissolves the natural and given character of institutions, particularly of that basic social institution, the family. Human society is indeed composed largely of institutions that our choices and customs have framed, and that have varied among cultures. But nominalism denies given natural norms by which institutions can be judged as more or less in harmony with the needs of mankind's common nature, and makes all institutions arbitrary. As Sir Ernest Barker warned, "Once oppose Nature to Convention, and the whole inherited tradition of the ages goes by the board."[10] But that result means little to the nominalist mind that knows not nature.

Nominalism today goes beyond Ockham's absolutes (substances and accidents), to dissolve substances in order to "remold them nearer to the heart's desire." Plastics are produced by breaking down natural substances to their constituent elements, which then are recombined in different ways to become new and previously unknown substances. Genetic engineering, carried far enough, aspires to do something similar. The nominalist method of understanding reality reduces human beings to collections of cells, and cells to collections of chemicals, because parts are ultimately more real than the wholes that they form. Therefore, it is permissible to remake human nature.

Ockham's doctrine of the univocity of being, with its concomitant denial of higher and lower orders of beings, puts all beings on the same level. It also leads some among us to consider it sheer arrogance for human beings to claim superiority to other animals. It further leaves some human beings feeling free to engender other human beings in glass for such purposes as artificial insemination or experimenting on fetuses in the hope of discovering remedies for the diseases that afflict still other persons.

The reduction of reality to individuality, proposed by Ockham in his logician's innocence, has at long last flowered not only in the moral equality of appetites remarked on by George Will. It has also led to the reduction of all assertions of moral truth to mere personal opinions that no one need accept as binding on himself. In the course of the twentieth century these consequences made their way into American law as constitutional rights that are specified nowhere in the text of the Constitution but are discerned in the idea of ordered liberty, which belongs to all persons alike.

The late Justice Harry A. Blackmun neither was nor pretended to be a philosopher and if charged with being an intellectual descendant of William of Ockham would doubtless have replied with a puzzled stare. As an example of his philosophical ignorance, in the opinion he wrote for the Court in *Roe v. Wade*,[11] he said "We need not resolve the difficult question of when life begins. When those trained in the respective disciplines of medicine, philosophy, and theology are unable to arrive at any consensus, the judiciary at this point in the development of man's knowledge is not in a position to speculate as to the answer."

Having said that, Blackmun proceeded to declare for the Court that a woman's right to choose to abort, that is, to kill the child in her womb, was, "founded in the Fourteenth Amendment's concept of personal liberty," as being, "fundamental," or, "implicit in the concept of ordered liberty." He admitted that "the Constitution does not explicitly mention any right of privacy," but cited a line of cases in which the Court had implicitly recognized such a right. For a judge, apparently, that is argument enough.

The essence of the declared right, however, is the freedom to choose. The heart of contemporary liberalism is the proposition that the fundamental human right is personal autonomy. This connotes not merely the ability to make choices, but that it is choice that makes an action good. A choice is not good because of the goodness of the action chosen. On the contrary, an action is good because it is chosen.

Obviously not even the U.S. Supreme Court can make that a universal proposition, since it would leave criminals free to destroy civilization, if only they were sincere in their belief in the rightness of their choices. We therefore must allow the Supreme Court to tell us which actions are covered by personal autonomy and which ones may be limited by compelling state interests. But Justice Blackmun was willing to go far in upholding the right to choose.

He was also willing to go far in subordinating the family to the state. Three years after *Roe v. Wade*, he wrote the opinion of the Court in *Planned Parenthood of Central Missouri v. Danforth*,[12] in which he declared unconstitutional a provision of a Missouri law that acknowledged a husband's right to prevent his wife, pregnant by him, from aborting the child which was his as much as hers. Speaking for the Court, Blackmun stated that, "we cannot hold that the State has the constitutional authority to give the spouse unilaterally the ability to prohibit the wife from terminating her pregnancy, when the State itself lacks that right." The idea that the right of a husband to forbid the abortion of his child could only be an authority delegated to him by the State should have provoked a roar of protest from coast to coast, but it did not. To the nominalist mind, only individuals are real, but relations are not real, including the relations between husband and wife and father and child.

Blackmun's nominalism appears most fully in a case already mentioned, *Bowers v. Hardwick*. This case concerned a Georgia law that made homosexual sodomy a crime. By a 5-4 majority the Court declined to hold the law unconstitutional. Blackmun wrote an opinion for the four dissenters wherein he cited a series of cases in which the Court had found that "a certain private sphere of individual liberty will be kept largely beyond the reach of government."

The heart of his argument is that "we protect the rights contained in that sphere not because they contribute in some direct and material way to the general public welfare, but because they form so central a part of the individual's life." Thus, "We protect the decision to marry precisely because marriage is an association that promotes a way of life. . . . We protect the decision whether to have a child because parenthood alters so dramatically an individual's self-definition. . . . And we protect the family because it contributes so powerfully to the happiness of individuals, not because of a preference for stereotypical households." With these words Blackmun denies that the family is a basic institution of society on whose health and well-being the common welfare depends, reducing it to a way of satisfying individual desires for happiness.

What counts for Blackmun is the centrality of individual choice:

> The fact that individuals define themselves in a significant way through their intimate sexual relationships with others suggests, in a Nation as diverse as ours, that there may be many "right" ways of conducting those relationships, and that much of the richness of a relationship will come from the freedom an individual has to *choose* the form and nature of those intensely personal bonds. . . . The Court claims that its decision today merely refuses to recognize a fundamental right to engage in homosexual sodomy; what the Court really has refused to recognize is the fundamental interest all individuals have in controlling the nature of their intimate associations with others.

Is it unfair to see hovering behind Justice Blackmun the ghost of a medieval friar? I think not. To be sure, the modern mind is the product of many earlier minds. But we are still suffering from several centuries of highly defective epistemology, and William of Ockham certainly has had something to do with that.

NOTES

1. Frederick Copleston, S.J., *A History of Philosophy*, vol. 3 (New York: Doubleday Image Books, 1963).
2. Philotheus Boehner, O.F.M., ed., *Philosophical Writings* (Indianapolis: Hackett, 1990).

3. *Bowers v. Hardwick,* 478 U.S. 186 (1986).
4. David A. J. Richards, *Toleration and the Constitution* (Cambridge, UK: Oxford University Press, 1986).
5. David Lindley, *The End of Physics: The Myth of a Unified Theory* (New York: Basic Books, 1993).
6. Thomas Hobbes, *Leviathan,* ed. Michael Oakeshott (Maldon, Mass.: Blackwell, n.d.)
7. Crane Brinton, *English Political Thought in the Nineteenth Century* (New York: Harper & Bros., 1962).
8. David Hume, *Treatise of Human Nature,* book 3, section 5.
9. George F. Will, *Statecraft as Soulcraft* (New York: Simon & Schuster, 1983).
10. Ernest Barker, *Greek Political Theory: Plato and His Predecessors* (New York: Barnes & Noble, 4th ed., 1951).
11. *Roe v. Wade,* 410 U.S. 113 (1973).
12. *Planned Parenthood of Central Missouri v. Danforth,* 410 U.S. 52 (1976).

3

The Death of the Legalized Constitution and the Specter of Judicial Review

Keith E. Whittington

Between the years 1990 and 2000, the Supreme Court struck down twenty-eight acts of Congress. This does not even include the numerous acts of state and local governments that the Court has also rejected on constitutional grounds over the past few years. The cases that the Court has decided recently cover a range of issues—from the regulation of pornography on cable television to partial birth abortion to Miranda warnings to school prayer to national regulation of state governments and officials. Its decisions cannot be reliably characterized as either conservative or liberal, with different coalitions of justices able to form majorities to strike down laws from across the political spectrum. Despite the mixed messages it sends on substantive issues, the Court is consistent in its remarkable boldness. It aggressively strikes down acts of the other branches of the national government as well as acts of the individual states. The current Supreme Court has exercised its power of judicial review at a historically unprecedented pace. It does so in defense of relatively uncontroversial aspects of the constitutional text, but is equally willing to do so in defense of its own controversial precedents—even when several members of the Court believe those precedents were wrongly decided. And the Court does all this with barely a word of apology or a hint of modesty.

John Marshall referred to the power of judicial review as an "awful responsibility" that the Court was sometimes obliged to use.[1] But notably, during the time that John Marshall served as Chief Justice of the United States, the Court found only one obscure provision of one federal statute unconstitutional—and even that ruling was of little consequence and actually reduced the powers of the Court in the short term. Between the creation of the Supreme Court under the U.S. Constitution and the Civil War, the Court only explicitly found two acts of Congress unconstitutional.

One, a provision of the Judiciary Act in *Marbury v. Madison*, was relatively trivial.[2] The other, the Missouri Compromise in *Dred Scott v. Sanford*, had already been superceded by subsequent federal laws.[3] The pace picked up significantly after the Civil War, culminating in the great conflict between the Supreme Court and the administration of Franklin Roosevelt during the Great Depression, in which the Court backed off decades of its own earlier rulings and gave its approval to the New Deal. The "switch in time" of Justice Owen Roberts also helped sink Roosevelt's plan to pack the Court, perceived by many to be a great threat to judicial independence.

Since the New Deal, the Court has had periods of unusual activism—most notably in the late 1960s and early 1970s.[4] Even then, however, the Court generally stayed out of the way of Congress, even as it aggressively went after the practices of a number of states (especially those in the South). The Warren Court was reminded of the risks of obstructing Congress in the summer of 1958, when legislation critical of the Court was barely defeated in the aftermath of judicial decisions expanding the protections of suspected domestic Communists. When speaking to Congress, the Court has generally been careful to pay its respects, to explain with great sadness the absolute necessity of its rejecting federal law, to indicate the great deference that the Court properly owes to an equal branch of the U.S. government. The twentieth century has exposed both the vulnerability and the power of the Court. The Court-packing plan seemed to show its vulnerability in the face of a concerted national majority. The Warren era seemed to show its strength to take action even on the most controversial social issues of the day.

The twentieth century has also called into question the foundations and purposes of the Court's power of judicial review. Where did the Court obtain this great power, and how is it supposed to be used? We once more-or-less agreed on the answers to those questions. Now, we no longer do. For many of us, this is simply a power that the Court has. We open the newspaper and read about what the Court has done today. We may ask ourselves whether the Court was right, by our own lights, in having done those things. We rarely pause to ask by what right the Court has done them. We may be stimulated to do so, as we have in the past, when the Court issues a ruling that we find particularly distasteful—as many have found the Court's decisions on abortion, for example.[5] But such cases are rare. What is disturbing is that the Court no longer bothers to think about those questions, either. And many of us who do spend time thinking about such matters find it increasingly difficult to reach agreement on any possible answers. The constitutional system that gave rise to the power of judicial review and in which it made sense is dead. Yet the power of judicial review lives on, a specter hovering over the body politic. Let us look a bit more closely at why this is the case.

The Constitution arose out of the perceived failure of the Articles of Confederation to provide adequate powers to the national government to pursue national interests and to secure sufficient protections for individual rights against democracy as it was practiced in the states. Although the Founders were immediately interested in creating a stronger government than had existed under the Articles of Confederation, they were also concerned with creating a limited government and preventing the abuse of political power. We might imagine three constitutional strategies for limiting government. Each of these strategies would have different implications for how judicial review might be justified and used.

The first strategy can be regarded as structural. The structural approach places little reliance on the judiciary to limit the power of the government and protect liberty. Rather, as the name implies, this approach relies on the structure of government itself to control political power. This was famously the constitutional strategy favored by the Federalists. When those who opposed the ratification of the new Constitution complained that the proposed constitution lacked a Bill of Rights—something that had become standard for state constitutions and had a history in British constitutional traditions—Alexander Hamilton responded in the New York newspapers (in articles that would eventually become known as *The Federalist Papers*) that the entire Constitution was a Bill of Rights.[6] We will return to his argument in a moment. But part of his point was that the entire Constitution was designed to secure liberty. The original, unamended Constitution did not primarily rely on a rights strategy for protecting liberty, however. It sought to protect liberty through such devices as the separation of powers and the design of the electoral system. These were the elements of the Constitution that James Madison emphasized.

In sharp contrast to many political systems, the American constitutional system seeks to divide political power, spreading political power across many hands rather than consolidating power and entrusting it to any single actor or institution. The American system of federalism created multiple independent levels of government, each exercising their own powers and their own political judgments. Within the national government itself, the Constitution creates separate branches—a feature of the Constitution that has been particularly visible to us with the rise of divided party government since the late 1960s. Even Congress itself is divided into two separate chambers that must cooperate in order to pass legislation. As Madison explained, power is made to counteract power, ambition to counteract ambition.[7] Similarly, the Federalists hoped to use the very size of the new nation to their advantage, designing an electoral system that forced diverse interests to cooperate and work together to elect officials and make policy.[8] The structural solution to political tyranny takes the existing social diversity and channels it into political diversity. In order to prevent majority tyranny, the great danger of democratic government, the Federalists sought to prevent the rise of any natural majorities. Successful political majorities would be large and diverse, not narrow and self-interested.

A second constitutional strategy also pursued by the Founders—in this case emphasized by both the Federalists and their anti-Federalist opponents—can be called a legalistic strategy. The legalistic strategy does carve out an important role for the judiciary, and this was the element of the Constitution that was emphasized by Chief Justice John Marshall in his opinions for the Court and in his early justification for judicial review. The legalistic strategy points to two elements of the U.S. Constitution. First is the concept of enumerated powers. The new federal government can only exercise the powers that had been specifically delegated to it by the Constitution. It was not to be a government of general jurisdiction like the preexisting state governments, capable of undertaking any action that government officials thought would be in the public good. The federal government could only undertake those actions that the Constitution had specifically entrusted to it, such as the detailed list of powers given to Congress in Section Eight of Article One of the Constitution. The national government had a limited grant of legal authority. As Marshall argued in his 1803 opinion in *Marbury v. Madison*, the federal government is the agent of the people, created to fulfill certain important but limited tasks. Marshall was particularly taken with the fact that the United States had a written Constitution. The powers of the national government were consciously considered, specified, and written down by the Constitution's drafters. The judiciary plays a role in identifying where those boundaries on government power lie and insuring that political officials do not go beyond them.

The second element of this legalistic strategy is the Bill of Rights and the written limits on government power. Hamilton thought the addition of a Bill of Rights to the U.S. Constitution would undermine the enumeration strategy. A listing of specific prohibitions on government power, a listing of rights, would imply that government had the power to do everything else not specifically prohibited to it. This had been the traditional function of Bills of Rights in Britain and in the states—they carved out exceptions to the otherwise unlimited powers of governments of general jurisdiction. Even the original Philadelphia Constitution adopted this approach in some instances, such as excluding ex post facto laws from the national legislative power and prohibiting the state governments from impairing the obligations of contracts. But a Bill of Rights can also be understood as a backstop to the enumerated powers rather than a substitute, and in any case they rely on a similar understanding of how political power should be limited. The Bill of Rights expresses legal limits on government power—limits that are clear in the text, known to government and citizens, and enforceable in court. The written Constitution, in both its enumerated powers and its rights provisions, acts as a contract or charter, simultaneously creating and delimiting the government's legal authority to act.

A final constitutional strategy can be called principled, rather than structural or legalistic. The principled strategy relies less on specific political and legal institutions than on the articulation and acceptance of correct philosophical principles. What distinguishes a constitutional government from an unconstitutional government, by this approach, is not the existence of checks and balances or legal limitations but a sincere commitment to liberal, democratic principles. In historic and comparative terms, this is no small thing. Clearly there are many countries in the world that can boast formal constitutional institutions and elaborate constitutional guarantees of rights—the Soviet constitution famously included long, detailed lists of individual rights that put American constitutions to shame—but what they lack is a real commitment to the principles of limited government and popular sovereignty. Those who hold political power regard other principles and values as more important than those of liberal constitutionalism—whether they are the values of class advancement, national strength, economic rationalization, cultural or ethnic conformity, religious fidelity, or just the immediate self-interest of the ruling elite.

Some have called this the "thin Constitution."[9] What they regard as important in the Constitution is not the thick details of the government structure—it really does not matter whether the president has attained the age of thirty-five years or whether states have equal representation in the Senate—but the ideals embodied in such foundational documents of the American political tradition as the Declaration of Independence, the Preamble to the Constitution, and the Gettysburg Address. What people know and value are not the vast body of constitutional rules of concern only to the lawyers, but the basic principles of liberty, equality, justice, and democracy. This may also be regarded as the moral Constitution. This is not the Constitution of structure and rules, but the Constitution of moral ideals. We understand what the Constitution requires not by consulting the law books or the history books, but by consulting moral philosophy and engaging in ethical inquiry. Ronald Dworkin has been a notable advocate of reading the Constitution morally, and as a constitutional scholar has been markedly more interested in a handful of textual majestic generalities than the structural or legal details of the Constitution.[10] A central question for us to consider is what role the judiciary should play in the context of the moral Constitution.

Judicial review is most clearly implicated in the legalistic constitutional strategy. It makes a great deal of sense to have such an institution as judicial review in the context of a legalized Constitution.[11] The Supreme Court is above all a court, staffed by lawyers and conducting its business in accord with the familiar procedures of appellate courts. Unlike the abstract constitutional review of some European political systems in which general questions of constitutional meaning are referred to a special court for clarification, American-style judicial review only arises as part of the regular judicial effort to resolve a court case or controversy. To the extent that the Constitution is a form of law, it can be interpreted and applied by lawyers employing traditional legal skills and tools. To the extent that the Constitution is a kind of charter of the government, it is useful for that charter to be interpreted and enforced by someone standing outside the government. As a political structure, the Constitution may be a machine that can go of itself. As a set of rules constraining government officials, the Constitution requires a magistrate to ensure that the rules are followed. But as I stated earlier, we have long since witnessed the death of the legalized Constitution. Let me say a bit more about that.

In order for this strategy to work the legalized Constitution requires two things—faithful interpreters and applicable conditions. Those conditions have largely failed, and they had failed at least by the time of the New Deal early in the twentieth century. First, the legalized Constitution requires faithful interpreters. The legalized Constitution is not self-enforcing. Somebody has to recognize the legal limits on the government and care enough to enforce those limits. This is the problem of the constitution of the Soviet Union. Although the rights listed in the Soviet Constitution may be admirable enough, in practice there was no desire on the part of the Soviet state to enforce those rights and no institution with the will or the power to insist that the formal commitments of the Constitution be respected. Notably, the requirement of faithful interpreters is much less essential to the structural constitutional strategy. Once we establish a president and a Congress and identify the rules by which individuals are chosen to fill those offices, then power really does tend to check power and ambition check ambition. The effect is hardly perfect. Power can be accumulated and abused despite structural safeguards, and the political structures described in a constitutional text may not correspond to the exercise of political power in reality. But by spreading power across multiple institutions, the structural Constitution does tend to force political officials to cooperate in order to get things done. And in cooperating, they must take into account diverse interests and compromise. They cannot ride roughshod over the interests of others because those others have political power and their support is necessary to get things done. The need for cooperation in the contemporary political system is most obvious when different political parties control the legislative and executive branches of the government. The alternative to bipartisan cooperation is gridlock. But the fragmentation of political power under the American Constitution ensures that this is still often the case even under the "unified government" of single party.[12] The structural Constitution is an empowering document—both in the sense of empowering a newly re-created national government and in the sense of empowering diverse political officials and interests.[13] By contrast, the legalized Constitution requires external enforcement mechanisms. Political officials will not naturally recognize the limits to their own power and voluntarily refrain from pursuing policies that exceed their authority, especially if those policies are popular or might help them win reelection. Political power encourages its own use.

The legalized Constitution requires not merely that *someone* care about the constitutional rules, but that *lots* of people—with political power—care about the constitutional rules. We have been very fortunate that our leaders have generally cared about the constitutional rules. Government officials may overlook constitutional rules, or disagree about their content, or regard the maintenance of constitutional rules to be somebody else's primary responsibility. They do not, however, deny the authority of the constitutional rules. It has not been considered a legitimate response in American politics to suspend the Constitution when it conflicts with our political goals, as it has been in so many other nations where liberal constitutional traditions are less firmly rooted. Our leaders have generally at least tried to be faithful constitutional interpreters, willing to learn about and abide by the constitutional rules even when they are inconvenient. Our nineteenth-century political debates are full of such talk. Presidents, congressmen, candidates for office, and politically active citizens routinely debated the intricacies of the Constitution and regarded constitutional issues as important to their own political decision making. Even now, the Constitution is universally regarded to be something that matters. Unconstitutional laws are recognized to be null and void. The United States does not have either the formal or informal equivalent of Canada's constitutional "notwithstanding" clause by which government policies can be enacted and enforced despite their inconsistency with constitutional requirements.

Nonetheless, this first condition of the legalized Constitution has failed, even if it has failed in relatively subtle ways. In the first place, government officials may still believe that they are bound by the Constitution, but they no longer believe that they have a primary responsibility for understanding and applying the Constitution correctly. Faithfully interpreting the Constitution is not their job. It is, at most, the specialized job of the judiciary. One of President Franklin Roosevelt's congressional supporters once expressed doubts about whether proposed legislation was constitutional and would be accepted by the courts. FDR famously advised the congressman to resolve all his doubts in favor of the legislation and leave the issue to the courts.[14] Politicians should do what they think best on policy grounds. Let someone else worry about whether the results can be squared with the Constitution. Although this attitude accepts a place for the legalized Constitution, it encourages a gradual corruption of the constitutional order. It urges officials to cut constitutional corners and wait and see whether anyone important notices. It encourages government to push the limits of its powers, and let others worry about the consequences for the system as a whole. It leads government officials away from thinking in constitutional terms. The burden of constitutional fidelity is displaced.

At the same time, political and legal elites lost faith in the belief that the Constitution could be faithfully interpreted. FDR himself was steeped in a new Progressive and Realist tradition that said that the Constitution was a living creature that evolved over time, changing and responding to the needs of the present. A living Constitution avoided the possibility that the Constitution might become dated and outmoded. A living Constitution was always in tune with the times. In escaping the rigidity of a fixed Constitution, however, this approach tends to render the Constitution "perfect." The Constitution is "perfect" precisely because it is never in the way. The Constitution is agreeable to the extent that it agrees with "us." The Founding strategy of the legalized Constitution assumed that government power could be chained down by constitutional rules. In the early twentieth century, political leaders came to believe that the Constitution was not a set of chains to bind them but a tool to be used by them. They did not reject the idea of constitutionalism. But they no longer understood constitutionalism in the same way as the Founders did.

The rise of the belief in a living Constitution was closely connected to a loss of faith in uncontroversial legal rules. The legalized Constitution assumed that some issues could be set outside of politics. We could recognize the limits of government power—we could faithfully interpret the constitutional rules—even if we disagreed over policy and politics. Constitutional violations could occur either through innocent error or through a transitory fit of emotion. Dispassionate and skillful judges could be expected to recognize the constitutional violation that elected officials might have overlooked in the heat of the political moment. In the early twentieth century, the very idea of neutral legal interpretation came under fire. Judges and other constitutional interpreters were no longer regarded as above politics. Their decisions were the very essence of politics. To FDR, his problem was not with the Constitution or even with the judges, but with the Republican judges. What he needed were more judges who thought like him. His Court-packing proposal was designed to achieve just that—to put a new generation of progressive-minded judges who shared with the president an understanding of what the needs of government were in the modern era. Such judgments could be very context specific, responding to a particular and aberrational abuse of power by politicized judges. A distinctive feature of twentieth century legal thought is that such politicization is now widely regarded as inescapable rather than aberrational, at least in regards to the fundamental constitutional texts that most concern the Supreme Court and us.[15]

The early twentieth century also tested and broke the second condition of the legalized Constitution—its assumption of an applicable social and political environment. In particular, industrialization and related changes in the economy and society called into question the assumption that the federal government could be one of strictly limited powers and that neutral observers could distinguish between policies made for the common good and policies made to benefit special interests.[16] The very idea of majority tyranny assumes that we know when the actions of the majority are tyrannical. Majority-rule—democracy—necessarily accepts the fact that there are political winners and losers, and that majorities make political winners. The goal of the Constitution is to identify some actions of the majority as benefiting themselves at the expense of the minority, as exploiting the minority. Debtor relief legislation was an immediate example of the democratic problem in the eyes of the Federalists. In the Confederation period, most voters were debtors rather than creditors—more people borrow money than lend it out. When debts became burdensome, many voters wanted government to relieve their burden and many states responded by passing laws eliminating or sharply reducing private debts. The lenders were out of luck (and money), political losers in a fair democratic process. The legalized Constitution was to lay down substantive rules preventing such things from happening, and assumed that neutral observers could distinguish such debtor relief laws from, for example, reasonable bankruptcy legislation.[17]

There were always disputes on the margins, but through most of the nineteenth century there was at least general agreement on how the lines should be drawn. By the early twentieth century, that was no longer true. It had been assumed that legislation designed to benefit debtors or laborers or farmers at the expense of creditors or employers or manufacturers was not for the truly common good but for the private good of the political majority. In the context of the new industrial economy, it was no longer so clear how to distinguish the private from the public good. Laws benefiting laborers could reasonably, if controversially, be regarded to be in the public good. A legislatively mandated minimum wage might transfer wealth from capitalists to laborers, but at the same time it might be preventing unjust exploitation in the economic arena or stabilizing and expanding the economy as a whole by securing a mass consumer market. The lines between the private and the public blurred. The rules could no longer be faithfully and uncontroversially applied. We no longer could tell what rights people had and when laws violated them. For every claimed rights violation, others could plausibly argue that no rights had been violated. At least at the constitutional level, where rights had necessarily been defined in a general way, there was no recognizably neutral perspective from which to challenge important actions of the government.[18] The legalized Constitution collapsed.

The collapse of the legalized Constitution has, or should have, rather dramatic consequences for the theory of judicial review, and probably its practice as well. The institution of judicial review was deeply tied to the legalized

Constitution. The Court is a legal body. The U.S. Constitution does not specify any particular qualifications for judges, but federal judges have always been lawyers. For many decades, the American Bar Association has played a prominent role in evaluating the qualifications of potential federal judges, and unsurprisingly professional legal skills play a far greater role in those evaluations than moral astuteness, philosophical sophistication, or political statesmanship. Unlike other countries, the United States does not have a distinctive institution to resolve constitutional disputes. Instead, constitutional controversies arise as a (small) part of the normal judicial caseload, and judges spend much of their time resolving normal legal disputes.

A legalized Constitution provides legal rules for judicial application to cases. Constitutions can serve many functions, and those functions are reflected in the different constitutional strategies. Constitutions may create a political order or offer important lessons about political values. Constitutions may also act as a fundamental law, laying down legally enforceable rules constraining government. John Marshall emphasized this dimension of the Constitution in order to justify judicial review. Judicial review was justified because the courts had a special responsibility "to say what the law is," and the Constitution was the fundamental, supreme law in the American legal system.[19] The legalized Constitution was written, specific, clear, and authoritative. It provided legal rules for judicial application. The interpretive effort of the Court is tied to the legalized Constitution. From the beginning, the Court has claimed to interpret the Constitution as a legal text, and it continues to act as if this were the case. Judicial opinions are filled with the traditional accoutrements of Anglo-American legal interpretation. The authority of the judicial interpretation of the Constitution for other government officials is said to derive from the logical imperative of the judicial conclusions. There are few believers in the possibility of a merely mechanical jurisprudence, and it is evident that constitutional interpretations can be controversial. Nonetheless, Marshall's initial plea that judges could not be expected to "close their eyes on the Constitution, and see only the law" still has force.[20] If the Constitution is not primarily a legal document providing legal rules, then the court's authority as an interpreter of laws no longer has any particular implication for a power of judicial review. If constitutional questions are continuous with normal legal questions, then an institution such as judicial review is sensible. If constitutional questions are distinctive and not particularly legalistic, then the peculiar authority of the courts for resolving constitutional controversies becomes rather tenuous.

Judicial review is an artifact. We have found it, and we have put it on a pedestal. But it exists out of its original intellectual and political context. Judicial review has outlived its original form and haunts us from beyond the grave of the legalized Constitution. The practice remains, but it no longer makes sense. At least, it does not make sense in the traditional ways in which it once made sense. *If*, as I have argued, the legalized Constitution is dead, and *if* judicial review has been traditionally tied to the legalized Constitution, and *if* no other basis for judicial review can be found, then the continuing exercise of such an important political power by the Supreme Court is deeply problematic. The practice of judicial review continues, and has even grown. The question becomes whether a logic found in a different constitutional strategy could justify this continuing practice.

So, where else might a justification for something like modern judicial review be found? As noted earlier, the structural constitutional strategy does not leave much space for judicial review. It does leave some, however. There is often a temptation for political officials constrained by the constitutional structure to attempt to undermine it or render those structures a bit less constraining. Although the Constitution may generally pit interest against interest, politicians may also collude to advance their general interests over those of others or to short-circuit constitutional structures in order to achieve immediate political goals. Congress and the president may find it in their immediate interest to circumvent the usual legislative process in order to create a legislative veto or a line-item veto, for example. Similarly, constitutional structures may not work as their designers expected. Political parties have helped overcome the constitutional division of the legislative and executive branches. The states in the twentieth century have proven less able to resist the expansion of the national government than the structure of federalism presumed. The Court may well have a role in shoring up the structures established by the Constitution.

We can imagine some form of judicial review being justified in terms of a structural constitutional strategy, but not a very active Court and not one that behaves much like our present Court. The initially more promising option may lie in the idea of a principled Constitution. Like the legalized Constitution, the principled Constitution emphasizes the substantive limits on what government can do and recognizes those limits as being external to the government itself and not simply self-enforcing. In fact, it would seem to be the principled Constitution that holds the most appeal for constitutional scholars on both the left and the right since the early days of the Warren Court and apparently for many of the justices themselves.

I do not want to attempt a complete argument here about why the principled Constitution is inadequate to sustaining an active judicial review. Allow me to simply suggest some of the problems with this approach. First, the judiciary would seem to have no special authority in regard to principles. In the context of legal rules, the courts can reasonably claim an institutional expertise and authority to act as legal interpreters, even of the fundamental law. By contrast, there is nothing that distinguishes the judiciary in relation to political principles. The judicial claim on constitutional principles is either residual or ad hoc. The tradition of the legalized Constitution has created a ready presumption that the courts speak for the Constitution, but there is no logical connection between the quite distinct strategies of the legalized Constitution and the principled Constitution. The mere fact that both are constitutional does not suggest that both belong in the courts. Constitutional scholars who are advocates of both the principled Constitution and judicial review have in recent decades attempted to draw connections between the two, for example by positing that the courts are a unique forum of principled deliberation in the American political system. Such efforts are hampered by the fact that they are reactions to recent developments rather than inherent features of the constitutional system. Judicial institutions that developed for legal purposes are pressed into service for other purposes, and it is not surprising that the there is not a strong fit between the institution and its newly posited mission.

Constitutional principles are inherently controversial, and this works against the authority of the courts for resolving constitutional disputes. The legalized Constitution assumes that constitutional violations will be relatively rare and arise from error, transitory ill-temper, or political bad faith. Judges can correct these constitutional violations because they need only recall the relevant constitutional rule to expose the violation and chastise the violator. By contrast, there may be little agreement on the meaning of the principled Constitution and what might constitute a violation. Although as individuals we may have judgments as to the best understanding and realization of liberty or equality or justice, such concepts are likely to be open to controversy and reconsideration at the level of society. It might well be obvious to us as individuals what the correct answer might be to various hard constitutional questions, but it is evident that those answers are not at all obvious to us as a political community. Although we may bemoan the loss of constitutional consensus in our society, our present condition of constitutional dissensus can hardly be ignored or wished away. A judicial decision will not eliminate the underlying controversy over the appropriate constitutional principle to guide the polity, except by fiat. If the controversy is to be settled by fiat, the courts are a particularly problematic institution to render such a decision in a democracy. If there is continuing, reasonable, and significant disagreement about the substantive content of constitutional principles, then it would seem more appropriate that these disputes be resolved politically and democratically.[21] Indeed, resolving such disagreements is an inherently political task. Such disputes require the creation of new law rather than the interpretation and application of previously existing law and prior political agreements. In fact, American politics routinely organizes around such questions as the justice of the death penalty or abortion or slavery in order to resolve them. Advocates of judicial review in such contexts require some explanation as to why such decisions are better and more appropriately rendered by the courts rather than in the broader political arena that is also deliberating and acting on such questions. In the context of the principled Constitution, the question must be why constitutional politics is better conducted in the courthouse than in the legislature.[22]

The apparent death of the legalized Constitution raises the problem of justifying judicial review in more stark terms than is generally recognized. Certainly it means that we cannot simply point to history as justification enough for the present practice. The fact that the power of judicial review was asserted and accepted early in the nation's history hardly justifies the current practice of judicial review. It was the existence of the legalized Constitution that made judicial review justifiable at the time of *Marbury*, and it is precisely the death of the legalized Constitution that breaks our link to that earlier practice. Similarly, we should not simply assume that the power of judicial review will or should continue simply because it is part of our inherited constitutional tradition. The advocates of the living Constitution were right to take note of the fact that constitutional understandings and institutions change over time. Other aspects of the original Constitution and constitutional practice have fallen into disfavor and been altered.

The core problem of justifying judicial review discussed here is somewhat different than the usual subjects of scholarly debate over the past several decades. Judicial review has been a subject of substantial normative theorizing and consideration since the early days of the Warren Court and before. That theorizing has been centrally defined in terms of what Alexander Bickel called the "countermajoritarian difficulty," the problem in a democracy of justifying an institution that is not itself electorally accountable striking down the laws passed by representatives of a majority of the American people.[23] This feature of judicial review does pose a real theoretical difficulty and has appropriately occupied scholarly attention. The problem created by the death of the legalized Constitution, however, is that it removes the single most plausible response to the difficulty. The countermajoritarian difficulty can seem rather artificial because courts and other unelected institutions routinely exercise governing powers and because the Constitution does not establish a narrowly majoritarian political system but rather a constitutional system that places certain impediments before majority power. The central concern created by the death of the legalized Constitution is less the countermajoritarian problem per se than the philosopher-king problem. The great difficulty with judicial review in the current context is not that it frustrates the will of democratic majorities, but that it places judges over the citizenry as arbiters of contested political principle. In the absence of the legalized Constitution, judicial review empowers judges to act not as judges but as constitutional founders. The necessary debate is not over whether judicial review is best understood as countermajoritarian or whether other political values can take priority over majoritarianism, but whether judges should be empowered to make the basic political decisions regarding the governing principles of our society.

In an effort to overcome the countermajoritarian principle, constitutional theorists have often focused on specifying the best interpretation of the Constitution. Judges can be authorized to act against other government officials on behalf of the best understanding of constitutional requirements. It is essential to recognize at this point, however, that there is no general agreement as to the best interpretation of the Constitution. Demonstrating to one's own satisfaction that one has gotten the right answer to the hard constitutional questions will not, under present circumstances, satisfy others that those answers are in fact warranted and are not simply political impositions. Constitutional theory must take account of the existence of those basic disagreements and consider what should be done given those continued disagreements. It would seem that two options seem most attractive. One would be the long and difficult task of reconstructing the legalized Constitution, which would necessarily be both an intellectual and a political project. The other option would be a sharp reduction in judicial power, recognizing the troubling nature of judicial review beyond the bounds of the legalized Constitution. The point is not that the exercise of the power of judicial review is never appropriate. It is simply that the exercise of that power is appropriate only within the contours of the legalized Constitution.

The justification for judicial review should now be central to our thinking about constitutional government. It is an important and impressive power, and is being exercised in increasing comfort and boldness. Unlike other exercises of political power in the American system, the basis for the power of judicial review is not obvious. Judges at the federal level cannot point to their electoral mandates and democratic pedigrees to justify their actions. They were not selected for the explicit purpose of serving the people's interest. They still claim to be performing a more specific and limited task, one that is merely incidental to their primary responsibility of saying what the law is. Even though this answer to the legitimacy question is increasingly implausible, the Court no longer bothers to examine it critically or explain the basis of its power. The justices increasingly assume their power, and trust that others will assume it as well. They trust that they can simply exercise that power and that others will respond by asking whether they exercised it wisely or foolishly—but not by asking whether the justices should be exercising such a power at all and on what basis the justices claim the right to set aside the deliberate decisions of our elected representatives. But questioning and understanding the basis and authority for the use of political power is at the very heart of the constitutional tradition. It is a question we should take seriously.

NOTES

1. *McCulloch v. Maryland*, 17 U.S. 316, 400 (1819).
2. *Marbury v. Madison*, 5 U.S. 137 (1803).

3. *Dred Scott v. Sandford*, 60 U.S. 393 (1856). Mark Graber has persuasively argued that the Court effectively set constitutional limits on Congress in several other, uncontroversial cases relating to land claims during the antebellum period. Mark A. Graber, "Naked Land Transfers and American Constitutional Development," *Vanderbilt Law Review* 53 (2000): 71.

4. Gregory A. Caldeira and Donald J. McCrone, "Of Time and Judicial Activism: A Study of the U.S. Supreme Court, 1800–1973," in *Supreme Court Activism and Restraint*, ed. Stephen Halpern and Charles Lamb (Lexington, Mass.: Lexington Books, 1982).

5. See *The End of Democracy? The Judicial Usurpation of Politics*, ed. Mitchell Muncy (Dallas, Tx.: Spence Publishing, 1997).

6. Alexander Hamilton, James Madison, and John Jay, *The Federalist Papers*, ed. Clinton Rossiter (New York: Mentor, 1961), 84.

7. Madison, *The Federalist Papers*, 51.

8. See Madison, *The Federalist Papers*, 10.

9. Mark V. Tushnet, *Taking the Constitution Away from the Courts* (Princeton: Princeton University Press, 1999).

10. See Ronald Dworkin, *Freedom's Law* (Cambridge: Harvard University Press, 1996).

11. On the "legalization" of the Constitution, see also Stephen M. Griffin, *American Constitutionalism* (Princeton: Princeton University Press, 1996), 11–18; Steven D. Smith, *The Constitution and the Pride of Reason* (New York: Oxford University Press, 1998), 31–47.

12. See David Mayhew, *Divided We Govern* (New Haven: Yale University Press, 1991); Keith Krehbiel, *Pivotal Politics* (Chicago: University of Chicago Press, 1998).

13. The "structural constitution" extends well beyond the formal features of the constitutional text itself and includes various constitutive institutions that have grown up around that text, such as the Senate filibuster.

14. Franklin D. Roosevelt, *Public Papers and Addresses of Franklin D. Roosevelt*, ed. Samuel I. Rosenman, vol. 4 (New York: Random House, 1938): 297–98.

15. See especially, Smith, *The Constitution and the Pride of Reason* 73–151; Louis Michael Seidman and Mark V. Tushnet, *Remnants of Belief* (New York: Oxford University Press, 1996).

16. See also, Howard Gillman, *The Constitution Besieged* (Durham, N.C.: Duke University Press, 1993); Howard Gillman, "The Collapse of Constitutional Originalism and the Rise of the Notion of the 'Living Constitution' in the Course of American State-Building," *Studies in American Political Development* 11 (1997): 191; Cass R. Sunstein, *The Partial Constitution* (Cambridge: Harvard University Press, 1993), 15–194.

17. See also, Jennifer Nedelsky, *Private Property and the Limits of American Constitutionalism* (Chicago: University of Chicago Press, 1990).

18. Of course, some constitutional provisions could still be regarded as having a fairly obvious meaning, but such provisions were also relatively unlikely to be violated by government officials and require enforcement by judges (though, unfortunately, there are always exceptions). The crisis of constitutional neutrality, however, means that many people think that the Constitution has been violated but there is no agreement on how it has been violated.

19. *Marbury v. Madison*, 5 U.S. 137, 177 (1803). See also, Keith E. Whittington, *Constitutional Interpretation* (Lawrence: University Press of Kansas, 1999), 50–61.

20. *Marbury v. Madison*, 5 U.S. 137, 178 (1803).

21. See also, Jeremy Waldron, *Law and Disagreement* (New York: Oxford University Press, 1999).

22. See also, Keith E. Whittington, *Constitutional Construction* (Cambridge: Harvard University Press, 1999); Bruce Ackerman, *We the People* (Cambridge: Harvard University Press, 1991).

23. Alexander M. Bickel, *The Least Dangerous Branch* (Indianapolis: Bobbs-Merrill, 1962), 16.

II

CULTURAL CONTROVERSIES AND THE COURTS: ABORTION, HOMOSEXUALITY, CHURCH, AND STATE

4

The Culture of Death, the Higher Law, and the Courts

Charles E. Rice

On December 13, 1995, Evangeline Aka and her unborn son died thirty hours after she was admitted to Jefferson Regional Medical Center in Pine Bluff for induction of labor. In 2001, the Arkansas Supreme Court upheld the suit for the wrongful death of the unborn child brought by Philip Aka, the husband and father, against the center.[1] The Court followed a law enacted a month previously which defined a viable fetus as a person for wrongful death actions.[2] Thirty-two states permit a wrongful death action for viable fetuses. Eight of them permit the action for a nonviable fetus.[3]

Mrs. Aka could have arranged to have her unborn son killed by abortion at any time before birth. This is so because the Supreme Court of the United States has decreed that the unborn are not persons and therefore have no constitutional rights.[4] So how can the child be a person so as to be protected against death by negligence, and a nonperson so as to be subject to execution at his mother's discretion? Or how, in twenty-four states, can it be both a constitutional right to kill an unborn child by abortion and a separate crime to kill that child in the course of killing or wounding his mother?[5] One should not expect consistency in this area. But how did the law get into such a fix and how ought citizens and judges react to it? We are living through what Francis J. Canavan, S.J., called "the fag end of the Enlightenment."[6] The Enlightenment refers to the efforts by philosophers and politicians, over the past three and more centuries, to build a society as if God did not exist. One result of those efforts is the influence in our culture of the idea that the intentional infliction of death is a legitimate and optional problem-solving technique. Legalized abortion and euthanasia provide examples of this. At Columbine High School in Littleton, Colorado, Santana High School in Santee, California, and elsewhere, teenagers seek a solution for their real or imagined grievances by executing their schoolmates.[7] After the Columbine shootings, President Clinton said, "[W]e must do more to reach out to our children and teach them to express their anger and to resolve their conflicts with words, not weapons."[8] As he said this, the high altitude bombing he had ordered in Kosovo was, in the words of North American Greek Orthodox Metropolitan Archbishop Pavlos, "bombing one of Europe's oldest Christian civilizations into oblivion."[9] As the late Cardinal John O'Connor said," "[I]t is difficult to see . . . why we seem to be virtually obliterating a country."[10]

The rising popularity of the death penalty reflects that consensus that intentional killing is an optional problem solver. A popular item in the pre-Christmas toy market in 2000 was Death Row Marv, a six-inch tall doll strapped to an electric chair. His neck, shoulders, waist, and wrists are movable. He comes with "the chair, wired helmet, floorboards, and electrocuting switch." The thirteen year-olds who are the targeted buyers are told in the advertisement: "Feel the burn as the electric buzz fills the room and he starts to shake and convulse. Experience the pain as the shaking continues and his eyes start to glow bright red. Enjoy the torment."[11] This is sick. But is there not also a real-life voyeurism, sponsored by the government and the media, in the spectacle accompanying the execution of Timothy McVeigh?

FOUNDATIONS OF THE CULTURE OF DEATH

The roots of these and other indicia of what John Paul II calls the "culture of death"[12] are traceable to three premises of the Enlightenment project: secularism, relativism, and individualism.[13] The secularist premise regards the existence of God as unknowable to reason. Father Canavan rightly traces this back to William of Ockham in the fourteenth century: "It is because of him that we feel that we never really know the nature of anything and therefore cannot grasp an objective standard of good and evil."[14] The replacement religion is secular humanism, which "sees man as a product of this world—of evolution and human history—and acknowledges no supernatural purposes."[15] The Supreme Court requires that government at every level must maintain neutrality between theism and nontheism.[16] This neutrality, however, is illusory, masking a practical hostility to theistic religion and especially to Christianity. When the Supreme Court ruled in 2000 that public high school football players and fans could not be allowed voluntarily to join in a pregame prayer, Chief Justice Rehnquist observed in dissent that "the Court's opinion . . . bristles with hostility to all things religious in public life."[17] In *Boy Scouts of America v. Dale*,[18] where the Court held that New Jersey could not violate the Boy Scouts "right of expressive association" by requiring the Scouts to appoint an avowedly homosexual scoutmaster, Justice John Paul Stevens, in a dissent joined by Justices Souter, Ginsburg, and Breyer, delivered what could fairly be regarded as a disparagement of Catholic teaching: "Unfavorable opinions about homosexuals 'have ancient roots.' Like equally atavistic opinions about certain racial groups, those roots have been nourished by sectarian doctrine."[19]

With respect to relativism, American universities have no shortage of professors who are absolutely sure that they cannot be sure of anything. Relativism, of course, is absurd. The statement that all things are relative must mean that that statement itself is relative. This is nothing new. "Since Descartes declared the only thing we can be sure of is our own existence as conscious beings—*cogito ergo sum*—modern philosophers have held with him that we know nothing but our own subjective states."[20] "Descartes," observed John Paul II, "inaugurated the *great authropocentric shift in philosophy.* 'I think therefore I am' . . . is the motto of modern rationalism. All the rationalism of the last centuries can be considered a continuation and expansion of Cartesian positions."[21] Alston Chase commented on the impact of a Harvard education on the sixteen year-old freshman, Theodore Kaczynski, who later became the Unabomber:

> "Rather than inculcate traditional values [the dominant professors] sought to undermine them. Soon, 'Thou shalt not utter a value judgment' became the mantra for Harvard freshmen in dorm bull sessions as well as in term papers. Postivism triumphed. Superficially, the positivist message appeared to be an optimistic one, concerning the perfectibility of science and the inevitability of progress. It taught that reason was a liberating force and faith mere superstition: the advance of science would eventually produce a complete understanding of nature. But positivism also taught that all the accumulated non-scientific knowledge of the past including the great religions and philosophies had been at best merely an expression of 'cultural mores' and at worst nonsense. Life had no purpose and morality no justification."[22]

The jurisprudence of a relativist culture has to be some form of legal positivism. Hans Kelsen, the foremost analytical positivist of the twentieth century, adhered to "philosophical relativism," which "advocates the empirical doctrine that reality exists only within human knowledge, and that, as the object of knowledge, reality is relative to the knowing subject. The absolute, the thing in itself, is beyond human experience; it is inaccessible to human knowledge and therefore unknowable."[23] He rejected "philosophical absolutism," the "metaphysical view that there is an absolute reality, i.e., a reality that exists independently of human knowledge."[24]

Kelsen regarded law as a system of coercive rules, or "legal norms," prescribed by the legislator in accord with the basic norm of the community. The legislator decides what is that basic norm and what legal norms would be in accord with it. There is no moral restriction on the content of legal norms. "Any content whatsoever can be legal; there is no human behavior which could not function as the content of a legal norm."[25] For Kelsen, the positive law—that is, a legal norm—cannot be criticized as unjust. This is so because, for Kelsen, justice "is not ascertainable by rational knowledge at all. Rather, from the standpoint of rational knowledge, there are only interests and conflicts of interests. . . . Justice is an irrational ideal."[26] After World War II, Kelsen acknowledged that "from the point of view of the science of law, the law under the Nazi government was law. We may regret it, but we cannot deny that it was law."[27]

Enlightenment relativism has had a substantial impact on the constitutional freedoms of speech and religion:

> Eric Voegelin has written that the principles of the Enlightenment. . . "seek to enthrone the Newtonian methods of science as the only valid method of arriving at truth.". . . [This] had enormous implications for a theory of freedom of speech. The criteria by which words should be judged shifted from their moral and spiritual content to their utility as objects of science. In effect, words corresponded to scientific data. . . . [A]s in science the freedom to consider all data was the precondition to progress.
>
> When this philosophy of science was applied to constitutional jurisprudence there could be almost no constitutional justification for the regulation of speech and expression. . . . [T]here did not yet exist all the scientific tools by which we could make a definite choice between good and bad data; better to allow almost all speech than to risk eliminating what would be later found as an advancement. . . . [T]hese sentiments . . . became the . . . justification for an almost unlimited expansion of the right to freedom of expression and an almost complete purging of religion from prominent areas of public life. Religion had to be purged from public life because, with the enshrinement of 'reason' as the guide of man, the experiences which inspired religious symbolisms were deemed unscientific [and] 'irrational' because they cannot be understood in scientific categories. Religion was valuable . . . only as a visible device of social utility which compelled men to act in an orderly fashion.[28]

Individualism is the third Enlightenment premise that defines our culture. Aristotle, St. Thomas Aquinas, and others recognized that man is social by nature. Enlightenment thinkers, instead, postulated a mythical "state of nature," in which all individuals were autonomous. They were sociable rather than social by nature.[29] Those autonomous individuals formed the state through the social contract. The purpose of the social contract, for Hobbes, was to achieve security; for Locke it was to provide a common judge and to protect rights; for Rousseau, it was to carry out the general will. Two points are important here. First, the State derives its authority, in the social contract, not vertically from nature and the plan of God but horizontally from the people. "The Declaration of the Rights of Man at the end of the eighteenth century," wrote Hannah Arendt, "was a turning point in history. It meant nothing more nor less than that from then on Man, and not God's command or the customs of history, should be the source of Law."[30] Second, the human person is seen as an isolated autonomous individual having relation to others, not by his nature, but only to the extent that he chooses to consent to that relation. That is the origin of pro-choice. Planned Parenthood did not think it up.

> The theories of the social contract . . . were elaborated at the end of the 17th century (cf. Hobbes): that which would bring harmony among men was a law recognized by reason and commanding respect by an enlightened prince who incarnates the general will. Here, too, when the common reference to values and ultimately to God is lost, society will then appear merely as an ensemble of individuals placed side by side, and the contract which ties them together will necessarily be perceived as an accord among those who have the power to impose their will on others. . . . By a dialectic within modernity, one passes from the affirmation of the rights of freedom, detached from any objective reference to a common truth, to the destruction of the very foundations of this freedom. The "enlightened despot" of the social contract theorists became the tyrannical state, in fact totalitarian, which disposes of the life of its weakest members, from an unborn baby to an elderly person, in the name of a public usefulness which is really only the interest of a few.[31]

Not surprisingly, these Enlightenment premises affected the cultural and legal treatment of one of the most basic human functions, the generation of new life. Until the 1930 Anglican Lambeth Conference, no Christian denomination had ever said that contraception could ever be objectively right.[32] The Lambeth declaration of 1930 was guarded, emphasizing its "strong condemnation of the use of any methods of birth control from selfishness, luxury, or mere convenience. The conference further records its abhorrence of the sinful practice of abortion."[33] Pope Pius XI responded with his 1930 encyclical, *Casti Connibii*. Catholics, moreover, were not alone in their opposition to the new course:

> It is impossible to reconcile the doctrine of the divine institution of marriage with any modernistic plan for the mechanical regulation or suppression of human birth. The church must either reject the plain teachings of the Bible or reject schemes for the "scientific" production of human souls. Carried to its logical conclusion, the committee's report [approving the use of contraceptives] if carried into effect would sound the death-knell of marriage as a holy institution, by establishing degrading practices which would encourage indiscriminate immorality. The suggestion that the use of legalized contraceptives would be "careful and restrained" is preposterous.[34]

We cannot understand what John Paul II calls "the culture of death" except in the context of the contraceptive ethic. As John Paul observed in *Evangelium Vitae:*

> [T]he pro-abortion culture is especially strong precisely where the Church's teaching on contraception is rejected. Certainly, from the moral point of view,

> contraception and abortion are *specifically* different evils: the former contradicts the full truth of the sexual act as the proper expression of conjugal love, while the latter destroys the life of a human being. . . . But despite their differences of nature and moral gravity, contraception and abortion are often closely connected, as fruits of the same tree. It is true that in many cases contraception and even abortion are practiced under the pressure of real-life difficulties, which nonetheless can never exonerate from striving to observe God's law fully. Still, in very many other instances such practices are rooted in a hedonistic mentality unwilling to accept responsibility in matters of sexuality, and they imply a self-centered concept of freedom, which regards procreation as an obstacle to personal fulfillment. The life which could result from a sexual encounter thus becomes an enemy to be avoided at all costs, and abortion becomes the only possible decisive response to contraception. The close connection between . . . contraception and . . . abortion . . . is being demonstrated in an alarming way by the development of chemical products, intrauterine devices, and vaccines which, distributed with the same ease as contraceptives, really act as abortifacients in the very early stages of the development of the life of the new human being. . . . [T]here exists in contemporary culture a certain Promethean attitude which leads people to think that they can control life and death by taking the decisions about them into their own hands.[35]

The contraceptive mentality facilitates also the acceptance of euthanasia. Contracepting couples "claim a power which belongs solely to God: the power to decide, in *a final analysis*, the coming into existence of a human person. They assume the qualification not of being cooperators in God's creative power, but the ultimate depositories of the source of human life."[36] If one makes himself the arbiter of the "coming into existence" of human life, it will be no surprise if he makes himself also the arbiter of the ending of life, through abortion, euthanasia, and suicide. Moreover, four decades of contraception have left the United States with a diminishing pool of workers to support a growing number of the elderly. "The population is rapidly growing older and will continue to do so in the next half-century. . . . In 1900, there were 10 times as many children below 18 as there were adults over 65. By 2030, there will be slightly more people over 65 than under 18. In fact, the population is aging because both fertility and mortality rates are below their long-term historic averages. Unless fertility rates increase, the population will not become younger even after the boomers have left the scene."[37] "Euthanasia," said John Paul, "one of the more alarming symptoms of the 'culture of death,' . . . in prosperous societies, marked by [a] preoccupation with efficiency which sees . . . elderly and disabled people as intolerable and too burdensome. These people are . . . isolated by their families and by society, which are organized . . . on . . . criteria of productive efficiency, according to which a hopelessly impaired life no longer has any value."[38]

The contraceptive ethic denies the intrinsic relation between sex and procreation. In the nature of things one reason why sex is reserved for marriage, why marriage is permanent, and why marriage is heterosexual is that sex is inherently connected with procreation and the natural way to raise children is in a family founded on a permanent marriage between a man and a woman. The contraceptive society cannot coherently reject promiscuity, divorce, and homosexual activity without denying itself. And the legitimization of pornography is predictable in that society. In *Humanae Vitae*, Pope Paul VI warned that the acceptance of contraception would lead to the treatment of women as sex objects: "[M]an, growing used to the employment of anti-conceptive practices, may finally lose respect for the woman and, no longer caring for her physical and psychological equilibrium, may come to the point of considering her as a mere instrument of selfish enjoyment, and no longer as his respected and beloved companion."[39] Nor is it surprising that a contraceptive society is receptive to in vitro fertilization and other forms of laboratory production of human beings, including cloning.[40]

CONSTITUTIONAL CHANGE AS ENABLER OF THE CULTURE OF DEATH

The basic holding of *Roe v. Wade*,[41] which overturned the abortion laws of every state, is that the life of the unborn child has no constitutional protection because "the word 'person' as used in the Fourteenth Amendment, does not include the unborn." *Roe v. Wade*[42] would not have occurred without the cultural developments discussed above.[43] A contributing factor, however, was the change in the character of the Constitution that had occurred over the preceding century. In the original design of the Constitution, the government of the United States—the federal government—was limited to its delegated powers and the states possessed all governmental powers except those they had delegated to the government of the United States. Thus, in 1833 the Supreme Court held that the provisions of the Bill of Rights did not apply to the states.[44] The Civil War began a trend to centralize power in Washington, a trend which was reinforced by the Spanish-American War and economic developments in the late nineteenth century. In 1913 the Sixteenth Amendment gave Congress unlimited power to tax incomes, the Seventeenth made United States Senators popularly elected and the Federal Reserve banking system[45] took the power to regulate the currency out of the hands of Congress. The Constitution delegates to Congress the power "[t]o coin Money [and] regulate the Value thereof, and of foreign Coin."[46] After 1913 Congressmen in both houses were able to bribe the voters with promised appropriations of the tax paying voters' own money, and the value of that money would be in the hands of bankers rather than of the people and their representatives.[47] World War I, the Depression, the New Deal, World

War II, the Cold War, and the hot wars in Korea and Vietnam accelerated the centralization of power in Washington.

In light of this increase of federal power, it is not surprising that as early as the 1920s the Supreme Court began to remove constitutional obstacles to the increase of federal power and to increase its own power relative to Congress, the Executive, and especially the states. The Court interpreted the Commerce Clause expansively to confer on Congress a virtually unlimited jurisdiction to regulate activities "affecting interstate commerce."[48] In its interpretation of the General Welfare Clause, which gives Congress "Power to lay and collect Taxes, Duties, Imposts, and Excises, to pay the Debts and provide for the common Defence and general Welfare of the United States,"[49] the Court conferred on Congress an open-ended power to appropriate and, in aid of the appropriation, to regulate any private activity receiving federal funds.[40] Although the Supreme Court has more recently imposed some restrictions on the commerce power,[51] we are unlikely to see any permanent and extensive rollback of federal power in these areas.

The most significant expansion of federal and Supreme Court power, however, occurred through the Court's misinterpretation of the Fourteenth Amendment. The Supreme Court "has perverted the Fourteenth Amendment. . . . *First,* the Court has undermined the federal structure by fastening the Bill of Rights upon the states through the fraudulent doctrine of incorporation. It has further eroded state autonomy, *second,* by interpreting provisions of the Bill of Rights as if their general language embodied detailed statutory schemes, thus depriving the states of their traditional authority to define the incidents of those natural and civil rights that are due every person. *Third,* the Court has given an unwarranted imprimatur to egalitarian doctrines through. . . the equal protection clause, once again depriving the states of their traditional authority to make reasonable legislative classifications in support of legitimate public policies."[52] [Emphasis added.]

The incorporation doctrine is the reason why high school football players cannot pray before a game, why pornographic materials have virtual tenure in public libraries, and why it is nearly impossible for a public figure to recover damages when he is defamed.[53] As Judge Robert Bork put it,

> "During the nineteenth century, the Court often made up its own Constitution, most notoriously in the 1857 decision in *Dred Scott v. Sanford*. Chief Justice Roger Taney's opinion for the Court found a constitutional right, good against the federal government, to own slaves. But it wasn't until this century, when the Court invented the theory that the Bill of Rights limited states as well as the federal government, that the opportunities for judicial government exploded. The First Amendment speech clause has been made a guarantor of moral chaos, while its religion clauses have been reshaped to banish religious symbolism from public life. The Court invented a right of privacy and used it to cre-

ate a wholly specious right to abortion. The list of such incursions into the legitimate sphere of democratic control goes on and on."[54]

The old Constitution is not there any more. The division of powers between the states and a limited federal government has given way to a centralized government of practically unlimited powers. The separation of powers, and checks and balances—among the branches of the federal government is moribund as a guarantor of liberty, including the right to life. In the original design, the Constitution itself was a bill of rights. The division of powers among governments and the separation of powers among government branches erected a practical check upon abuse by any of them. Today, the right to life and other personal rights are dependent, for their existence as well as protection, on the dictates of unelected Supreme Court Justices, practically unrestrained by anything except their own wills. The Constitution was a great work, "the greatest single contribution ever made to Government as an applied science."[55] It is no reflection on the framers of that instrument that the form of government it created could not survive the collapse of its moral and cultural foundation.

A MATTER OF RECONVERSION

Technological advances, including early abortifacients by chemistry and palliative care that can be used to mask in some cases the "terminal sedation" of vegetative and other patients, are moving abortion and euthanasia beyond effective reach of the law.[56] The law is an educator. But the law also reflects the culture in which it lives. Absent a profound cultural change, there is no realistic hope of restoring full constitutional protection for the right to life, especially with respect to the unborn. Legal and political efforts to restore the right to life remain important primarily for educational purposes. But the defining contest is in culture and religion, a battleground favorable to the pro-life effort. The pro-life objective should be the reconversion of the American people to the conviction that "the laws of Nature and of Nature's God" control and that the human person has a transcendent right to life precisely because that life is a gift of God.

THE NATURAL LAW AND THE JUDGES

Where does all this leave the judge? St. Thomas Aquinas thought that "It is better 'that all things be regulated by law than left to be decided by judges.'"[57] But he also insisted that unjust laws are "acts of violence rather than laws."[58] A human law that "deflects from the law of nature" is unjust and "is no longer a law but a perversion of law."[59]

After World War II, West German courts applied natural law principles in some cases to hold some Nazi laws invalid. As Gustav Radbruch said:

> "For the soldier an order is an order; for the jurist, the law is the law. But the soldier's duty to obey an order is at an end if he knows that the order will result in a crime. But the jurist, since the last natural law men in his profession died off a hundred years or so ago, has known no such exception and no such excuse for the citizen's not submitting to the law. The law is valid simply because it is the law; and it is law if it has the power to assert itself under ordinary conditions. Such an attitude towards the law and its validity [i.e., positivism] rendered both lawyers and people impotent in the face of even the most capricious, criminal, or cruel of laws. Ultimately, this view that only where there is power is there law is nothing but an affirmation that might makes right. [Actually] law is the quest for justice . . . if certain laws deliberately deny this quest for justice (for example, by arbitrarily granting or denying men their human rights) they are null and void; the people are not to obey them, and jurists must find the courage to brand them unlawful."[60]

An appellate court at Frankfurt rejected the claim of physicians who killed prisoners in medical experiments that they were immune to prosecution because their actions were authorized by the law of the Third Reich:

> Law must be defined as an ordinance or precept devised in the service of justice [citing Radbruch]. *Whenever the conflict between an enacted law and true justice reaches unendurable proportions*, the enacted law must yield to justice, and be considered a "lawless law." . . . An accused may not justify his conduct by appealing to an existing law if this law offended against certain self-evident precepts of the natural law.[61]

What about courts in the United States? The duty of any judge, anywhere, is to apply the law. This applies to the Constitution, which is, after all, a law. Numerous provisions of the Constitution embody natural law principles, including the guarantees in the Fifth and Fourteenth Amendments against deprivation of life, liberty, or property "without due process of law"; the Fourteenth Amendment's command that no state shall "deny to any person within its jurisdiction the equal protection of the laws"; the Ninth Amendment's declaration that "the enumeration in the Constitution, of certain rights, shall not be construed to deny or disparage others retained by the people"; and the prohibition in Article I, Section 10, of the enactment by any state of an "ex post facto law or law impairing the obligation of contracts."

The judge, however, has no warrant to import his own natural law or other views of what the law ought to be into the Constitution. Justice Joseph Story, who served on the Supreme Court from 1811 to 1845, described the traditional principles that govern constitutional interpretation:

The first and fundamental rule in the interpretation of all instruments is, to construe them according to the sense of the terms, and the intention of the parties. . . . Where the words are plain and clear, and the sense distinct and perfect arising on them, there is generally no necessity to have recourse to other means of interpretation. It is only when there is some ambiguity or doubt arising from other sources that interpretation has its proper office.

In construing the Constitution of the United States, we are, in the first instance, to consider what are its nature and objects, its scope and design, as apparent from the structure of the instrument, viewed as a whole, and also viewed in its component parts. Where its words are plain, clear, and determinate they require no interpretation; and it should, therefore, be admitted, if at all, with great caution, and only from necessity, either to escape some absurd consequence, or to guard against some fatal evil. Where the words admit of two senses each of which is conformable to common usage, that sense is to be adopted which without departing from the literal import of the words, best harmonizes with the nature and objects, the scope and design, of the instrument.[62]

Judge Robert H. Bork would appear to agree. He draws a distinction, however, between the judge as citizen, who "must seek moral truth" and the judge as judge, who "must be . . . a legal positivist":

The formulation and expression of moral truths as positive law is, in our system of government, a system based on consent, a task confided to the people and their elected representatives. The judge, when he judges, must be, it is his sworn duty to be, a legal positivist. When he acts as a citizen, he, like all other citizens, must not be a legal positivist, but must seek moral truth. Otherwise, there is no way for anybody to say what the law should be, what should be enacted and what repealed. Or, at least, there would be no way other than to express one's personal interests, which no one with a differing interest is likely to find in the least persuasive.[63] The highest political truth for a judge is the Constitution of the United States, but if a statute does not contravene the Constitution, it contains the "truth" the judge must apply, because the people govern.[64]

There is no need to rely on natural law principles to reject *Roe v. Wade*. The framers of the Fourteenth Amendment did not have the status of the unborn child in mind but they intended to ensure that, "in the eyes of the Constitution, every human being within its sphere. . . from the President to the slave, is a person."[65] One purpose of the Fourteenth Amendment was to overturn the *Dred Scott* case,[66] in which the Supreme Court held that the free descendants of slaves were not citizens and said that slaves were property rather than persons.

Roe v. Wade can rightly be criticized by commentators, and disregarded by Supreme Court justices, as a misinterpretation of the Fourteenth Amendment, regardless of whether *Roe* is a violation of a higher law of natural justice. But if a formal constitutional amendment were adopted to legalize abortion, or if an amendment were adopted to repeal the Thirteenth Amendment and legalize slavery, then even a Supreme Court justice would face the choice of applying the letter of the Constitution or the higher law.

The Supreme Court addressed the natural law issue as early as 1798. In *Calder v. Bull*,[67] Justice Samuel Chase said that if a state enacted an ex post facto law, it would be invalid even if it had not been prohibited by the Constitution of the United States or the constitution of that state: "There are certain vital principles in our free Republican governments, which will . . . overrule an apparent and flagrant abuse of legislative power; as to authorize manifest injustice by positive law; or to take away that security for personal liberty, or private property, for the protection whereof the government was established. An *act* of the Legislature (for I cannot call it a law) contrary to the great first principles of the social compact, cannot be considered a rightful exercise of legislative authority."[68]

Justice James Iredell responded: "If . . . the Legislature of the Union, or the Legislature of any member of the Union, shall pass a law, within the general scope of their constitutional power, the court cannot pronounce it to be void, merely because it is in their judgment contrary to the principles of natural justice. *The ideas of natural justice are regulated by no fixed standard: the ablest and the purest men have differed upon the subject*; and all that the court could properly say, in such an event, would be, that the Legislature (possessed of an equal right of opinion) had passed an act which, in the opinion of the judges, was inconsistent with the abstract principles of natural justice."[69] [Emphasis added.]

"Chase's views, not Iredell's, . . . were in the mainstream of late eighteenth-century American jurisprudence. It is surely significant that Iredell was alone on the Court in his express criticism of Chase on this point."[70] Professor Edward S. Corwin neatly summarized the early recognition of controlling supra-constitutional principles:

> The attribution of supremacy to the Constitution on the ground solely of its rootage in popular will represents, . . . a comparatively late outgrowth of American constitutional theory. Earlier the supremacy accorded to constitutions was ascribed less to their putative source than to their supposed content, to their embodiment of essential and unchanging justice. . . . *There are*, it is predicated, *certain principles of right and justice which are entitled to prevail of their own intrinsic excellence, altogether regardless of the attitude of those who wield the physical resources of the community. Such principles were made by no human hands; indeed, if they did not antedate deity itself, they still so express its nature as to bind and control it. They are external to all Will as such and interpenetrate all Reason as such. They are eternal and immutable. In relation to such principles, human laws are, when entitled to obedience save as to matters indifferent, merely a record or transcript, and their enactment an act not of will or power but one of discovery and declaration.* The Ninth Amendment of the Constitution of the United States, in its stipulation that 'the enumeration of certain rights in this Constitution shall not prejudice other rights not so enumerated,' illustrates this theory perfectly, except that the prin-

ciples of transcendental justice have been here translated into terms of personal and private rights. The relation of such rights, nevertheless, to governmental power is the same as that of the principles from which they spring and which they reflect. They owe nothing to their recognition in the Constitution—such recognition was necessary if the Constitution was to be regarded as complete. Thus the legality of the Constitution, its supremacy, and its claim to be worshipped, alike find common standing ground on the belief in a law superior to the will of human governors.[71]

Ultimately, however, Justice Iredell's view, rejecting the supervening authority of natural law, prevailed in the American courts.[72] An enacted law, otherwise constitutional, will not be struck down, to borrow George Mason's phrase, on the ground that "[a]ll acts of legislature apparently contrary to natural right and justice are, in our laws, and must be in the nature of things, considered as void."[73] Nor should natural law arguments be used to fashion novel constructions of constitutional provisions. The how-not-to book on the use of natural law in constitutional cases was written by Justices William Brennan and Thurgood Marshall. They routinely asserted the invalidity of the death penalty, "for whatever crime and under all circumstances," on the ground that it violates the Eighth Amendment's prohibition against "cruel and unusual punishments."[74] One minor flaw in their reasoning is that the explicit recognition of the death penalty in the Fifth Amendment establishes that the Eighth Amendment, adopted at the same time as the Fifth, does not prohibit that penalty. Brennan and Marshall were not using natural law there as a standard higher than the Constitution itself. Rather, their analysis purported to interpret the Eighth Amendment. Their reconstruction of it according to their private version of natural law, in contradiction to the Fifth Amendment, was an attempted judicial amendment of the Constitution.

Judges may fairly be said to have a natural law duty, reinforced by their oath, to interpret and apply, rather than remake, the law. Laws in serious conflict with natural law principles would commonly run afoul of provisions of the Constitution itself, such those relating to due process, equal protection, and the like. A judge would have no need to resort to natural law to justify his refusal to enforce such an unconstitutional law. In principle, however, the Constitution itself and laws enacted pursuant to it are subject to the higher natural law and the law of God. If the Thirteenth Amendment were repealed and slavery were reinstituted, a judge ought to refuse to enforce it. His duty would be to apply "the laws of Nature and of Nature's God."[75] "Nevertheless, this responsibility offers no warrant for 'noninterpretive' judges to roam at large over the constitutional landscape, acting as a continuing constitutional convention in disregard of the text and the evident intent of the framers. Only rarely would a judge be entitled or obliged to rely on supraconstitutional principles to refuse to uphold or enforce an enacted law. As the German courts indicated after World War II, judges should take this step only when the conflict between the law or precedent and justice is 'intolerable' or 'unendurable.'

Such a conflict could occur with respect to *Roe v. Wade*, because that ruling authorizes the execution of a certainly innocent human being."[76]

A Supreme Court Justice need not reach that conflict with respect to *Roe v. Wade*, because the decision's denial of personhood to unborn human beings incorrectly interprets the Fourteenth Amendment. But what about a lower court judge who is required by Supreme Court precedent to authorize an abortion for a minor or to authorize her to make the pro-abortion decision?[77] When Probate Judge Randall J. Hekman, in Grand Rapids, Michigan, was faced with that problem, he refused to allow the abortion and refused to assign the case to another judge. Judge Hekman's explanation of his stand merits extended consideration:

> The idea of judges putting themselves above the law should be repugnant to all citizens. . . . But are there ever instances in which, for the sake of justice, judges should disobey the law? . . . What if the law requires a judge to order the execution of a person known to be totally innocent? What if a judge is required by law to order Jewish people to concentration camps or gas chambers because the law says that Jews are non-persons? . . . Are these not all instances in which judges should take a stand against unjust laws for the sake of doing that which is ultimately right?
>
> Can the judges in these cases escape moral culpability either by obeying the law and saying they were "just following orders" or by disqualifying themselves so that other judges without their scruples can issue the unjust decrees? Certainly the "just following orders" defense did not work to excuse the Nazi war criminals–nor should it have worked.
>
> How about disqualification? If a judge steps aside from a case knowing . . . that another judge will be found who is . . . "unbiased" and who thus will enforce unjust law, the first judge does not absolve himself from his moral dilemma. The judge who is required by law to order the execution of an innocent man and deliberately gives the case to another judge remains a knowing and willing part of the ultimate injustice. However, if the case is taken out of the judge's grasp through the appeal process, he cannot morally be faulted: he has done what he could do.[78]

When a similar problem was faced by Nebraska Juvenile Court Judge Joseph W. Moylan, he resigned from the bench rather than accept the case.[79] Others have urged recusal as the proper response of a judge in such a situation.[80]

Under Supreme Court precedents, if the judge finds that the minor is immature, he is required to authorize or refuse the abortion in light of her best interests with no regard for the interests of the unborn child. If he finds that the minor is mature he is required to authorize her to decide whether to have the abortion.[81] That sort of case could involve the judge in proximate material cooperation in what, in the moral sense, is murder. He could recuse himself. Recusal would not be necessarily immoral in objective terms, but it is hardly an adequate response to the situation from the point of view of the unborn child who presumably would regard the identity of his killers as a matter of indifference. How can the judge, who has the case, justify stepping aside so that someone else can step in to authorize the murder? Nor does the obligation of the judicial oath change this conclusion. How can an oath that one takes before God oblige him to violate a negative precept of the Commandments, which negative precepts oblige without exception?[82]

I am not suggesting that judges have a roving commission to pick and choose what laws they will obey. An unjust law, as Aquinas says, is void and not law. However, if it is unjust as contrary to human good, because it is beyond the authority of the lawgiver, oppressive, or a serious denial of equality, one may be obliged to obey it if a greater evil would result from disobedience. For a judge to substitute his opinion for that of the legislature whenever he concludes that the law is unjust, would create the evil of instability in the law. However, the second type of unjust law, says Aquinas, is the law contrary to divine good in that it would compel one to violate the divine law. Such a law, he says, must never be obeyed.[83] Many enacted laws are unjust. But a judge would have no right to depart from his normal judicial duty just because he thinks the law is unjust, unless that normal duty would require him to be a proximate material cooperator in a violation of a negative prohibition of the Commandments.[84]

There are very few situations under our Constitution where this issue could arise at the Supreme Court level. You don't need to talk about the higher law to conclude that legalized abortion violates the Fifth and Fourteenth Amendments. But it could come up at the lower level in the implementation of orders involving abortion. Death penalty cases can also raise the issue.[85] Unlike abortion, however, the death penalty is not intrinsically wrong. Recusal could be a more appropriate response in such cases.

In the pre–Civil War period, no federal judge ever refused to enforce the Fugitive Slave Act of 1793 and the fugitive slave provisions of the Compromise of 1850.[86] If one had, how would he be regarded today? Nor did any even recuse himself. The underlying issue was left for resolution in *Dred Scott*. Since 1973, the nation could have profited from the example of judges in abortion cases refusing to recuse themselves, staying in place and refusing to cooperate in the execution of the innocent. Recusal is inadequate in the abortion context because it implies that the problem is with the judge—that he or she has private scruples. Instead, the problem is with the law.

The ultimate remedy for laws that implement the culture of death is to change that culture by building a culture of life. "What is urgently called for," said John Paul[87] "is a general mobilization of consciences and a united ethical effort to activate a great campaign in support of life. All together we must build a new culture of life. . . . . The first step toward this cultural transformation consists in forming consciences with regard to the incomparable and inviolable worth of every human life."[88]

NOTES

1. *Aka v. Jefferson Hospital Association*, 2001 Arkansas LEXIS 291.
2. Arkansas, Act 1265 of 20901 (approved April 4, 2001).
3. 2001 Arkansas LEXIS 291, n. 2.

4. *Roe v. Wade*, 410 U.S. 113 (1973).

5. See *Note*, "Fetal Homicide: Woman or Fetus as Victim? A Survey of Current State Approaches and Recommendations for Future State Application," *William & Mary Law Review* 41 (2000): 1845.

6. Francis Canavan, S.J., "Commentary," *Catholic Eye* (December 10, 1987):2.

7. See *New York Times*, Mar. 6, 2001, p. A1; *New York Times* (March 7, 2001):A1.

8. *Public Papers of the Presidents of the United States* Book I (1999):587.

9. Letter of Archbishop Pavlos to President Clinton, March 23, 1999; http://members.tripod.com.

10. Cardinal John O'Connor, Column, April 29, 1999, www.ny-archdiocese.org/cardinalcolumnsarticle.cpm?id=28.

11. Michelle Malkin, "Death Row Toy Debut," *Washington Times* (August 18, 2000):A21.

12. See generally, *Evangelium Vitae* (1993).

13. See generally, Heinrich Rommen, *The Natural Law* (Saint Louis, Mo.: B. Herder Book Co., 1947), ch. IV and V.

14. Francis Canavan, S.J., "In the Midnight Hour," *National Catholic Register* (June 8, 1982):4.

15. *The Humanist*, "Statement of Purpose" (May–June 1973):3.

16. *Torcaso v. Watkins*, 367 U.S. 488 (1961); *Abington School District v. Schempp*, 374 U.S. 203 (1963).

17. *Santa Fe Independent School District v. Doe*, 120 S. Ct. 2266, 2283 (2000).

18. 147 L.Ed.2d 554 (2000).

19. 147 L.Ed.2d at 593.

20. Cornelius J. Hagerty, C.S.C., *The Problem of Evil* (North Quincy, Mass.: Christopher Publishing House, 1978), 24.

21. Pope John Paul II, *Crossing the Threshold of Hope* (New York: Alfred A. Knopf, 1994), 51–52.

22. Alston Chase, "Harvard and the Making of the Unabomber," *The Atlantic Monthly* (June 2000):41, 50.

23. Hans Kelsen, *Essays in Legal and Moral Philosophy* Ota Weinberger, ed., (Dordrecht, Germany and Boston: Reidel Publishing Company, 1973), ix.

24. Hans Kelsen, "Absolutism and Relativism in Philosophy and Politics," *American Political Science Review* 42 (1948):906.

25. Hans Kelsen, "The Pure Theory of Law, Part II," *Law Quarterly Review* 51 (1935):517, 518–19.

26. Hans Kelsen, "The Pure Theory of Law, Part I, *Law Quarterly Review* 50 (1934):474, 482.

27. Hans Kelsen, *Das Naturrecht in der politischen Theorie*, F. M. Schmoelz, ed., (1963), 148, quoted in translation in F. A. Hayek, *Law, Legislation and Liberty* vol. 2 (Chicago: University of Chicago Press, 1976), 56.

28. William Smith, "The First Amendment and Progress," *Humanitas* (Summer 1987) 1, 5–6.

29. See Heinrich Rommen, *The Natural Law* (1947), ch. V.

30. Hannah Arendt, *The Origins of Totalitarianism* (New York: Harcourt Brace & World, 1966), 290.

31. Joseph Cardinal Ratzinger, "The Problem of Threats to Human Life," *The Pope Speaks* 36 (1991):334–35.

32. See *New York Times*, August 15, 1930, 1.
33. *New York Times*, August 15, 1930, 1, col. 6.
34. *Washington Post*, editorial, March 22, 1931.
35. *Evangelium Vitae*, 13, 15.
36. Pope John Paul II, *Discourse*, September 17, 1983, in *The Pope Speaks* 28 (1983):356, 356–57.
37. Samuel H. Preston, "Children Will Pay," *New York Times Magazine*, September 29, 1996, 97
38. *Evangelium Vitae*, 64.
39. Pope Paul VI, *Humanae Vitae* (1968), 17.
40. For information, contact American Life League, P.O. Box 1350, Stafford, VA 22554, (504) 659-4171.
41. 410 U.S. 113 (1973).
42. 410 U.S. at 158.
43. See generally, Charles E. Rice, *The Winning Side* (Mishawaka, In.: St. Brendan's Institute, 2000), 11–21; 89–96.
44. *Barron v. Baltimore*, 32 U.S. (7 Pet.) 243 (1833).
45. 38 Statutes at Large, Part I, Chapter 6 (63rd Cong., 2d Sess., 1913).
46. U.S. Constitution, Article I, Section 8, cl. 5.
47. See Robert Higgs, *Crisis and Leviathan* (New York: Oxford University Press, 1987), 113.
48. See *Wickard v. Filburn*, 317 U.S. 111 (1942); *Katzenbach v. McClung*, 379 U.S. 294 (1964); *Perez v. U.S.*, 402 U.S. 146 (1971).
49. U.S. Constitution, Article I, Section 8, cl. 1
50. See *Grove City v. Bell*, 465 U.S. 455 (1984).
51. See *U.S. v. Lopez*, 514 U.S. 549 (1995); *Printz v. U.S.* 521 U.S. 898 (1997); *U.S. v. Morrison*, 120 S. Ct. 1740 (2000),
52. James E. Bond, *No Easy Walk to Freedom* (Westport, Conn.: Praeger, 1997), 252.
53. See discussion in Charles E. Rice, *The Winning Side* (2000), 47–53.
54. Robert H. Bork, "Our Judicial Oligarchy," *First Things*, (November 1996):21, 23.
55. Viscount James Bryce, *The Study of American History* (Westport, Ct.: Greenwood Press, 1971, c1922), 53.
56. See Charles E. Rice, *The Winning Side* (2000), 59–74, 81–88.
57. St. Thomas Aquinas, I, II, Q. 95, Art. 1, quoting Aristotle, *Rhetoric*, i, l.
58. St. Thomas Aquinas, I, II, Q. 96, art. 4.
59. St. Thomas Aquinas, I, II, Q. 95, art. 2.
60. Quoted in Ernst von Hippel, "The Role of Natural Law in the Legal Decisions of the German Federal Republic," *Natural Law Forum* 4, 1959:106, 110.
61. von Hippel, "The Role of Natural Law" at 111 (emphasis added); see Charles E. Rice, "Some Reasons for a Restoration of Natural Law Jurisprudence," *Wake Forest Law Review* (1989):539, 555.
62. Joseph Story, *Commentaries on the Constitution of the United States* (1891), Book III, 400-44; Story's "Rules of Interpretation" comprise chapter V (397–456) of Book III of his *Commentaries*.
63. Robert H. Bork, "Natural Law and the Constitution," *First Things* (March 1992):16, 19.
64. Hadley Arkes, Russell Hittinger, William Bentley Ball, and Robert Bork, "Natural Law and the Law: An Exchange," *First Things* (May 1992) 45, 53; see also the criticism

of the Bork position in Russell Hittinger, "Liberalism and the American Natural Law Tradition," *Wake Forest Law Review* 25 (1990):429; William B. Ball, "The Tempting of Robert Bork: What's a Constitution without Natural Law?" *Crisis*, (June 1990):28; and Hadley Arkes, *Beyond the Constitution* (1990).

65. Cong. Glob, 37th Congress, 2d Session 1449 (1862) (Sen. Sumner); see discussion in brief, *amicus curiae*, Catholics United for Life, in *Webster v. Reproductive Health Services*, 492 U.S. 490 (1989), 14.

66. *Dred Scott v. Sanford*, 60 U.S. 393 (1857).

67. 3 U.S. 386 (1798).

68. 3 U.S. at 387–89.

69. 3 U.S. at 398–99.

70. Stephen B. Presser, *Recapturing the Constitution* (Washington, D.C.: Regnery Publishing, Inc., 1994), 121.

71. Edward S. Corwin, "The Higher Law Background of American Constitutional Law," *Harvard Law Review* 42 (1928):149, 152–53.

72. See *Dred Scott v. Sanford*, 60 U.S. (19 How.) 393 (1857); see discussion in Charles E. Rice, *50 Questions on the Natural Law* 2d ed. (San Francisco: Ignatius Press, 1999), 385–89.

73. *Robin v. Hardaway*, 2 Va. 109, 114 (1772).

74. See *Gregg v. Georgia*, 428 U.S. 153, 229, 231 (1976) (dissenting opinions of Brennan and Marshall).

75. Declaration of Independence (1776).

76. Charles E. Rice, *50 Questions on the Natural Law* 2d ed. (1999), 121.

77. See, *Planned Parenthood v. Casey*, 505 U.S. 833 (1992).

78. Randall J. Hekman, "Judging: By What Standard?", *Christian Legal Society Quarterly* 4(1983):19, 19–21.

79. Joseph W. Moylan, "A Pretty Drastic Step," *The Rescuer*, August–November 1994, 4, 5.

80. See Richard B. Saphire, "Religion & Rescusal," *Marquette Law Review* (1998):351; see also *Los Angeles Daily Journal*, November 8, 1995, 1, recounting the refusal of Judge John T. Noonan Jr., of the 9th Circuit U.S. Court of Appeals, to a request that he recuse himself from an abortion case on account of his Catholic faith. See also John H.Garvey and Amy V. Coney, "Catholic Judges in Capital Cases," *Marquette Law Review* 81 (1998): 303 .

81. See *Planned Parenthood v. Casey*, 505 U.S. 833 (1992).

82. Pope John Paul II, *Veritatis Splendor* (1993), 52.

83. St. Thomas Aquinas, I, II, Q. 96, Article 4.

84. See the discussion of formal and material cooperation in Charles E. Rice, *The Winning Side* (2000), 229–31.

85. See John H. Garvey and Amy V. Coney, "Catholic Judges in Capital Cases," *Marquette Law Review* (1998):303.

86. See discussion in Charles E. Rice, *50 Questions on the Natural Law* 2d ed., (1999), 28–29.

87. *Evangelium Vitae*.

88. Pope John Paul II, *Evangelium Vitae*, 95–96.

5

Who Owns the Right to Privacy?

Jeremy Rabkin

The right to privacy has a bad name among social conservatives. That is entirely understandable: very extreme abuses of law and policy have been justified over the past thirty years in the name of privacy. Nonetheless, conservatives have a stake in preserving (or restoring) broad constitutional protection for private life. In truth, conservatives have more of a stake in such protection than their political opponents.

Yet many conservatives have been so focused on the errors of liberal activist courts that they have come to think the best role for judges is the most modest and deferential. To take this view is to let constitutional debate turn exclusively on the errors of liberal activists. It is a view that assumes the Constitution has no particular relevance to the great social controversies sometimes called the "culture war."

I think this view is unwise at many levels. Conservatives ought to be arguing not so much for minimalist understandings of the Constitution as for reasonable understandings. And protection for private life is one of the central aims of the Constitution—at least as the Constitution was understood before the upheavals of the 1960s. Conservatives should be trying to conserve the better elements of our constitutional heritage.

WHY PRIVACY?

The right to privacy achieved notoriety with the Supreme Court's 1973 ruling in *Roe v. Wade*,[1] where privacy was held to be the grounding for a newly discovered right to abortion. But recognizing a right to privacy was not a necessary premise of the ruling in *Roe*. It was surely not a sufficient premise.

Whatever else a right to privacy may encompass, no one argues that it allows one person to kill another whenever the crime is perpetrated in a private setting. No one argues—in general—that a right to privacy would constrain government from protecting human life. The ruling in *Roe* rests on the Court's assertion that in the first and second trimesters of a pregnancy, the developing child is not human life—or at least, not human life worthy of legal protection. The Court reasoned that since there is dispute about the moral status of the fetus, government may not endorse any one theory of when life begins. This is, of course, a nonsequitur: if it were true that controversy disqualified government from acting, we would have vastly less government (and vastly less taxation to pay for what remained). Privacy was not the ground of this decision but at most a convenient label slapped onto the conclusion.

Even at the time, many scholars who supported the outcome of *Roe* conceded that Justice Blackmun's opinion was, in its own terms, unconvincing. Some scholars argued that the right to abortion should be justified instead on the grounds that restrictions on abortion could only be justified by theological dogma and the Constitution (they argued) prohibits government from enacting sectarian dogma into law. Others argued that full equality for women requires that they not be burdened with an unwanted pregnancy, since men are never burdened in this way. Therefore, some scholars argued, restrictions on abortion should be seen as violations of the Equal Protection guarantee in the Fourteenth Amendment. These arguments may not be much more convincing than those in *Roe*. These alternative arguments certainly do not convince me. But it remains notable that when proponents of abortion rights tried to come up with better arguments for *Roe,* they shrugged off the right to privacy and tried to rest their claims on altogether different grounds.

The Court itself experienced great difficulties in sticking with the privacy argument in *Roe*. Justice Blackmun's opinion in *Roe* had played on the association between privacy and intimacy. Thus, it tried to ground its conclusions about abortion on the Court's 1965 ruling in *Griswold v. Connecticut,*[2] where a right to privacy had been invoked to invalidate a state law prohibiting the sale of birth control devices even to married couples. The majority opinion in *Griswold* dwelled on the special intimacy of marital relations.

Yet a divided Court subsequently declined to extend this reasoning to invalidate laws against homosexual intimacy. The Court was indeed criticized for betraying its own doctrine in this later case, *Bowers v. Hardwick.* [3] But if this ruling betrayed *Roe*'s understanding of privacy, so did the uniform failure of federal courts to take up constitutional challenges to laws against private use of narcotics or against the use of medicines unapproved by the FDA.[4]

On the other hand, the Court's handling of other cases implied that *Roe*, itself, was not really about intimacy. Within a few years, the right to privacy was extended from a right to use contraceptives to a right to advertise their sale in public media.[5] By 1980, four justices of the Supreme Court were prepared to affirm that the right to privacy meant not only the right to seek an abortion but the right to have taxpayers fund the operation.[6] The doctrine had drifted far from any grounding in intimate relations.

Protection for intimacy, it turned out, was never much more than a convenient rhetorical ploy. The same four justices who held that government was required to fund abortion were, in other cases, quite insistent that government could not fund religious schools. Funding of religious schools, they argued, would compromise the government's obligation to maintain a neutral stance toward religion. Funding of religious schools, they claimed, would imply an endorsement of religion and government (they insisted) must never act in any way that might be seen as endorsing religion. Yet the same justices who voted to enforce neutrality with a demanding interpretation of the First Amendment's Establishment clause were also in favor of carving out special exemptions from otherwise valid law for favored religious minorities—such as the Amish[7] and followers of the Indian Peyote cult.[8]

These twists and turns are not so arbitrary as they seem, however. Stripped of lawyerly manipulation of precedents—which are too contrived and arbitrary in these cases to take seriously—liberal justices have followed a rather consistent impulse. They opposed even indirect aid to religion out of solicitude for those with unusual religion or no religion. They favored solicitude for unusual religions for the same reason. And they demanded public funding for abortion for the same reason—so that those who seek or those who favor abortion should not feel excluded.

Weird as it seems, there is even some logic in the Court's 1996 ruling in *Romer v. Evans*,[9] which declined to overrule *Hardwick* but nonetheless held that Colorado could not prohibit localities from adopting gay rights measures. On its face, the ruling seems to say that Colorado can, if it so chooses, impose criminal penalties for engaging in sexual intimacies with partners of the same sex, but the state cannot deny homosexuals the benefit of special antidiscrimination laws that would constrain the conduct of strangers. Gay rights measures typically ban a very wide range of private practices, including decisions about apartment rentals. So the ruling in *Evans* seems to say that the state remains free to regulate what people do at night in their bedrooms but must not give private landlords—or perhaps even private renters, seeking roommates—the right to choose who can share those bedrooms. The state, itself, can intrude into the most intimate practices, but it can't allow private individuals to make personal choices about the people they prefer to deal with.

Here, too, there is an underlying logic. Protecting intimacy, per se, was not really a central concern of the Court, but ensuring equality has been an overriding concern for many justices. To the majority of the justices, denying homosexuals the benefits of special state regulation in *Evans* seemed an intolerable injustice, because an affront to civic equality. Allowing state regulation of sexual intimacy might seem hard on homosexuals, but constraining state regulation in general was not the Court's priority.

One does not have to dwell on the tedious prose and twisted legal constructions of the Court's opinions to see the point. Equality is a very powerful rallying cry, especially for the political left. One might say it is the defining passion of the left. If you are concerned to equalize, you need a very powerful state. If you spend too much time worrying over privacy, you will hobble the state—and constrain the pursuit of equality.

That is the underlying logic. It is preached in one form or another in the best law schools and the best universities and on the editorial pages of the best newspapers. And many Supreme Court justices have lacked the self-confidence or the inclination to resist the trend of progressive opinion.

The same trend is certainly apparent in the Court's handling of cases that invoke the First Amendment to protect private groups. In the early 1960s, the Court held that southern states could not inquire into the membership of civil rights organizations like the National Association for the Advancement of Colored People (NAACP), as this would have a chilling effect on the ability of such organizations to recruit new members and thus constrain their capacity to engage in public advocacy.[10] But this right of free association seemed to disappear in the 1980s, when the Court held—in three different cases over the course of a decade—that states could prohibit private organizations from excluding women.[11] The justices did not seem to recognize any contradiction. They solemnly affirmed that forcing the Jaycees to admit women would not at all affect the advocacy aims of the organization—to promote the business concerns of young men.

The arguments in particular cases might seem strained, but again the overriding logic was clear. Protecting private organizations was good when it served the cause of equality. When the cause of equality seemed threatened by private membership practices, then protecting private organizations was bad. The pattern is very easy to follow once one grasps the controlling priorities.

The same impulse has carried the Court through a seemingly twisted trail on other First Amendment issues. Since the mid-1960s, the Court has sought to ensure broad First Amendment protection for pornography.[12] Even the use of four-letter words in public places—such as courtrooms—was thought to merit Free Speech protection, since "one man's vulgarity is another's lyric."[13] Even topless dancing, in the view of some justices, should receive First Amendment protection, since nudity is a form of expression.[14] Distinguished commentators endorsed such rulings on the ground that government should not impose the moral preferences of the majority—that is, make the minority of those who enthused over such fare feel excluded or rejected.[15]

When feminists began to demand speech controls, however, the Court took a different tack. The Court has struggled over the past two decades to refine and apply feminist doctrine on sexual harassment. The doctrine was grafted, by judicial fiat, onto civil rights legislation of the 1960s, which had been enacted in the prefeminist era when no one had any such idea. By the 1980s, the Court had come to think that lewd or offensive expression could create a hostile environment and the government could therefore hold private employers accountable for allowing it.[16] Even off-color banter—which is quite remote from pornographic depictions—may create a hostile environment in the view of many courts and commentators. So the Supreme Court has sanctioned broad pressure on employers to constrain the speech of employees.[17]

But again, this is not as contradictory as it looks. The Court had already sanctioned broad constraints on the speech of employers in the context of labor disputes. It has also sanctioned draconian curbs on the protest activity of anti-abortion protesters.[18] Free speech is good when it is identified with the cause of equality. When it is seen to conflict with regulation for the sake of equality, free speech protection can be readily reduced. Now, some of the same commentators who defended broad free speech claims in other contexts tell us that Congress must have the power to suppress speech in advance of elections. This is called campaign finance reform—and must be constitutional because it serves the cause of equality.

Conservatives often look at this pattern and suspect—or openly protest—that equality has become a code-word for sheer moral relativism. But this complaint, understandable as it is, misses the larger point. It may well be true that equality is invoked in ways that are inconsistent and confusing. It may well be true that those who wield this slogan often seek to undermine traditional moral standards for a whole host of reasons, some of which are only indirectly related to the cause of equality.

But the fact remains that equality is a powerful slogan. And people who dismiss it as a plea for moral relativism are blinding themselves to the depth of moral passion that the slogan can inspire. Whatever one might say about moral relativism as a philosophic theory, the facts of human nature are rather stubborn. Most people want to feel inspired by great causes, at least at some times and to some extent. Most people are easily stirred to indignation at what they see as wrongful. People who profess to be champions of tolerance or equality are at least as ready as others to be inspired by great causes—and stirred to indignation against those who resist them. Equality is the most powerful of the slogans that animates progressive visions of a properly engineered society. Equality stirs a very great deal of moralistic passion and energetic political advocacy.

I do not at all think that egalitarian passion must sweep everything before it. Quite clearly, that has not happened. The United States is less stirred—or less intimidated—by egalitarian rhetoric than most other Western countries. There is no significant socialist party here. There has, on the contrary, been a great resurgence of respect for free markets. Again, to an extent that is unmatched in any other Western country, Americans show much underlying respect for religion and religion remains in many ways a conservative force in America.

But if one wants to conceive contemporary political struggles as a "culture war," one must acknowledge that equality is a powerful slogan for liberal advocates. And their opponents must have equally broad slogans. Privacy or private life are powerful and should be. They summon much of what makes conservatives, in particular—and large portions of the American electorate, generally—suspicious of an overreaching state.

The Supreme Court's ruling in *Boy Scouts of America v. Dale* illustrates both the promise of this perspective—and the deplorable hesitancy of the Court's current approach to implementing it.

NOT JUST SEX: THE *DALE* CASE

The facts of the *Dale* case are straightforward. James Dale had long experience in scouting. In college, he became active in a gay rights organization and his activism was a subject of newspaper attention. A local chapter of the Boy Scouts decided this was enough to disqualify him from serving as a Scoutmaster. Dale charged discrimination and the Supreme Court of New Jersey held that the Boy Scouts had indeed violated a state law prohibiting discrimination on the basis of sexual orientation (among other things) in public accommodations. The U.S. Supreme Court subsequently held that the New Jersey ruling was in violation of BSA's First Amendment right to "freedom of association."

In fact, the Court could only summon five justices for this ruling and the four dissenters were quite insistent on the wrongness of the majority's ruling. For its part, the majority opinion was, if not quite apologetic in tone, at least very narrowly drawn. In fact, it is so narrow that it might seem designed to cover only this one special case.

Like previous rulings on freedom of association, the majority opinion in *Dale* identifies two strands of precedent supporting this right. One strand, says the Court, is rooted in protection for intimacy—citing *Griswold*. The other rests on First Amendment protection for the organizational needs of advocacy groups. The majority opinion pronounced the first set of precedents irrelevant to this case and relied instead on the free speech cases. But the reasoning is strangely blinkered on both lines of doctrine.

If one treats *Griswold* as the foundation for the right to privacy (as the *Dale* court does), then it seems natural to associate privacy with sex. But *Griswold* itself claimed to be elaborating or extending an existing body of precedents, which it grouped together under the then somewhat novel phrase, "right to privacy." None of the cases cited in *Griswold*, however, were about sexual practices. The idea of constitutional protection for sexual practices may have been a novelty of that case. But the notion that the state cannot interfere in broad categories of private decision—that was not new at all.

Among the cases cited for this proposition in *Griswold* were two from the 1920s. One of these precedents was *Meyer v. Nebraska,*[19] overturning a Nebraska law that prohibited the teaching of the German language. The other was *Pierce v. Society of Sisters,*[20] which sought to require all children to attend public schools—with the effect (and intention) of outlawing Catholic schools and other forms of private, religious education. At the time they were decided, these rulings were not controversial. *Pierce* was a unanimous decision, while only Justice Holmes dissented in *Meyer* (and not with great conviction). These cases were not controversial because they reflected the standard view of the Fourteenth Amendment at that time—that it was intended to establish certain broad and general limits on the regulatory power of the state.

Nobody pretended that schools were intimate places or that dealings between teachers and students in the classroom were especially intimate relations. Rather, the Court emphasized the broad powers of parents to determine the proper education and upbringing for their children and declaimed against the notion that the state could assert open-ended powers to constrain and direct the upbringing of children.

In truth, even the Court's expressed concerns about family life seem to have been a matter of rhetorical embellishment. The Court in that era was perfectly willing to question laws relating to labor practices and pricing practices of commercial firms. The Court took for granted that the Constitution provided broad protection for private life—for private property and private contracts, as much as for private associations. It is not clear that the result in *Meyer* and *Pierce* would have been any different if the Court had simply focused on the disputed statutes as arbitrary interference with the right of private individuals to freely contract with others for services—even if the services had not involved the teaching of young people.

Since that time, we have grown accustomed to a much larger role for government in regulating economic transactions. It may no longer be politically feasible for the Court to resurrect the full range of restrictive doctrines with which it sought to constrain economic regulation before the 1930s. But whatever may be true for commercial firms in the wider economy, nonprofit social organizations still have considerable claims to constitutional protection from overreaching government. The decision in *Dale* does little to advance such claims, however.

Even the First Amendment argument invoked by the majority in *Dale* was set out in very narrow terms. The majority found that the Boy Scouts regarded opposition to homosexuality as central to the point of view they wished to promote. The majority opinion by Chief Justice Rehnquist thus reasoned that requiring the Boy Scouts to admit homosexuals would undermine their capacity to advocate their viewpoint. Putting the argument in these terms invited the dissenters to protest—as they did—that the Boy Scouts had actually shied away from discussing homosexuality and James Dale might well have participated as a scoutmaster without undermining the general advocacy position of the Boy Scouts.

Yet all of this wrangling is surely beside the point. The Boy Scouts should have the right to determine their own membership—period. It shouldn't be up to judges to decide which membership rules would or wouldn't affect the organization's advocacy. If the government can tell the Boy Scouts to admit homosexuals, it can just as well tell them to admit female scouts. Female scouts certainly have aptitude for most of the same activities pursued by the Boy Scouts. The whole history of the Girl Scouts proves the point. But Co-ed Scouts wouldn't be Boy Scouts. Maybe Co-ed Scouts would be better. But why is this a decision for the government rather than the Boy Scouts, themselves?

Even if one views the issue with a focus on free speech, it is silly to pretend that free speech can be adequately protected by safeguarding actual advocacy. No one argues that free speech protection extends only to immediate political advocacy, addressed to voters in the next election. Everyone agrees that free speech protection should extend to the writings of Plato and Aristotle and John C. Calhoun—as to Darwin and Einstein and all of their critics, however remote they may seem from contemporary political debate. We cannot adequately protect political advocacy without safeguarding a broader right to receive and exchange information and learning on all subjects.

In fact, we can't adequately protect political advocacy without protecting the institutions that preserve and renew learning in a broad range of fields. Surely the First Amendment is relevant to universities and research institutions. It is also relevant to private book clubs. If the government can tell the Boy Scouts whom to admit to membership—whenever courts are satisfied that such compulsory membership does not diminish the ability to advocate their views—then it is equally plausible for the government to tell these other organizations which people they can and can't exclude. Perhaps advanced degrees in relevant subjects are not that necessary, nor knowledge of foreign languages, and so on.

The point isn't that we will slide down a slippery slope to totalitarian control without constitutional limitations. The point is simply that government intrusion in these areas, even of a relatively modest level, will already trigger First Amendment concerns. Free speech means more than the last words in a tirade. It means the whole background of private inquiry and discussion that makes it possible to have serious public debate. At some point, however, one must wonder whether it makes sense to view the issue in terms of free speech rather than a more general right of private association—without having to trace out any direct line of connection between the internal life of the organization and its public advocacy.

The same sort of argument applies to constitutional guarantees of religious freedom. The Boy Scouts claim that their organizational purpose requires them to exclude professed atheists as well as self-declared homosexuals. In previous litigation, the exclusion of atheists has also been challenged. Some commentators have argued that the Scout policy on homosexuality also has a religious basis and might thus be protected under the Free Exercise clause of the First Amendment. This argument was not pressed in *Dale* and therefore not addressed by the Supreme Court. But it is worth thinking through, because it raises similar problems to those we have seen with the free speech argument.

The central problem is that, just as they don't really set themselves up as an advocacy organization, the Boy Scouts don't set themselves up as a religious institution. The Scouting movement has recruited tens of millions of boys from a great variety of religious faiths. It does not try to convert them to the same faith. It does not endorse, much less try to inculcate, any detailed or specific theology. For the Boy Scouts to claim an exemption from nondiscrimination laws on religious grounds, they might well have to position themselves as something they really are not or have not wanted to be.

I am skeptical, in fact, that any entity, even a particular religious sect, should be able to claim a special exemption from otherwise valid laws on the grounds that the Free Exercise clause of the First Amendment guarantees such special exemptions. The Court flirted briefly with this notion but seems to have abandoned it now. Among the many difficulties with such exemptions is that they require courts to inquire whether a particular religious faith is sincerely held by those claiming the exemption and whether that faith really does or does not require such an exemption. This is not a proper role for judges. But it is reasonable to inquire whether government has any business imposing certain constraints on private organizations.

The Court in *Pierce* did not think to inquire whether Catholics had a particular need for special Catholic schools. The Court in *Meyer* did not think to inquire whether the students in that particular school (which happened to be serving a German Menonite community, where students were taught to pray in German) had a particular need for instruction in German language. The Court disdained to be dragged into haggling for particular excuses. It put the burden on the government to show that it had any need to intrude on private education.

After all, the situation of the Boy Scouts is not unusual. The Scouts affirm certain very general religious tenets without claiming to be a religious movement. What should we say about the Salvation Army? Or the Young Mens Christian Association? Must they claim to be sectarian organizations or actual churches to qualify for broad protection against government interference? What if they want to limit their leadership to professing Christians? Is it the government's place to say this is unnecessary?

The Supreme Court could do a lot more to protect private organizations. It would have to develop its doctrines in more ambitious terms. But a start in this direction is not politically infeasible. In the past decade, the Court has resurrected broad doctrines of federalism—even in the teeth of egalitarian clamor. It is not bringing back the severe limits on federal authority enforced before the 1930s but it is indicating a willingness to defend some lines, even when Congress claims that discrimination requires a federal response. The Court could do the same for private organizations, as it has now begun to do for state governments.

But would conservatives be right to cheer? I think they would.

NOT LIBERAL ACTIVISM OF THE RIGHT

Conservatives should first stop pretending that opposition to liberal activism requires them to embrace a populist outlook that opposes all constitutional constraints. The Constitution is about constraints on government. Conservatives who think their quarrel is with the Constitution itself should probably stop thinking about American politics and turn their thoughts toward emigration.

Populist rhetoric is fun but it is a bit silly for social conservatives. We are not the majority. When Rev. Jerry Falwell tried to sell his proposals under the banner of the Moral Majority, he provoked quite hostile reactions from most Americans—even though most of the individual points in his program (with the arguable exception of controls on abortion) had broad support. Americans recoil from moral authoritarianism in politics. Falwell himself bowed to the prevailing tide of opinion when he renamed his advocacy organization the Liberty Foundation. When Rev. Pat Robertson subsequently organized the Christian Coalition, he did not claim to represent the majority and focused much of his advocacy on protecting the concerns of religious conservatives as a beleaguered minority.

No group should try to read its own policy agenda into the Constitution, merely because it would be convenient to have courts impose that agenda. But calling for broader constitutional protection of private organizations is not a call for open-ended judicial activism. It is certainly no more activist than many other doctrines that now have wide support—even among conservatives.

Thus, almost everyone now seems comfortable with the notion that courts will enforce guarantees of free speech and religious freedom against overreaching by state and local governments. Yet the First Amendment, where these guarantees appear, is plainly addressed to Congress. ("Congress shall make no law . . . abridging the freedom of speech. . . .") The Supreme Court has long held that the Fourteenth Amendment imposes similar restrictions on state and local governments. But the actual language of the Fourteenth Amendment does not say a word about religious freedom or freedom of speech. Where regulation by state and local governments is concerned, it is no more activist to defend private organizations on broader terms of private rights of association than it is to defend them on the basis of religious freedom or free speech.

It was only in the 1960s that the Supreme Court began to treat guarantees of the Bill of Rights as directly applicable to the states through some mysterious process of incorporation into the Fourteenth Amendment. For nearly a full century before the 1960s this doctrine was repeatedly urged on the Court—and rejected by almost all justices. What earlier justices thought was that the Fourteenth Amendment offered a broad guarantee against arbitrary interference with private life. The justices were not agreed on the meaning of the Fourteenth Amendment guarantee of "the privileges and immunities of citizens"—as even the drafters of the Fourteenth Amendment seem to have been rather hazy on the meaning of this phrase.

The guarantee against deprivation of "life, liberty, and property without due process" was thus made to carry meanings that might have been intended for this prior clause. Since the 1930s, the following clause, guaranteeing "equal protection of the laws," has often been invoked by the Court to deal with claims that might, in earlier times, have been addressed under the due process clause. Even if technical doctrines have shifted over time, it is not a recent or strained notion that the Fourteen Amendment provides broad protections against state interference with private life.

At the same time, we must acknowledge that original intent cannot, by itself, provide the proper answer to all constitutional questions. Even Judge Robert Bork, one of the strongest advocates for a jurisprudence of original intent, acknowledges that today's Supreme Court could not now return to the original intent of the Commerce clause. Since the 1930s, a great mass of federal legislation has been enacted under liberalized interpretations of the congressional power to regulate commerce among the states. As Bork concedes, no Court would dare to strike all of this down, nor would it be proper to put the country through such a court-ordered upheaval.

Once one acknowledges that some changes are here to stay, however, it is necessary to think about complementary adjustments. Justices Scalia and Thomas, for example, are the two most ardent champions of original intent jurisprudence on the current Court. They are also the most insistent advocates of the doctrine that government should be forbidden to impose racial preferences, even for the sake of affirmative action. This doctrine is not quite in accord with original intent. Yet it may still be an entirely justifiable response to a constitutional landscape now transformed by other departures from original intent. In a world where government is permitted much broader regulatory authority than the Framers intended, it is reasonable to make more room for countering protections.

Perhaps what most disturbs skeptics is that claims to constitutional protection for private association are so open-ended that they are an invitation to wide-ranging judicial activism. But this concern shows how much the whole subject has been thrown into confusion by the overreaching of contemporary public policy—and the passivity of contemporary judicial doctrine.

Government certainly must control many kinds of private activity. Controlling private conduct is, after all, the central purpose of government. Core government responsibilities—protecting against threats to life and health and property—don't become private matters, beyond the reach of the law, simply because they arise in private settings. A violent assault in a private home or a small prayer chapel is as much a crime as one that occurs on a public street.

But the law already limits many types of regulation to public settings, where transactions occur among relative strangers. Laws against "discrimination" are a prime example. No civil rights law seeks to control invitations to private dinner parties. The law invoked against the Boy Scouts in *Dale* covered public accommodations. Virtually all laws against discrimination are framed in this way, at least when safeguarding the availability of general services to the public. The precise issue in *Dale* was whether New Jersey could define the Boy Scouts—with troops that are often rather small and often meet in private homes—as a public accommodation.

The general issue is whether laws that don't apply universally can be applied arbitrarily—allowing some parts of society to shelter under statutory exemptions or limitations while exposing others to direct regulatory controls. Prohibitions on employment discrimination generally exempt churches from their jurisdiction. What gives government the constitutional authority to offer exemptions to religious bodies while denying such exemptions to other private organizations?

Given decades of acceptance for broad regulation of business activity, reasonable constitutional doctrine in this area may have to distinguish nonprofit organizations from commercial firms. Perhaps the obvious bright line is whether a particular organization has been recognized as a charitable or educational institution, qualifying for tax-exempt status. Reasonable people may have reasonable disagreements about where to draw the line in particular cases. But it is hardly an extreme or unreasonable claim that the internal affairs of private organizations—however we define this category—deserve general protection against arbitrary governmental interference. At the least, government should be required to meet some showing of a compelling public interest before it can interfere with the membership practices of private organizations.

For courts to enforce this sort of protection requires no more activist initiative than courts already exercise in areas of constitutional law where the judicial role is widely accepted. It is no more, for example, than courts now do when facing free speech challenges to regulations of protest activity. Under current First Amendment doctrine, courts allow government to regulate the time, place, and manner of protest rallies or marches, but only if such regulation is applied in a reasonably even-handed manner and justified by compelling public concerns. What these qualifications should mean in particular cases is often a matter of reasonable dispute; but courts have the last word in such disputes.

In fact, the question is not whether courts can properly settle every possible dispute about the associational rights of private organizations. Few organizations are likely to litigate these issues because few organizations have the resources to pursue determined constitutional challenges. The question is whether the Supreme Court will give some encouragement or reinforcement to the general notion that private organizations deserve at least some presumption of constitutional protection for their own internal practices. The general idea is already in statutory law and in public consciousness—which is why nondiscrimination laws focus on public accommodations and do not try to reach hiring practices of religious institutions. The issue, then, is whether the Court will give more dignity or authority to a protective impulse that already has considerable recognition.

The Constitution is not just a rule for courts but a framework for political life. Some provisions—like the Second Amendment guarantee of the right to bear arms—have had great impact on contemporary political debate, with almost no assistance from court decisions. Appeals to the right of private association have much political promise on their own. They don't need elaborate judicial monitoring to have an effect. But they would probably carry more weight if given some formal endorsement by the Supreme Court. And the majority opinion in *Dale* was, at the least, a missed opportunity to provide that kind of endorsement.

Can conservative advocates advance this appeal in contemporary political debate? I certainly hope so. I do not see anything in our own beliefs that should inhibit us from trying to advance this line of constitutional argument. Unlike populist appeals to the claims of transient majorities, an appeal to the rights of private groups is not something conservatives need to regard with misgivings or ambivalence. Appeals to the rights of private organizations do not rest on mere tactical concessions or compromises with contemporary liberal opinion. Arguments about the rights of private groups are not inherently related to nominalism or relativism or individualism.

The firmest and best ground for recognizing the rights of private organizations is inherently conservative: some of the most important aims of social life—such as inculcating high moral and religious standards—cannot be adequately performed by government. Certainly, in a large and diverse country, government faces real limits on its capacity to inspire and direct the conscience of individual citizens. That is, I would think, a simple statement of fact and not an ideological premise. So private organizations are particularly important, because they can still do a good deal where government cannot.

This is hardly a new or recent insight. In medieval Europe, the great historic struggles between Church and State were above all about the Church's claim to govern itself without political interference from the holders of state power. If we are a going to use terms like "culture war," we should recall the precise origin of the term, Bismarck's *Kulturkampf* was precisely about whether the Prussian state could interfere with the internal organization of the Catholic Church in Prussia. Bismarck's policy, designed to impose modern "culture" on a "foreign" Church, was widely supported by German liberals of the 1870s. But the Church successfully resisted this attack by appealing to older and deeper notions about the necessary limits of state authority. It was an appeal to some of the oldest and noblest traditions of Western political life. And it remains a pertinent appeal in contemporary American politics, where efforts to extend state control are inspired by a secular religion of egalitarian moralism.

One can say, without exaggeration, that the U.S. Constitution was designed to prevent government from launching a culture war against churches and other private organizations. Conservatives should have no difficulty in embracing this understanding. They need only have confidence in their own principles to do so. But it would be nice to have more help from the Supreme Court.

NOTES

1. *Roe v. Wade*, 410 U.S. 113 (1973).
2. *Griswold v. Connecticut*, 381 U.S. 479 (1965).
3. *Bowers v. Hardwick*, 478 U.S. 186 (1986).
4. See the chapter on drugs in David A. J. Richards, *Sex, Drugs, Death and the Law*, (Totewa, N.J.: Rowman & Littlefield, 1982).
5. *Carey v. Population Services International*, 431 U.S. 678 (1977).
6. *Maher v. Roe*, 432 U.S. 464 (1977).
7. *Wisconsin v. Yoder*, 406 U.S. 208 (1972).
8. *Employment Division v. Smith*, 494 U.S. 872 (1990).
9. *Romer v. Evans*, 517 U.S. 620.
10. *NAACP v. Alabama*, 357 U.S. 449 (1958); *NAACP v. Button*, 371 U.S. 415 (1963).
11. *Roberts v. Jaycees*, 468 U.S. 609 (1984); *Board of Directors of Rotary International v. Rotary Club of Duarte*, 481 U.S. 537 (1987); *New York State Club Association, Inc. v. City of New York*, 487 U.S. 1 (1989).

12. *Manual Enterprises, Inc. v. Day,* 370 U.S. 478 (1962); *Jacobellis v. Ohio*, 378 U.S. 184 (1964); *Memoirs v. Massachusetts,* 383 U.S. 413 (1966).

13. *Cohen v. California,* 403 U.S. 15 (1971).

14. *Barnes v. Glen Theatre,* 501 U.S. 560 (1991) (5-4 ruling against topless dancing).

15. See, for example, Ronald Dworkin, "Liberalism" and "Do We Have a Right to Pornography," in *A Matter of Principle,* (Cambridge, Mass.: Harvard University Press, 1985).

16. *Meritor Savings Bank v. Vinson,* 477 U.S. 57 (1986).

17. *Harris v. Forklift,* 510 U.S. 17 (1993); *Faragher v. Boca Raton,* 118 S.Ct. 2275 (1998); *Burlington Industries v. Ellerth,* 118 S.Ct. 2257 (1998).

18. *Madsen v. Women's Heath Center,* 512 U.S. 735 (1994); *Hill v. Colorado,* 530 U.S. 730 (2000).

19. *Meyer v. Nebraska,* 262 U.S. 390 (1923).

20. *Pierce v. Society Sisters,* 268 U.S. 510 (1925).

6

Tolerance and American Constitutionalism: The Case of Gay Rights

Murray Dry

The title of this book reminds me of the first sentence of Justice Scalia's dissent in *Romer v. Evans*. "The Court has mistaken a *Kulturkampf* for a fit of spite." In that case, the Supreme Court held that Colorado's state's referendum, known as Amendment 2, which repealed all laws and regulations protecting homosexuals from the law books, violated the fourteenth amendment to the Constitution. According the Justice Scalia, that decision conflicted with *Bowers v. Hardwick*, in which the Court upheld Georgia's criminal sodomy law as applied to homosexuals, and placed

> the prestige of this institution behind the proposition that opposition to homosexuality is as reprehensible as racial or religious bias. Whether it is or is not is *precisely* the cultural debate that gave rise to the Colorado amendment (and to the preferential laws against which the amendment was directed). Since the Constitution of the United States says nothing about this subject, it is left to be resolved by normal democratic means, including the democratic adoption of provisions in state constitutions. This Court has no business imposing upon all Americans the resolution favored by the elite class from which the Members of this institution are selected, pronouncing that "animosity" toward homosexuality . . . is evil."[1]

Justice Scalia's remarks thus reveal that part of the culture wars in America today involves the question of toleration toward homosexuals. Have the American courts, and especially the U.S. Supreme Court, been overreaching their authority in decisions that invalidate laws and referenda in the name of matters such as privacy, liberty, or equal protection? This is certainly Justice Scalia's position.

Judge Robert Bork apparently shares that view. In an essay entitled, "Our Judicial Oligarachy," published in *First Things* in November 1996, he identified Justices Scalia and Thomas as the only Supreme Court Justices who "attempt to give the Constitution the meaning it had for those who adopted it."[2] Judge Bork criticized the Court's decision in *Romer v. Evans* decision and concluded his essay by calling for a constitutional amendment, either to provide for a congressional override of Supreme Court decisions or to deprive the courts of the power of constitutional review. That issue of *First Things* was devoted to the question, 'The End of Democracy? Judicial Usurpation of Politics." It became famous, or infamous, for the following editorial board statement: "The question here explored, in full awareness of its far-reaching consequences, is whether we have reached or are reaching the point where conscientious citizens can no longer give moral assent to the existing regime."[3] In a subsequent issue of the journal, Judge Bork wrote a brief letter reaffirming his "criticism of the judiciary's usurpation of democratic power" but sharply disassociated himself from that editorial position.[4]

In this chapter, I want to address the concerns of Justice Scalia and Judge Bork as applied to judicial decisions concerning homosexuality. My argument is that American constitutionalism supports the principle of toleration and that courts as well as the political branches of government have a role to play in establishing that principle. I will first discuss toleration and its relation to the principles of American government. Then I will consider the work of the courts in American constitutionalism. Finally, I will examine the major judicial decisions regarding homosexuality.

TOLERATION AND THE AMERICAN POLITICAL REGIME

John Locke's *A Letter Concerning Toleration* is the most important textual source, for both the American founders and for the Supreme Court today, for the importance of the principle of toleration. Deeming it "above all things necessary to distinguish exactly the business of civil government from that of religion, and to settle the just bounds that lie between the one and the other," Locke distinguishes that which concerns men's souls from that which concerns the Commonwealth.

> The Commonwealth seems to me to be a society of men constituted only for the procuring, preserving, and advancing of their own civil interests. Civil interests I call, life, liberty, health and indolency of body; and the Possession of outward things, such as money, lands, houses, furniture, and the like.[5]

A church is later defined as a "voluntary society of men, joining themselves together of their own accord, in order to the public worshipping of God, in such a manner as they judge acceptable to him, and effectual to the salvation of their souls."[6] As a result of this division, government has a monopoly over the coercive powers and they may legitimately be employed in matters pertaining to civil concerns; churches, on the other hand, are free to engage in their activities, subject to their not contravening the civil law. The duty of toleration requires the government to leave religion alone in matters that are indifferent to the civil protection of life, liberty, and estate. Every church is also under a duty of toleration with respect to the rights of each person. As a private association, however, a church need not tolerate someone who offends against its laws: the remedy is "the sentence of excommunication" but it "carr[ies] with it no rough usage, or word or action, whereby the ejected person may any wise be damnified in body or estate."[7]

Locke's *Letter* was an important source for both Jefferson and Madison, who succeeded in establishing religious freedom in Virginia in 1785. In his Bill for Establishing Religious Freedom, Jefferson wrote "it is time enough for the rightful purposes of civil government for its officers to interfere when principles break out into overt acts against peace and good order."[8] In his "Memorial and Remonstrance Against Religious Assessments," Madison wrote that a just government "will be best supported by protecting every citizen in the enjoyment of his religion with the same equal hand which protects his person and his property; by neither invading the equal rights of any sect, nor suffering any sect to invade those of another."[9]

Since I am linking Madison's understanding of government to Locke's, I should acknowledge that Madison made sure that the word "toleration" did not appear in the Virginia Declaration of Rights. George Mason's draft contained the words "that all men should enjoy the fullest toleration in the exercise of religion." Madison proposed different language, which Mason and the Convention accepted in part, and the final version asserted that "all men are equally entitled to the free exercise of religion," without any reference to toleration.[10] As Eva Brann pointed out in her fine essay on Madison's Memorial, toleration "implie[d] not a right to religious liberty but a privilege granted." Brann goes on to note that Locke, "by a typical cunning twist, shifts the meaning of the term" from "granted" to "required": toleration is now "required of the magistrate toward all churches . . . ." While Madison "balked at the term 'toleration' in fundamental law," [11] Locke's use of "toleration" reflects the importance of individual rights for legitimate government. Furthermore, it alters the balance of power between a citizen and his regime, since the converse of an individual right is a governmental duty not to infringe on it. For the purpose of considering the rights of homosexuals under American constitutionalism, Locke's discussion of the limits of governmental authority is more important than is his discussion of the right of religious freedom.

The American founders also studied Montesquieu's *Spirit of the Laws* and frequently cited him on federalism and the separation of powers. Throughout his work, Montesquieu supports the mildness of moderate governments.

In book 12, he discusses the laws that form political liberty in relation to the citizen. He mentions four kinds of crimes—against religion, mores, the public tranquility, and security—but the effect of his discussion is to limit criminal law to the fourth category.[12] Then in a separate chapter, entitled "On the crime against nature," Montesquieu considers homosexuality along with magic and heresy. He puts them together because all three were punished by burning. This is what he says about homosexuality:

> Do not clear the way for this crime, let it be proscribed by an exact police, as are all the violations of mores, and one will immediately see nature defend her rights or take them back. Gentle, pleasing, charming, nature has scattered pleasures with a liberal hand; and by overwhelming us with delights, she prepares us with our children through whom we are born again, as it were, for satisfactions greater even than those delights.[13]

The reference to an exact police in conjunction with mores, manners, and morals refers to fines, shame, and constraint as modes of punishment. But Montesquieu's moving account of the natural pleasures of procreation must make us wonder whether he thinks any severe measures need to be taken.[14]

Locke and Montesquieu also emphasize the right of property, or commercial freedom. Montesquieu writes that commerce "cures destructive prejudices," and "everywhere there is commerce there are gentle mores."[15] The American founders agreed on the importance of property, which supports gentle mores and toleration.

American hostility to homosexuality comes largely from the Puritan legacy. No one appreciated the Puritan contribution to American freedom more than Alexis de Tocqueville. But Tocqueville separates the good that he thinks religion can do for the mores of a democratic people from the Puritans' severe criminal laws. Tocqueville celebrates a recast Puritanism, a form of Christianity that provides order to the moral world, but "when it arrives at the political world, it halts; trembling, it leaves off the use of its most formidable faculties." Tocqueville observes Americans "seeking with an almost equal ardor material wealth and moral satisfactions, Heaven in the other world and well-being and freedom in this one."[16] While he thinks the moralist has a role to play in tempering the pursuit of well-being, Tocqueville praises religion for not attempting to ally with politics to limit the Americans' love of material wealth and freedom.[17]

The question is, how should we understand the dictates of morality, especially in relation to sexual relations and activities, and what role, if any, is there for law, criminal or civil, as an enforcer of morality? If we follow Locke, Montesquieu, and Tocqueville, I think we should start with an appreciation of the distinction between the public and the private spheres. Government's use of law to enforce morality should be connected in some clear way to the fundamental purposes of liberal democracy. Does homosexual behavior threaten the mores of the American people in a way that justifies criminal sanctions, the denial of civil rights, or forms of shunning or exclusion? Montesquieu appears to support the latter sanctions, especially if it could be shown that homosexuality poses a threat to the dominant mores of the people. If sexual orientation were a matter of choice, or if children or adolescents were susceptible of being turned toward homosexuality by advocates, that might conceivably justify public acts to reinforce support for heterosexuality and the nuclear family.

At this point I draw on Richard Posner's book, *Sex and Reason*[18] to make the case for toleration. According to Posner, the evidence strongly suggests that homosexuality is largely determined rather than chosen. The best estimate of the number of "real" homosexuals—that is excluding opportunistic occurrences—is between 2 to 5 percent of the male population and considerably less of the female population. The removal of disabilities does not seem to change these numbers. It is not easy to convert a homosexual to heterosexuality or heterosexual to homosexual.[19]

This is my brief for toleration as a principle of American constitutionalism and for its application to homosexuals. Toleration is not the only principle of American constitutionalism, however. The related principles of freedom of speech and association allow individuals and private associations to express their own opinions and to shun those they dislike. Two of the cases I discuss below reveal this conflict between toleration and freedom of speech and association.

TOLERATION AND JUDICIAL POWER

I turn now to judicial power and its relationship to the principle of toleration. It is one thing to make the case for toleration and hope to persuade citizens and lawmakers to draw the proper conclusions. What happens, however, when the majority's position, as reflected in the laws, supports the subordination or exclusion of a group of individuals—such as blacks, women, or homosexuals—from certain rights? How much does it matter whether the opinion in support of a differential treatment is defensible or indefensible, from the perspective of the judicial power? I mention blacks and women because it took judicial decisions to secure their rights, not because I think the analogy of any one to the other is perfect.

Critics of the exercise of judicial power in the areas of birth control, abortion, and homosexuality charge the courts and their defenders with obliterating the distinction between law making and law finding. Justice Scalia holds that the Constitution's clauses, no matter how general the language, can be reduced to a clear meaning. In *Planned Parenthood of Southeastern Pennsylvania v. Casey,* the Court affirmed a woman's right to terminate a pregnancy before viability while scrapping the Roe trimester for Justice O'-Connor's "undue burden" test.[20] Justice Scalia, in a partial dissent, characterized the Court's Joint Opinion as calling "reasoned judgment" what "turns out to be nothing but philosophical predilection and moral intuition."[21] The courts have gotten into the people's business, according Justice Scalia.

> As long as this Court thought (and the people thought) that we Justices were doing essentially lawyers' work up here—reading text and discerning our society's traditional understanding of that text—the public pretty much left us alone. Texts and traditions are facts to study, not convictions to demonstrate about. But if in reality our process of constitutional adjudication consists primarily of making value judgments; if we can ignore a long and clear tradition clarifying an ambiguous text, [if our] pronouncements of constitutional law rests primarily on value judgments, then a free and intelligent people's attitude toward us can be expected to be (ought to be) quite different. The people know that their value judgments are quite as good as those taught in any law school—maybe better.[22]

Judging is simply a matter of studying the facts of text and traditions and doing one's legal sums, in other words. Justice Scalia's rules-based approach to the due process clause is to look to tradition, and to look at the most specific level possible. He elaborated his views in an earlier case, in which a man, Michael H., sought visitation rights, claiming he was the natural father of a child born to Carole D, who was married to Gerald D.[23] The Court rejected his claim and Justice Scalia wrote an opinion stating the judgment. His distinctive interpretation of the liberty that the due process protects did not gain the assent of Justices Kennedy and O'Connor. The dispute was between a parenthood claim, backed by a blood test that supported the claim with a 98.07 percent probability, and a statute's presumption that a child born to a married woman is legitimately the child of the marriage. Justice Brennan, in dissent, argued for the traditional support for parenthood. Justice Scalia and the majority supported the unitary family tradition. In his footnote, Justice Scalia wrote:

> Though the dissent has no basis for the level of generality it would select, we do: We refer to the most specific level at which a relevant tradition protecting or denying protection to, the asserted right can be identified. If [there] were no societal tradition either way, regarding the rights of the natural father of a child adulterously conceived, we would have to consult, and [if possible] reason from, the tradition regarding natural fathers in general. But there is such a more specific tradition, and it unqualifiedly denies protection to such a parent. [Because] general traditions provide such imprecise guidance, they permit judges to dictate rather than discern the society's views. [Although] assuredly having the virtue (if it be that) of leaving judges free to decide as they think best when the unanticipated occurs, a rule of law that binds neither by text nor by any particular, identifiable tradition, is no rule of law at all.[24]

Justice O'Connor, joined by Justice Kennedy, expressly dissented from that footnote. As evidence that the Court has not always followed such an approach, she cited *Griswold*[25] and *Eisenstadt*[26] Even more telling, she added: "On occasion, the Court has characterized relevant traditions protecting asserted rights at levels of generality that might not be 'the most specific level' available.[27]

Writing in *Federalist 78*, Alexander Hamilton notes that an independent judiciary is "a safeguard against the effects of occasional ill humors in society," which may extend to the injury of private rights by "unjust and partial laws. Here also the firmness of the judicial magistracy is of vast importance in mitigating the severity and confining the operation of such laws."[28] That sounds like judicial interpretation based on principles, not rules. Likewise, Justice Marshall's magisterial opinion in *McCulloch v. Maryland*, after pronouncing that 'it is a constitution we are expounding," not a prolix legal code, proceeds to make a distinction between great and substantive powers and instrumental powers that allow him, along with his interpretation of necessary as useful or convenient, to establish a liberal construction for the enumeration of powers.[29] On Justice Scalia's reasoning, had the Court known of the Federal Convention's brief discussion of banks and charters of incorporation, which resulted in the decision to not include the power,[30] strict construction would have been the necessary conclusion.

Surely Justice Marshall's famous line about expounding a constitution in light of the general language that is in the instrument tells against any simple approach to its meaning. Likewise, Hamilton seemed to count on the kind of judicial statesmanship that Justice Scalia claims is illegitimate in his *Casey* dissent. Careful reasoning about complex legal issues need not be a matter of visceral gut reactions, as we associate with value judgments.

JUDICIAL DECISIONS CONCERNING RIGHTS OF HOMOSEXUALS

I turn now to an overview of judicial decisions regarding rights of homosexuals. I will begin with the two major Supreme Court decisions, mentioned above: *Bowers v. Hardwick*[31]and *Romer v. Evans*.[32] I will then discuss two Supreme Court decisions involving the free speech rights of private associations and the fourth circuit court's decision upholding the military's "Don't ask, Don't tell" policy regarding gays in the military. Finally, I will discuss my own state of Vermont's same-sex marriage case, which was decided on state constitutional grounds and led to the passage of Vermont's Civil Union statute.

Bowers v. Hardwick

Georgia's statute defined sodomy as "any sexual act involving the sex organs of one person and the mouth or anus of another."[33] The penalty was imprisonment of from one to twenty years. Michael Hardwick was arrested in his apartment after a police officer followed him home to arrest him for drinking in public. Allowed into the apartment by a guest, the officer caught sight of Hardwick engaged in oral sex with another man. The two men were arrested for violating the sodomy law (Hardwick for public drinking also), kept in jail for twelve hours, and then released. Hardwick brought suit in federal district court, alleging that since he was a practicing homosexual, this law put him in imminent danger of arrest. The district court dismissed his claim, but the Court of Appeals, citing the *Griswold, Eisenstadt,* and *Stanley*[34] privacy cases, reversed, holding that the statute violated Hardwick's fundamental rights. The Supreme Court reversed the Court of Appeals, 5-4; Justice White wrote the majority opinion denying that there was a fundamental right to engage in homosexual sodomy.[35]

Since Hardwick was not prosecuted, and since there had apparently not been a prosecution under this law for at least forty years, the Court could have simply dismissed the case as moot. Posner thinks the majority chose to decide the case in order to put a clear stop to the scope of the right of privacy, which had expanded from marital use of contraceptives to a single person's use, to a woman's decision to terminate an unwanted pregnancy before viability.[36] Justice White distinguished those cases as pertaining to "a fundamental individual right to decide whether or not to beget or bear a child."[37] The cases also concerned the sexual activities of consenting adults in places of privacy.

Justice White framed the issue in terms of a right to engage in homosexual sodomy and relied on the notion of liberties that are "deeply rooted in this Nation's history and tradition" to conclude that this one was not.[38] His reliance on the historical practice of criminal sodomy laws reflected Justice Scalia's emphasis on the most specific level to illustrate what due process means. Justice Blackmun, in dissent, framed the issue in terms of a fundamental right for an adult to engage in private, consensual sexual conduct.[39] To Justice White's contention that a right to voluntary sexual conduct between consenting adults would include "adultery, incest, and other sexual crimes," Justice Blackmun responded by distinguishing the cases; adultery violates a contract and is likely to injure third parties and that the problematic character of true consent in incest cases justifies the prohibition.[40]

The dissenting Justices also called into question the majority's willingness to restrict the law to homosexuals, since the broad language covered sex acts by heterosexuals as well, including married couples. Can the Court justify reading a special animus against homosexuals into a law that on its face reflects an animus towards certain forms of sexuality? And, if the Court can do that, on the grounds that the law otherwise would be unconstitutional and the legislative intent was to keep as much as possible, can the people of Georgia discriminate against homosexuals in that manner? Is the ban on homosexuality from Leviticus a sufficient grounding for criminal laws under the American Constitution?

Given the weight the majority places on tradition to justify the law, one wonders whether any of the five Justices would have reconsidered had they known, as Posner points out, that traditionally sodomy did not include the specific act for which Hardwick had been arrested.[41]

Justice Powell provided the fifth vote in this case. He indicated that while he did not think that a fundamental right was involved, he did think that the potential for a penalty of up to twenty years for "a single act of sodomy, even in the private setting of a home," raised an Eighth Amendment "cruel and unusual punishment" issue.[42] After retiring from the Court, Justice Powell indicated that he had changed his mind about this case.[43] Powell's opinion reminds us that the Court could only do what it did with the knowledge that the law was not being enforced. The strongest defense of the law amounts to reducing its significance to an expression of popular disgust at the way homosexuals engage in sex. Of course the possibility of continued harassment was present, but the circumstances under which an officer witnessed the act of sodomy were unusual.

Romer v. Evans

This case originated when the people of Colorado passed Amendment 2 on November 3, 1992. The margin was 53 to 47 percent. Thus a constitutional referendum invalidated the antidiscrimination laws and regulations of the state as well as of the local governments in Denver, Boulder, and Aspen. Since the case was decided on a summary judgment in the district court, the state courts never determined whether the Amendment meant that homosexuals could be fired or in any other way discriminated against by the state government. But, notwithstanding Justice Scalia's contention that the Amendment "does no more than deny special rights,"[44] the Amendment clearly allowed—and one might say encouraged—private employers and owners of housing to discriminate against homosexuals statewide. It is an interesting irony that conservatives, who generally support federalism, supported a populist constitutional device that strips local governments of the right to resolve civil rights matters in their own way.

Justice Kennedy wrote the court opinion in the 7-2 decision; only Justices Scalia and Thomas dissented. As the majority saw the issue, there was a vast disproportion between any legitimate government interest and the means chosen. That is, the associational rights of persons whose religious beliefs hold that homosexuality is wrong surely would justify some limitation on the application of civil rights protection in employment and housing. We know this as the "Mrs. Murphy's boarding house" exception to Title 2 of the 1964 Civil Rights Act, which outlawed discrimination in places of public accommodations. As for the claim that the state needed to conserve resources to fight discrimination against other groups, there was no evidence to support the alleged budget drains. The Court thus concluded that "Amendment 2 classifies homosexuals not to further a proper legislative end but to make them unequal to everyone else. This Colorado cannot do. A State cannot so deem a class of persons a stranger to its laws."[45]

Justice Scalia's claim that the *Bowers* decision justifies the Amendment is not persuasive. First, Justice Scalia seems to rely on the principle that the greater implies the lesser, but that is not always the case. States may choose to outlaw the sale of alcohol, but if they make these activities legal, they cannot restrict advertising that is accurate and does not deceive.[46] Second, *Bowers* is problematic as a precedent precisely because it looks like the law would not have been allowed to stand if the state had proceeded with its prosecution. Whatever harm the *Bowers* decision may do to homosexuals in Georgia, it does not stand for the proposition that they can be prosecuted. Colorado's Amendment 2 was not going to be limited to a symbolic statement of hostility to homosexuals; it removed from state or local governmental control any protection against discrimination in housing or employment or places of public accommodation.

Military and Homosexuals: "Don't Ask, Don't Tell"

Our government's current policy toward homosexuals in the military was enacted into law in November 1993 and is known as "Don't ask, Don't tell." This policy was fully considered by the fourth circuit court of appeals, sitting en banc, in the case of *Thomasson v. Perry*.[47] The Supreme Court denied certiorari.[48] Judge Wilkinson wrote the court opinion in the 9-4 decision. He reviewed the extensive discussions between the executive and legislative branches. This started with President Clinton's expressed intent to end discrimination on the basis of sexual orientation in the military, included nine days of congressional hearings, and ended with a statute that did not accept the president's initial proposal.

Finding that "success in combat requires military units that are characterized by high morale, good order, and discipline, and unit cohesion," Congress concluded that "the prohibition against homosexual conduct is a long standing element of military law that continues to be necessary in the unique circumstances of military service." Therefore, service members "who demonstrate 'a propensity or intent to engage in homosexual acts [ ] create an unacceptable risk to the high standards of morale, good order, and discipline, and unit cohesion that are the essence of military capability." The statute provided three grounds for separation from the military: engaging in or attempting to engage in a homosexual act; marrying or attempting to marry a person of the same sex; or stating that one is a homosexual, unless he or she can demonstrate that "he or she is not a person who engages in, attempts to engage in, has a propensity to engage in, or intends to engage in homosexual acts."[49]

In early May 1994, Lieutenant Paul Thomasson, a ten-year veteran in the navy with a stellar performance record, sent a letter to four admirals declaring "I am gay," and expressing his strong disagreement with the military's policy. This led to a Board of Inquiry hearing and to his honorable discharge from the navy. Thomasson challenged his dismissal on equal protection, due process, and first amendment grounds. The district court granted summary judgment for the government.[50]

Emphasizing the duty of Congress and the president to provide for defense, Judge Wilkinson quoted the Congressional finding that "the maintenance of military unit cohesion,—which is the key to combat capability—must remain paramount over the desires of a single individual or group."[51] Another congressional statement described military life as "spartan, primitive, and characterized by forced intimacy with little or no privacy." And General H. Norman Schwarzkopf testified that "the introduction of an open homosexual into a small unit immediately polarizes that unit and destroys the very bonding that is so important for the unit's survival in time of war."[52]

That addressed the due process objections to the policy. As for the first amendment, Judge Wilkinson gave two replies. First, the policy covers not speech itself but speech that establishes a rebuttable presumption that an individual engages in or intends to engage in homosexual acts. Second, the meaning of "the freedom of speech" is narrower in the military than it is in civilian life.[53]

Dissenting Judge Hall attempted to rebut the majority's reliance on cohesion and morale by quoting similar language that was used to justify racial segregation of the armed services in the 1940s.[54] He did not note that the troops were integrated by an executive order of President Truman in 1947, not by a judicial decision. Judge Hall also cited testimony from someone serving under Thomasson to the effect that "his sexual orientation had no adverse effect on myself or on the Navy."[55]

That evidence, and Posner's discussion of the "givenness" of homosexuality, might suggest a reconsideration of congressional policy. Because of the importance of the military mission, and the need for cohesiveness and the lack of privacy, the circuit court's deference to Congress and the president was warranted. The Supreme Court took the same position with regard to the male only registration law, in light of the legislative restraints on women in combat.[56]

Two Free Speech and Associational Rights Cases: *Hurley* and the *Boy Scouts of America*

The last two federal cases involve the freedom of speech and right of association versus the right of homosexuals to be free from discrimination. In the first case,[57] the South Boston Allied War Veterans' Council refused to allow the Irish American Gay, Lesbian, and Bisexual Group of Boston (GLIB) to march as a unit with their own banners in the St. Patrick's Day parade in Boston. In the second case,[58] the Boy Scouts of America, in Monmouth County, New Jersey, removed James Dale, a model scout who had been appointed assistant scoutmaster of Troop 73, when they learned that Dale was an active, and activist, homosexual. The highest state courts upheld public accommodations statutes as applied to the private associations in each case. The Supreme Court reversed, unanimously in the parade case and 5-4 in the Boy Scouts case. The determining issue for the majority in each case was the expressive right of the private association. The second case was close because four Justices did not think the Boy Scouts had established a clear position regarding homosexuality.

In the *Hurley* case, Justice Souter wrote the court opinion. The state court had said that the St. Patrick's Day parade took virtually all comers and had no particularized message. Hurley, speaking for the veterans' council, argued that they had excluded the Klu Klux Klan and an antibusing group, but that argument did not seem necessary. The whole purpose of a parade, Justice Souter said, was to express a message collectively. Respondent GLIB's participation as a unit in the parade was also for the sake of expression. While the public accommodations law did not regulate speech on its face, its application in this case implicated speech.

> Since every participating unit affects the message conveyed by the private organizers, the state courts' application of the statute produced an order essentially requiring petitioners to alter the expressive content of their parade. Although the state courts spoke of the parade as a place of public accommodation, . . . once the expressive character of both the parade and the marching GLIB contingent is understood, it becomes apparent that the state courts' application of the statute had the effect of declaring the sponsors' speech itself to be a public accommodation.[59]

Individuals were not denied the right to participate in the parade on the basis of their sexual orientation. The Council objected to the group's message that homosexuals are present and by implication are granted equal dignity and respect. GLIB can gain permission to march in its own parade, under neutral criteria for selection.

In the second case, *Boy Scouts of America v. Dale*, decided in 2000, the individual who was ousted from the Scouts had been a model scout from the age of eight, when he first joined, to the age of eighteen, when he became an eagle scout. A year later he was accepted into adult membership and appointed assistant scoutmaster for Troop 73. But when he went away to school, to Rutgers in 1990, Dale acknowledged to himself and others that he was gay, became copresident of the Lesbian Gay Alliance and advocated the need for gay role models. When the Monmouth County leadership learned of this they revoked Dale's membership. In reply to Dale's inquiry, Council Executive James Kay wrote to say that the Boy Scouts "specifically forbid membership to homosexuals."[60] Dale sued under the state's public accommodations law and the New Jersey Supreme Court affirmed the judgment in his favor. In addressing the Hurley precedent, the state supreme court said that reinstating Dale did not require the Boy Scouts to express any message.

The U.S. Supreme Court, in a 5-4 decision, reversed. Chief Justice Rehnquist delivered the court opinion, which Justices O'Connor, Scalia, Kennedy, and Thomas joined. The Chief Justice recited the Boy Scouts' mission statement, which includes the words: "To keep myself physically strong, mentally awake, and morally straight."[61] Acknowledging that the meaning of "morally straight" was not clear with respect to homosexuality, the Chief Justice deferred to the Boy Scouts. He also cited a 1978 policy statement by the Boy Scouts' Executive Committee: "We do not believe that homosexuality and leadership in Scouting are appropriate. We will continue to select only those who in our judgment meet our standards and qualifications for leadership."[62] For the majority, this put the case on logical all fours with *Hurley*: ". . . the presence of Dale as an assistant scoutmaster would just as surely interfere with the Boy Scouts' choice not to propound a point of view contrary to its beliefs."[63]

Justice Stevens, in dissent, did not interpret the policy statement in 1978, or any later statement, as definitive. The full interview included remarks suggesting that the Boy Scouts would have to reconsider their position if a law prohibited employment discrimination. That is arguably different from the associational right the Boy Scouts claim here. Justice Stevens insisted that the Scouts were on notice but did nothing to clarify their position on the meaning of "morally straight" and "clean." Justice Souter's short dissent makes the same point; to qualify for the *Hurley* right, the Boy Scouts need to be clear in expressing their policy of opposition to homosexuality.

The case is difficult because one strongly suspects that the Boy Scouts could have maintained their general position against homosexual advocacy without losing this model scout. They could have made it clear to Dale that he was not to discuss sexual orientation in his capacity as an eagle scout.

The case for a strict "Don't ask, Don't tell" policy seems less persuasive in this setting than in the military. As for the constitutional merits, however, the majority's position seems right. The Boy Scouts have the right to insist that their message is not in any way compromised, and if they did not make themselves clear about being morally straight before the *Dale* case, they have now. This policy may be reconsidered, as the Boy Scouts are reportedly losing financial support and some public schools have refused to allow them to use their facilities.

Baker v. State

I turn now to Vermont's same-sex marriage case of *Baker v. State.*[64] In 1997, three couples sued in Chittenden Superior court, alleging the right to have same-sex unions recognized by the state as marriages. Judge Levitt upheld the State's marriage statutes; the state interest in "furthering the link between procreation and child rearing" justified limiting marriage to a man and a woman.[65] On appeal, the Vermont Supreme Court unanimously reversed. Chief Justice Amestoy, writing for the Court, relied on the State Constitution's Common Benefits clause in deciding the case. That clause, in pertinent part, reads: "That government is, or ought to be, instituted for the common benefit, protection, and security of the people, nation, or community, and not for the particular emolument or advantage of any single person, family, or set of persons, who are a part only of that community."[66]

The Court then held that the state is "constitutionally required to extend to same-sex couples the common benefits and protections that flow from marriage under Vermont law. Whether this ultimately takes the form of inclusion within the marriage laws themselves or a parallel 'domestic partnership' system or some equivalent statutory alternative, rests with the Legislature."[7]

The Chief Justice noted the state's "legitimate and longstanding interest in promoting a permanent commitment between couples for the security of their children." Then he pointed out that "many opposite sex couples marry for reasons unrelated to procreation, that some couples never intend to have children, and other couples are incapable of having children." In addition, many children are being raised by "same-sex parents," and "increasing numbers of children are being conceived by such parents through a variety of assisted-reproductive techniques." Furthermore, "the Vermont legislature has not only recognized this reality, but has acted affirmatively to remove legal barriers so that same-sex couples may legally adopt and rear the children conceived through such efforts." The Chief Justice then cited a provision of the Vermont statutes that allows the partner of a biological parent to adopt if it is in the child's best interest, without reference to sex.[68] The statute represented a legislative affirmation of a previous Vermont Supreme Court decision in 1993. The state law had provided that in the event of adoption the natural parents would lose all parental rights. There was a step-parent exception: the spouse of a natural parent could adopt without the natural parent's giving up parental rights. In the 1993 case, Deborah wanted to legally adopt Jane's children without Jane losing her parental rights. Writing for a unanimous court, Justice Johnson said "we are mindful that the state's primary concern is to promote the welfare of children . . . and the application of the statute should implement that purpose."[69] Noting that an unmarried person can adopt, the Court concluded that it would be contrary to the spirit of the law to interpret it to prevent Deborah from adopting in this case.

By pointing out the ways in which Vermont state law had already treated same-sex couples as parents with rights and responsibilities for children, Chief Justice Amestoy suggested that the Court's decision was only an extension of that trend.

Moreover, by emphasizing the matter of benefits, and by leaving it to the Legislature to decide what had to be done to equalize them, the Court made the legislature a continuing partner in the matter. For these reasons, I think the Vermont Supreme Court cannot fairly be charged with inappropriate judicial activism in this case. The general nature of the common benefits clause had already been fleshed out in judicial and then in legislative decisions on this subject.[70]

The Chief Justice's argument was the most conservative of the three presented in this case. Justice Dooley applied "strict scrutiny" to get to the same result.[71] Justice Johnson dissented in part, because she would have granted full relief and enjoined town officials from denying a marriage license on the basis of the sex of the applicants. She viewed the marriage statutes as examples of sex classifications, which were thus subject to strict scrutiny.[72] This is how the Hawaii Supreme Court viewed the issue. As Chief Justice Amestoy pointed out at the end of his opinion, the Hawaii Supreme Court decision mandating same-sex marriage under the state constitution produced a constitutional amendment defining marriage as between a man and a woman and thus repealing the state court's decision.[73]

The Vermont Supreme Court's decision galvanized the state into a full-scale debate, which included two days of public hearings. The legislature, with the support of Governor Howard Dean, passed a full Civil Union bill on April 26, 2000. The bill provides same-sex couples with all the privileges and responsibilities of marriage, without the name and its symbolic significance. The Civil Union Bill, Act 91, was an important issue in the state elections in November 2000. Opponents of the Act ran on the slogan "Take Back Vermont" (Supporters adopted the slogan, "Take Vermont Forward"). They only succeeded in defeating a few legislative supporters of Civil Unions. Governor Dean, a Democrat, defeated his Republican challenger, Ruth Dwyer, who advocated repeal of Civil Unions, by a 60 to 40 percent margin. Sixteen months after the Supreme Court's decision, the people of Vermont and their lawmakers have participated fully in deliberations about the subject and are generally satisfied with the result.

CONCLUSION

I conclude that in their treatment of the rights of homosexuals, the courts have been responsible partners in the maintenance of American constitutional democracy. The only apparent exception to that statement is the *Hardwick* case, but it was tacitly overruled in *Romer*. If a state law criminalizing homosexual behavior ever gets into court, the Supreme Court would strike it down under the kind of reasonableness test it employed in *Romer*. The courts have been nudging legislatures toward toleration, but they have also respected legitimate reasons for treating homosexuals differently from heterosexuals. They give the military and private associations a wide berth, while subjecting government regulations to a reasonable scrutiny, one that looks for reasons that continue to make sense, in light of the totality of our laws and mores. The Vermont Supreme Court drew on the legislature's recognition that same-sex couples can make good parents. Other states may disagree, and the Federal Defense of Marriage Act reserves that decision to the states.[74] At some time the Supreme Court will have to decide whether this Act satisfies the Constitution's Full Faith and Credit clause. Since the Vermont Supreme Court, under the "adequate and independent state grounds" doctrine, was able to interpret its state Constitution without reference to federal constitutional (equal protection) law, Congress should be permitted to leave it to the several states to decide how they want to treat either same-sex marriages or civil unions.

I have argued that judicial interpretation of constitutional principles is not merely fact finding, as Justice Scalia implies, but an exercise in reasoning about purposes and means. As for Justice Scalia's remark about the Court's *Romer* decision, I think these cases reflect culture wars that have their source in religious convictions—and in some cases, the legislative and judicial (*Bowers*) or the popular (*Romer*) action was based on spite. In the other cases, rights are legitimately in conflict. The Court supported freedom of speech and associational right over the homosexual's right to tolerance in *Hurley* and *Dale*, and it supported the military's judgment, backed by Congress, of its special requirements in *Thomasson*. And the Vermont Supreme Court drew on prior legislative support for homosexuals as parents to interpret its own constitution to require something like civil unions. Except for *Bowers*, these majority opinions reflect how both Publius and Chief Justice Marshall understood expounding the Constitution.

NOTES

1. *Romer v. Evans*, 134 L. ed. 2d 855, 868–9 (1996).
2. *First Things*, 67 (November 1996):21
3. *First Things*, 18

4. See the Correspondence section in the January 1997 edition, 2.

5. *A Letter Concerning Toleration,* ed. James H. Tulley (Indianapolis, In.: Hackett Publishing Company Inc., 1983), 26.

6. *A Letter Concerning Toleration*, 28

7. *A Letter Concerning Toleration*, 30

8. *The Portable Thomas Jefferson,* ed. Merrill D. Peterson (New York: Viking Press, 1975), 252–3.

9. "Memorial and Remonstrance Against Religious Assessments," in *The Papers of James Madison,* ed. Robert A. Rutland and William M.E. Rachal (Chicago and London, University of Chicago Press, 1973) volume 8, Eighth Resolution, 302.

10. See Gailland Hunt, "James Madison and Religious Liberty," in *Annual Report of the American Historical Society,* 1901 vol. I, (Washington, Government Printing Office, 1902), 166–167.

11. "Madison's Memorial and Remonstrance: A Model of American Eloquence," in *The Past-Present: Selected Essays of Eva Brann* (St. John's College, 1997), 225.

12. Montesquieu, *The Spirit of the Laws,* ed. Anne Cohler, Basia Miller, and Harold Stone (Cambridge, Cambridge University Press, 1989) book 12, chapter 4, 189–91. Crimes of the third category are "a simple breach of police," by which Montesquieu has noncriminal, or civil, sanctions in mind, 191.

13. *The Spirit of the Laws*, book 12, chapter 6, 194.

14. Montesquieu seems to say that homosexuality brings its own mild punishment, or deprivation, which is an inability to procreate. The Vermont "same sex marriage" case, discussed below, draws on a case involving one woman's desire to adopt the natural child of her female partner; see infra text at note 68.

15. *The Spirit of the Laws*, book 20, chapter 1, 338.

16. *Democracy in America,* trans. Harvey Mansfield and Delba Winthrop, (Chicago, University of Chicago Press, 2000) vol. I, part one, chapter 2, 43.

17. *The Spirit of the Laws*, vol. I, part two, chapter 9, 278–88

18. Richard Posner, *Sex and Reason*, (Cambridge, Mass.: Harvard University Press, 1992).

19. *Democracy in America*, 291–303.

20. *Planned Parenthood of Southeastern Pennsylvania v. Casey*, 505 U.S. 833 (1992).

21. *Planned Parenthood of Southeastern Pennsylvania v. Casey*, at 1000.

22. *Planned Parenthood of Southeastern Pennsylvania v. Casey*, 1000–1001.

23. *Michael H. v. Gerald D.* 491 U.S. 110, (1989).

24. *Michael H. v. Gerald D.* at 127 note 6.

25. *Griswold v. Connecticut*, 381 U.S. 479 (1965).

26. *Eisenstadt v. Baird*, 405 U.S. 438 (1972).

27. *Eisenstadt v. Baird*, 132. Justice O'Connor referred to *Loving v. Virginia,* among other cases. In *Loving,* the Court overturned the state's anti-miscegenation law. Justice Scalia replied to the Joint Opinion's reference to Loving in Casey by asserting that "the tradition in that case was contradicted by a text—an Equal Protection Clause that explicitly establishes racial equality as a constitutional value." see Casey, at 980, note 1. Of course, the equal protection clause did not clearly prohibit racial classifications. see Bickel, "The Original Understanding and the Segregation Decision 69 *Harvard Law Review* 1 (1955). The traditional hostility to homosexuals, was ratified in *Bowers v. Hardwick,* which will be discussed below.

28. *The Federalist Papers*, ed. Clinton Rossiter, new introduction by Charles Kesler (New York: Mentor, 1999)., 438.

29. *Wheaton* 316 (1819): 407, 411–20.

30. Max Farrand, ed. *Records of the Federal Convention,* revised edition in 4 volumes (New Haven, Yale University Press, 1937), volume II, 615–616.

31. *Bowers v. Hardwick*, 478 U.S. 186 (1986).

32. *Romer v. Evans*, 134 L Ed 2d 855 (1996).

33. The text of the statute, in relevant part, is in Justice White's court opinion, 478 U.S. 186, 187 footnote 1. The facts in this case, as presented in the text, come from Posner, supra, n18, p. 340 (see his note 40).

34. *Stanley v. Georgia* 394 U.S. 557 (1969).

35. *Stanley v. Georgia* at 191.

36. Posner, supra, note 18, 341–42.

37. 478 U.S. 186, 190

38. 478 U.S. at 194; the quote comes from Justice Cardozo's opinion in *Palko v. Connecticut* 302 U.S. 319 (1937).

39. *Palko v. Connecticut* at p. 209.

40. *Palko v. Connecticut* at 209, note 4, replying to Justice White's remarks at 196.

41. Posner at supra note 16, p. 343.

42. 478 U.S. 186, 197–98.

43. See John C. Jefferies Jr., *Justice Lewis F. Powell Jr.* (New York: Charles Scribner's Sons 1994) 530.

44. This was the State's position, which Justice Kennedy stated at 134 L Ed 2d 855, 862 and Justice Scalia quoted at 869.

45. *Romer v. Evans*, at 868.

46. *Rubin v. Coors Brewing Company* 514 U.S. 476 (1995) and *44 Liquormart, Inc. v. Rhode Island* 134 L Ed. 2d 711 (1996).

47. 80 F. 3d 915 (1996).

48. 519 U.S. 948 (1996).

49. 134 L Ed 2d 855, 920 (internal quotations omitted).

50. *Romer v. Evans*, 920, 921.

51. *Romer v. Evans*, 927.

52. *Romer v. Evans*, 929.

53. *Romer v. Evans*, 931-933.

54. *Romer v. Evans*, 953.

55. *Romer v. Evans*, 952.

56. *Rostker v. Goldberg* 453 U.S. 57 (1981).

57. *Hurley v. Irish-American Gay Lesbian and Bisexual Group of Boston* 515 U.S. 557 (1995).

58. *Boy Scouts of America and Monmouth Council v. James Dale* 147 L Ed. 2d 554 (2000).

59. 515 U.S. 557, 572–573.

60. 147 L Ed. 2d 554, 561.

61. *Boy Scouts of America v. Dale*, 563.

62. *Boy Scouts of America v. Dale*, 565.

63. *Boy Scouts of America v. Dale*, 567.

64. 1999 Vt Lexis 406 (1999).

65. *Baker v State,* Chittenden Superior Court, No. S1009-97, 17.

66. Vermont Constitution, chapter I, art. 7, quoted in Chief Justice Amestoy's opinion in *Baker v. State* at 5.

67. *Baker v. State,* Vermont Lexis 405, at 5.

68. *Baker v. State,* 42–43. The statute is 15A V.S.A. section 1–102(b).

69. *In re B.L.V.B.* 160 Vt 368, 371 1993.

70. The Vermont Supreme Court's decision in *Brigham v. State* in 1997 (166 Vt 249), which used the same "common benefits" clause to overturn state funding of public education largely on the basis of local property taxes is a harder case to defend. That is because federal case law went the other way and there was no previous legislative or judicial action to support the decision.

71. *Brigham v. State,* 71ff.

72. *Brigham v. State,* 94, 119–120.

73. *Brigham v. State,* 63–64.

74. "No State, territory, or possession of the United States, or Indian tribe, shall be required to give effect to any public act, record, or judicial proceeding of any other State, territory, possession, or tribe respecting a relationship between persons of the same sex that is treated as a marriage under the laws of such other State, territory, possession, or tribe, or a right or claim arising from such relationship." 104 H.R. 3396; P.L.104–199 section 2a; 110 Stat 2419; 28 U.S.C.S. section 1738c.

7

Religious Freedom Without Religious Neutrality: Our Once and Future Constitutional Common Sense

Graham Walker

This chapter makes several potentially astonishing claims—astonishing, at least, to those who are accustomed to the prevailing consensus on the subject of religion and government in America. Among the surprising claims I make are the following: that the issue of religious freedom is distinct and separable from the debate over whether or not government should be religiously neutral; that religious liberty is, in fact, compatible with certain forms of government patronage of a preferred religion or set of religions; that this is a good thing, since avoiding government patronage of preferred religions (that is, the attempt at governmental religious neutrality) is a demonstrable impossibility; and, finally, that the U.S. Constitution is both highly principled and highly realistic, and therefore it requires protection for the free exercise of religion but does not require governmental neutrality with respect to religion.

Of all these claims the last—that neutrality is not constitutionally required—is the most immediately intelligible and thus the most immediately controversial. As I will explain, there are two reasons why the Constitution does not require governmental neutrality toward religion: a textual reason and a logical reason. The textual reason, in brief, is that the Constitution permits, indeed protects, religious establishments where they exist below the federal level; and obviously no religious establishment is religiously neutral. Also, as a textual matter, the Constitution permits noncoercive patronage of religion by even the federal government, so long as it does not entail the coercive and fiscal measures that accompanied "an establishment of religion" at the time the First Amendment to the Constitution was ratified.

The logical reason why religious neutrality is not constitutionally required is different from the textual reason. The logical reason is that governmental neutrality is impossible, and the Constitution does not require the attainment of an impossible state of affairs. What makes governmental neutrality impossible is not that people cannot want it, but that they cannot achieve it. Even worse, governmental religious neutrality is not an ideal that can be "approximated," as one might approximate justice, because the more successful the approximation, the less neutral the result. How can this be? It is simply that a policy of neutrality itself inexorably functions as a form of religious establishment. This is empirically observable. I am tempted to call it the iron law of religious neutrality. To say that something is unattainable is not, of course, to say that public policy makers cannot try to attain it. But it is unwise to do so, and much harm has been done in the pursuit of this particular impossibility.

I will pursue these claims shortly in greater detail, but it is worth noting first that the issues they raise seem more important than ever in light of the March 2001 decision by the Sixth U.S. Court of Appeals regarding the Ohio state motto and, especially, in light of the controversy surrounding President Bush's "faith-based initiative." This presidential initiative enjoys considerable popular support because of a widely-felt sentiment. Many Americans apparently agree that if the federal government is in the business of conducting social service grant competitions, it is unfair to disqualify religious organizations from eligibility, especially when these organizations sometimes have the most effective programs and when most Americans are themselves rather religious. The faith-based initiative seems to be built on four principles as announced by the president himself, and as expressed by John DiIulio, his key advisor on the matter. First, the grant programs have to be all-inclusive in their eligibility policy, in that any and all religious-based groups may apply just as freely as nonreligious groups. Second, there has to be a secular alternative available whenever a religious organizations is also funded. Third, the federal government will not fund the specifically religious activities of these groups even though it may fund their activities in other ways. Fourth and finally, President Bush's key principle seems to be that these organizations must not be required or impelled to give up their religious identity or mission in order to participate.

Unlike the faith-based initiative, the Ohio motto case is clearly encompassed by the plain terms of the U.S. Constitution, as the Court of Appeals recognized. The facts were simple: The state of Ohio has as its official motto the text taken verbatim from Matthew 19:26, where Jesus says, "With God all things are possible." The act of the Ohio legislature that established this motto was, indeed, perfectly legitimate, for two reasons. First, it was an act of a state legislature, not an act of the federal government; second, the act did not violate the free exercise of religion. After all, no belief was compelled and no acquiescence was demanded of the citizens of Ohio (or of anyone else). They only had to look at the motto on the wall as they walked into state office buildings—or ignore it. They were not required to attest agreement with it, nor was any state benefit made contingent upon affirmation of it. There was some argument among the judges on the Court of Appeals as to whether the motto does or does not belong to the Christian religion in particular. Although many non-Christians could agree with the motto, those who knew the source of the statement pointed out that it is derived explicitly from the most authoritative source in Christianity, Jesus Christ himself. That fact, however, only makes its constitutional status more clear. The first amendment protects Ohio's decision to have a motto like this precisely *because* it is an identifiable and specifically religious motto, not *despite* its being particular to one religion or several religions. Looked at in this way, the state motto of Ohio is an expression (albeit a mild one) of an establishment of religion, and the First Amendment deprives the federal government of any power to legislate respecting an establishment of religion.

President Bush's faith-based initiative is a more complicated case. The complication is illustrated by the on-again, off-again fate of the Teen Challenge drug rehabilitation program. On frequent occasions during the fall 2000 campaign, candidate Bush praised the Teen Challenge program as one of the faith-based programs with an exceptionally successful record of freeing drug addicts from their addictions. He said that it ought, therefore, to be one of those organizations eligible to compete for federal drug rehabilitation funding. On the other hand, when the initiative was actually announced, one of President Bush's spokesmen said that Teen Challenge would not be eligible because its activities were pervasively religious. Within a few days, however, John DiIulio announced that, after some retooling of the program, Teen Challenge would be eligible after all. The vagaries of this initiative deserve careful attention. I believe that the faith-based initiative can be seen more clearly, and its knots untangled, if we view it in the light of broader constitutional principles concerning religion and government that I aim to delineate here. That is, we can assess the faith-based initiative properly if we understand how it is that the Constitution requires religious freedom but does not require religious neutrality.

NEUTRALITY VERSUS THE TEXT

In our day, the idea that government must be neutral on moral and religious matters is pervasively accepted. Conduct a thought experiment. What happens if you ask Americans questions like this: Does the Constitution permit the government to encourage religiosity and to promote proper morality in the citizens? Or does the Constitution forbid official efforts to praise piety and virtue and to discourage impiety and vice? Millions of Americans know the answer to these questions off the top of their heads. They know that virtue is strictly a private affair, and religion even more so. They take it as a self-evident truth that "government shouldn't legislate morality" and that there must be a wall of separation between religion and governmental agencies of all kinds. They believe that the Constitution is the bulwark of these self-evident truths. Such beliefs are not so much convictions as commonplaces. They are things not argued but taken for granted. To question these beliefs is to risk derision or worse, especially on most American university campuses.

Academic exponents of this prevailing view say the same thing, in a different tone of voice. Public authority, they aver, must not merely refrain from forcing citizens to agree with a favored moral or religious viewpoint (even their opponents agree with this). Public authority, they contend, must prescind from any action that would confer a governmental endorsement or public imprimatur on any particular moral or religious values.

This prevailing view, whether popular or academic, is wrong. The text of the U.S. Constitution, the logic of the structure established by the text, and the history of the text all stand against it. So does political wisdom, even apart from the constitutional text.

We may begin with the text and structure. There are four provisions in the text of the Constitution that affect religion. The most obvious are the first part of the First Amendment and the Article VI prohibition on religious tests for federal office. In addition, there is the Tenth Amendment, which declares that all the powers not enumerated and given to the national government are reserved to the states or the people. Finally, there is the first section of the Fourteenth Amendment, which prohibits not the federal government but the states from depriving U.S. citizens of their privileges or immunities and from depriving any person of liberty without due process of law.

The text of the First Amendment does not contain the words "separation of church and state," as many students are startled to discover. The first clause of the amendment says instead, "Congress shall make no law respecting an establishment of religion, or prohibiting the free exercise thereof." Taken in conjunction with the Tenth Amendment, this seems to have had a clear meaning to the ratifying generation, and to have a plain grammatical meaning even now: Congress shall make no law concerning, or with respect to, an establishment of religion. This certainly prohibits Congress from creating a national religious establishment. Just as plainly, it also prohibits Congress from enacting any legislation with respect to any establishment of religion wherever it might otherwise exist independently of Congressional action. In fact, establishments of religion, of various types, existed in many states and localities at the time of the adoption of the First Amendment, and this amendment shielded all of them from any interference by the federal Congress. This observation is certainly bolstered by the Tenth

Amendment, which reserves all unenumerated powers to the states and the people. The Constitution nowhere gives the national government the power to determine public policy respecting an establishment of religion by other governmental entities.

Even the Article VI prohibition on religious tests, if considered literally, permits a different interpretation from the one usually given now. Under the prevailing interpretation, the no religious tests provision of Article VI is supposed to be at least exemplary, and probably determinative, for government policy at all levels. Isaac Kramnick and R. Laurence Moore make this argument, asserting that the Article VI prohibition makes ours a decisively "Godless Constitution."[1] The prohibition is exemplary, they say, because by restricting the federal government in this way, the Constitution establishes a pattern or example to be followed at all other levels of government authority. They reason that since the federal government is superior in authority to other levels, other levels ought to model themselves after it in every respect. (Is it relevant here to note that most Americans probably doubt that the federal government has established a record to be emulated?)

There is, however, another way of looking at the Article VI prohibition on religious tests—in fact, a way of looking at it which prevailed for a very long time. Consider the state of Maryland, which for generations enforced a religious test for state office. Following the pattern set in colonial times, the 1776 Constitution of Maryland required office holders to affirm their belief in the Christian religion. This was, at the time, not terribly restrictive in practice and, in context, may be seen as something of an expression of religious pluralism, since it included both Catholics and Protestants who had nurtured successive antagonisms against one another throughout Maryland history. The religious test for office was retained in the Maryland Constitution through various adjustments, until the 1960s when the Maryland Constitution simply required state office holders to affirm their belief in God. So stated, the test excluded only atheists. In 1961 the U.S. Supreme Court announced that Maryland's religious test violated the federal Constitution.[2] By order of the Court, the test was therefore eliminated. The Court asserted, in effect, that Maryland had been violating the Constitution for 170 years, roughly from the adoption of the First Amendment. Or, in other words, seen in the longer scope of history, it took some 270 years for the nation to notice that this state had been defying American principles all along.

If this interpretation is too whimsical for words, it makes sense to take the text of Article VI as it stands, without imputing to it an unstated exemplary quality. After all, Maryland was hardly alone in employing religious tests for state office. Such tests for office were not uncommon in the thirteen colonies, and in those same communities once they became states. Religious tests for office also figured in local and municipal levels of government. And although Kramnick and Moore might wish that their personal aversion to religious tests were widely shared, there is in fact no literal conflict between a prohibition of such tests to the federal government and their retention by the states and localities. In this light, we should be able to recognize that Article VI is not necessarily exemplary. Those who were keen advocates of religious tests for office at the state level need not have been opponents, but could have been among the most vigorous of proponents of the Article VI prohibition at the federal level. This is because they would have seen it as a way of preserving their particular state religious tests, protecting them from dilution or threat at the federal level, where any religious test implemented might have come out differently from the ones in place in particular states. In keeping with the general thrust of the Tenth Amendment, someone who was a keen advocate for the state religious tests for office could also have been a keen advocate of the Article VI prohibition on federal religious tests. The question of whether to have religious tests for office—and what kind if any to have—is moot to the federal government because that is reserved to the states and their subdivisions.

NEUTRALITY VERSUS HISTORY

It shouldn't be surprising that while dealing with the text we have consulted history. History is not always determinative in constitutional matters, but it is always relevant. In this instance it is worth considering the several generations of Americans who fought for independence, and who ratified the Constitution and its early amendments. Those Americans surely did not understand themselves to be repudiating or delegitimizing their own institutions of self-government. They were repudiating the Crown but not their own ongoing practices. What were those practices with respect to religion and government? To modern sensibilities they were shocking indeed. In brief, Americans of the founding period pervasively practiced what our courts now call unconstitutional religious establishment.

Such practices are well-documented history, most recently confirmed and represented by the Library of Congress in its 1998 exhibit on "Religion and the Founding of the American Republic," and in the accompanying volume by the same title.[3] In the narrative portion of this text, historian James Hutson, Chief of the Library's Manuscript Division, discusses at length the historical evidence for the governmental religious practices of the late colonial period, of the Continental Congress, and of the new states and the federal government under the Constitution. Hutson shows that Americans through most of this period were accustomed to speaking of the religious functions of government in terms of the tasks of the magistrate. The magistrate was expected to act, in his official capacity, as a "nursing father" of the church. The phrase, drawn from the text of Isaiah 49:23, captured the prevailing view that local and state governmental authorities, while remaining institutionally distinct from the church, were expected to use their public powers to promote the well-being of the church and of true piety. The nursing father metaphor, Hutson shows, was widely employed in America from the seventeenth century to the early decades of the nineteenth century.[4]

It is not surprising that early Americans thought that public officials ought to promote piety, because they were an overwhelmingly religious people. This was so not only during the early colonial period and the Great Awakening, but also in the years preceding, and including, the War for Independence and its aftermath. Hutson points out that contrary to familiar claims (recited by Kramnick and Moore, among others), Christian piety was not shrinking but rather blossoming during this period.[5] Some historians in the mid-twentieth century evidently erred on this point by taking at face value reports from missionary societies, which, seeking funding increases from the home office, exaggerated ungodliness in pioneering communities. They may also have erred on this point by focusing on church membership figures rather than church attendance figures—the former understandably smaller than the latter among settlers on the move westward. A greater error still has been uncovered by feminist historians, who have documented religious participation by women, which burgeoned during the Revolutionary era and was often neglected in official tallies. In the society seeking and gaining independence from Britain, religion was in the "ascension rather than the declension," as Hutson puts it.[6]

It was this highly pious society that in October of 1774 consented together for common action independently of the authority of the Crown.[7] Though fragile, their unity as of that date was linguistic, religious, and cultural, but it was also politically institutionalized in a single Continental Congress. That Congress, which ultimately declared independence, vigorously prosecuted the war, and recommended the new Constitution for ratification, also zealously practiced the role of nursing father. Not content merely to employ a chaplain and begin its sessions with prayer, the Congress exhorted the public via a series of explicitly religious proclamations. As James Hutson notes, "For ten years, from its first fast day proclamation of June 12, 1775, until its final thanksgiving proclamation of August 3, 1784, Congress adopted and preached to the American people the political theology of the national covenant."[8] Issued regularly and emphatically, these proclamations sought "through the merits and mediation of Jesus Christ [to] obtain his pardon and forgiveness" (1776), and invited Americans to "join the penitent confession of their manifold sins . . . and their humble and earnest supplication that it may please God, through the merits of Jesus Christ, mercifully to forgive and blot them out of remembrance" (1777).[9] The policy of the Confederation Congress could hardly be called religiously neutral, but neither could it be accused of coercion in its patronage of Christian piety.[10]

The religious posture of that first national Congress carries implications unwelcome for those who favor official secularism. Some hope to evade such implications by insisting that everything changed in 1789 with the ratification of the Constitution, which had been commissioned and recommended by that Confederation Congress. This is a vain hope. The state constitutions (most modified around 1776) nearly all preserved potent features consistent with the nursing father theory even after 1789. Many state constitutions retained explicitly Christian tests for state office-holders, some incorporated tax schemes to support churches and religious education, and nearly all contained hortatory language that gave noncoercive rhetorical patronage to Christian piety.[11]

Even the newly established federal government, narrow in its jurisdiction, did not adopt a posture of religious neutrality. The day after the Bill of Rights was approved by the House of Representatives—including the portentous First Amendment—a motion was introduced to instruct President George Washington to proclaim "a day of public thanksgiving and prayer, to be observed by acknowledging, with grateful hearts, the many signal favors of Almighty God." Passed by both houses of Congress with only two objections, the motion was implemented with alacrity by President Washington.[12] Washington's own eagerness to affirm the new nation's dependance on piety and providence is well known, as are his religious proclamations. The same is true of second president John Adams.

Those made uneasy by the overt religiosity of Washington and Adams often prefer to focus on America's third president, Thomas Jefferson. They praise Jefferson for repudiating the nursing father theory, for recognizing the religious neutrality ostensibly required by the Constitution. Yet at the very period when Jefferson was declining to issue presidential religious proclamations, and penning his famous letter extolling a "wall of separation" to the Danbury Baptists, Jefferson was also attending explicitly Christian worship services regularly in the House Chamber of the U.S. Capitol. He was, in this same period, regularly dispatching the U.S. Marine Band—under his direct authority as chief executive—to accompany those worship services. He was, moreover, authorizing worship services, including the proclamation of the gospel and the serving of Holy Communion, in executive branch buildings including the War Office and the Treasury. As Hutson puts it, "It is no exaggeration to say that, on Sundays in Washington during Thomas Jefferson's presidency, the state became the church.[13] The Reverend Ethan Allen recorded an anecdote about Jefferson that, though uncorroborated, fits neatly with Jefferson's practices in these matters—though not with the portrait usually painted of him today. According to Allen, President Jefferson was walking to church one Sunday (probably headed for the Capitol), carrying "his large red prayer book under his arm when a friend querying him after their mutual good morning said which way are you walking Mr. Jefferson. To which he replied to Church, Sir. You going to Church Mr. J. You do not believe a word in it. Sir, said Mr. J. No Nation has ever yet existed or been governed without religion. Nor can be. The Christian religion is the best religion that has been given to man and I as chief Magistrate of this nation am bound to give it the sanction of my example. Good morning Sir."[14]

Jefferson's successor, James Madison, called the Father of the Constitution, is frequently invoked as the authority behind American religious neutralism. Those who portray Madison this way often emphasize Madison's "Detached Memoranda," unpublished reminiscences penned in 1817 after his second presidential term. Law review articles routinely cite Madison's private ruminations in support of the Supreme Court's dictum that the First Amendment "precludes government from conveying or attempting to convey a message that religion or a particular religious belief is favored or preferred."[15] Similarly, It has become common for legal scholars to argue that courts should rule unconstitutional every remaining public affirmation of piety—such as in the Pledge of Allegiance, in the national motto, on our coinage and currency, in the recognition of Christmas as a federal holiday, in governmental chaplaincies, in presidential inaugurals and in court proceedings themselves ("God save this honorable Court"). Their arguments regularly cite Madison's private "Detached Memoranda" as a basis for their constitutional claims.[16]

Yet such works either downplay or conveniently omit to mention that James Madison, as president, issued four thanksgiving day proclamations, officially calling Americans to days of "public humiliation and fasting and of prayer to Almighty God. . . . humble adoration to the Great Sovereign of the Universe, of confessing their sins and transgressions, and of strengthening their vows of repentance."[17] As James Hutson notes, "In his Detached Memoranda Madison criticized the religious policies he approved as a member of Congress and followed as president—the appointment of chaplains and the proclamations of days of fasting and thanksgiving."[18] While Madison's private regrets deserve our respectful attention, they do not expunge the constitutional authority that he, as president, considered sufficient to justify his official patronage of religion. To put the same point differently, Madison's unpublished reminiscences could serve as good arguments for amending the Constitution, but they do not determine the meaning of the text as it stands. In particular, these latter-day ruminations do not carry the official weight of Madison's own official actions as president—especially since such actions were repeated by presidents before and long after Madison.

The plain words of the Constitution, as they were understood at ratification and as they were put into practice by the statesmen who framed them, make it hard to sustain the supposed imperative of governmental religious neutrality. As Daniel L. Dreisbach has argued, the First Amendment's restrictions on establishment were understood as jurisdictional restrictions on the national government, not as substantive restrictions governing any and all governmental bodies. Like Yale law professor Akhil Reed Amar, Dreisbach argues that the establishment clause of the First Amendment has more in common with the Tenth Amendment than it has with any other part of the Bill of Rights.[19] Thomas Jefferson himself, Dreisbach argues, "believed the First Amendment erected two distinct walls of separation: one between the federal government and religious institutions, thereby preventing the establishment of a national church; and the other between the federal and state governments on matters pertaining to religion, thereby preventing the federal regime from interfering with religious establishments and practices endorsed by state governments."[20] This accords with the view of Chief Justice John Marshall, who declared for the Supreme Court that the guarantees in the Bill of Rights "contain no expression indicating an intention to apply them to the state governments."[21] Justice Joseph Story in his 1833 *Commentaries on the Constitution of the United States*, was only voicing the original consensus when he wrote that the First Amendment was intended "to exclude from the national government all power to act on the subject [of religion]. . . . The whole power over the subject of religion is left exclusively to the state governments, to be acted upon according to their own sense of justice and the state constitutions."[22]

Marshall and Story understood that Americans of the ratifying era were agreeing only to add a thin new top layer, above the ongoing political authority of the states and local communities. That top layer, a central or federal government, would have explicitly enumerated powers, with power over the issue of religious establishment pointedly excluded. Far from calling into question the legitimacy of local and state efforts to promote piety and virtue, this arrangement, it was thought, would have the opposite effect. Keeping the top layer thin would protect the thickness of bottom layer—the moral and religious jurisdictions of the states and of the people organized in local communities. It would strengthen local government patronage of piety precisely by preventing the new federal government from intruding into matters best controlled closer to home.

INCORPORATION VERSUS THE TEXT

Obviously, things have changed. The Supreme Court has turned away completely from this understanding of the place of religion in the constitutional order, and it began to do so about fifty years ago. In view of the more than 200-year history of the Constitution—and in view of the American state and local religious practices extending back almost 400 years—this is a relatively recent development.

During these recent fifty-odd years, the Supreme Court has employed the First Amendment as the major mechanism by which to invalidate the public promotion of virtue and piety. In 1947 the Court announced that the amendment demanded a "wall of separation between church and state," which must be kept "high and impregnable."[23] In keeping with this view, local schools have had to abandon their attempt to promote reverence for traditional morality by posting the Ten Commandments on the school wall.[24] Local schools have also had to give up on the attempt to make school children feel accountable for their behavior to a higher power by making them listen to a daily nonsectarian prayer opening the school day, or even by having an opening moment of silence.[25] The Court has similarly determined that it is constitutionally impermissible for a prayer to be officially offered at middle school commencement exercises, even though attendance at such exercises is voluntary.[26] Even student-led public prayer at high school football games is now impermissible.[27] All these practices fall afoul of the established principle, announced by the Court, that all governmental entities, at all levels, "must pursue a course of complete neutrality toward religion," and that all their policies must have "a secular purpose and effect."[28]

Under the new dispensation, the impact of the First Amendment is the similar even when the official promotion of virtue does not suffer from a fatal entanglement with religion. Because of this approach, local school boards have had to abandon their attempt to promote patriotism (by requiring school children to salute the American flag).[29] And for similar reasons, legislative efforts to condemn or penalize hateful speech have been thwarted.[30] According to the Supreme Court, the Constitution's First Amendment requires law and public authority at all levels to be content neutral in such matters.

Even in recent decisions considered favorable to religion, the constitutional principle established by the Court is hostile to the public affirmation of piety. The reason that public schools must now allow Bible studies and religious films on family life during off-hours on school premises is the same reason that public universities must retain funding for student-run religious newspapers: no public authority may engage in viewpoint discrimination.[31] Equal access to public forums is mandated not only by federal statute,[32] but also, we are told, by the First Amendment's (implied) requirement that public authority always adhere to a posture of neutrality. Such cases, lauded by religious conservatives, actually scuttle the original Constitution more profoundly than ever. Precisely to the degree that the religious prerogatives of private individuals are vindicated, the public affirmation of religious piety by state and local communities is subverted. The neutrality principle that affirms the former condemns the latter. Even influential conservative jurists support this progressive deconstruction of the original constitutional scheme.[33]

Nothing in the text of the Constitution changed in 1947 to precipitate the change that began then. The Supreme Court justified the change, however, by claiming that legislatures and courts had, until then, failed to see the religious implications of a textual change made back in 1865—the Fourteenth Amendment. The justices, and legal scholars who follow their work, call this the doctrine of incorporation. The first section of that amendment is said to incorporate many of the protections of the first nine amendments, now applying them as restrictions on state governments, not merely restrictions on Congress. Given the way the Court chose to interpret the First Amendment, it began dictating to the states and localities what their policy should be in religious matters—namely, a policy of neutrality.

Although this represented an astounding reversal of the original constitutional design, it is easy to understand the Supreme Court's captivity to a cascading set of logical propositions leading inexorably to its modern doctrines. Five propositions suffice to illustrate the sequence.

1. The First Amendment prevents Congress from creating a national religious establishment and requires Congress to protect the free exercise of religion.
2. Nonestablishment and freedom necessitate governmental religious neutrality.
3. The Fourteenth Amendment brings the states (and their subsidiary local governments) under the rules of the Bill of Rights.
4. Therefore, the states must refrain from creating state religious establishments and must protect the free exercise of religion.
5. Therefore, the states must practice governmental religious neutrality.

The two conclusions follow necessarily from the first three assertions. The problem is that the second and third of those assertions are faulty. Nonestablishment does not require neutrality because even the federal government can make its religious preferences known without establishing religious tests for office or tax levies for favored churches—in other words, without undertaking the practices that were the defining features of "an establishment of religion" at the time the Constitution was ratified. Free exercise of religion does not require neutrality because any government can make its religious preferences known without requiring citizens to agree, without penalizing them for their dissenting views, and without interfering with their worship services. Moreover, the Fourteenth Amendment does not bring the states unequivocally under the rules of the first ten amendments. No wonder it took the Supreme Court about eighty years to discover in the Fourteenth Amendment the basis for its novel claims.

To make this clear, it is important to concede—even to rejoice—that the Fourteenth Amendment does indeed curtail the jurisdiction of states. It denies them the power to restrict the liberties of individual citizens in ways that may previously have been legitimate.[34] According to Amar, this reasonably incorporates most of the rights and liberties listed in the first nine amendments, obliging the states to respect those liberties just as the federal government had always been obliged to do. But the Fourteenth Amendment could not reasonably incorporate either the Tenth Amendment or the establishment clause of the First Amendment. It would be nonsensical to do so, Amar argues. How could a state be forced to abide by provisions that prevent the federal government from intruding into a state jurisdiction? The establishment clause and the Tenth Amendment are thus in principle "unincorporable."[35] As Dreisbach puts it, "incorporating the nonestablishment provision . . . is as nonsensical as incorporating the Tenth Amendment."[36] The only intelligible possibility would be to insist on parallelism—that is, to hold that the Fourteenth Amendment prohibits the states from interfering with the religious jurisdictions of their constituent counties and towns (just as the First Amendment prohibited the federal government from interfering with the religious jurisdictions of the states). If this interpretation is intelligible but silly, we are left with the Supreme Court's current view of incorporation and the religion clauses, which, though unintelligible, is too consequential to be silly.

The point of these reflections is not that incorporation is mistaken. The Fourteenth Amendment indeed incorporates the liberties announced in the first nine amendments. But it only incorporates liberties: "nor shall any State deprive any person of . . . liberty . . . without due process of law." The free exercise of religion is a liberty enjoyed by an individual, but the jurisdictional framework set up by the establishment provision and by the Tenth Amendment is not. It is therefore not incorporated. States may no longer infringe religious liberty, but they still retain their original prerogatives concerning official patronage of religion, or lack thereof. Not surprisingly, this understanding of the establishment clause accords with constitutional history until roughly fifty years ago. Before that time, the Supreme Court never claimed that symbolic patronage of Christian piety at any governmental level, or even official sponsorship of churches and religious tests for office at the state level, were unconstitutional. Indeed, the long silence of the Court on such matters implied the view of establishment issues described above.

None of this means that state religious establishments would now be a good thing if they were once again permitted, rather than forbidden, by the Supreme Court. But it does mean that the moral and religious possibilities of American federalism are, properly understood, considerably broader than the Court—and most Americans, now see them to be. If even this modest conclusion would shock most modern Americans, it only illustrates how the novel legal imperatives imposed by the Court over the past fifty years have profoundly influenced American society.

AN INTELLECTUAL SEA-CHANGE

The Supreme Court's incorporation of the establishment clause may have been unintelligible, but that proved no obstacle to a self-confident Court, and the novelty went almost unnoticed by legal intellectuals at the time. During the period of the Court's innovations on religion, a sea-change was occurring in the American intellectual climate. Seen in broader perspective, the Court's rethinking of these matters was part of the larger reinterpretation of American identity underway among intellectuals, and quickly transmitted to ordinary Americans. As World War II drew to a close, America came to understand itself no longer as a complex constitutional mixture serving to protect both the traditional culture of virtue and the liberty of individuals. Perhaps because of its innate complexity, the structure established at the Founding had little appeal. Instead, Americans began to think of their country in simpler terms, as the embodiment of liberty taken as a prerogative of individuals only. Individual freedom became, in the prevailing mind, the architectonic principle of the whole. This freedom was understood not merely as freedom from coercion, but as freedom from influence—freedom from any influence emanating from some source other than the individual self. Given this conception of freedom, it is not hard to see how governmental neutrality on religion was said to be necessary in order to protect the prerogatives of the individual to be free from all unsought influences. Governmental influence on religious matters—even scrupulously noncoercive influence—was an obvious and identifiable influence. During the same decades that governmental religious influence was ruled out of order, the religious influence of families and communities was also, logically, under similar attack.

What accounts for this intellectual sea-change that drove the courts and was driven by them so decisively? It is not necessary, and maybe not possible, to give a conclusive answer to this question. But it is worth reflecting on the intellectual psychology of the Cold War, which was just getting underway as the Supreme Court upended the original constitutional rules. This psychology very much affected the intellectual classes. In that era Louis Hartz was beginning to argue that America had been a liberal country from the start, committed to the unfettered private discretion of the individual and hostile to any conception of the common good or any corresponding public truth.[37] As a socialist himself, Hartz was offering censure not praise. His opponents on the other side of the ideological divide reacted in a manner predictable given the Cold War climate of opinion. Patriotic intellectuals concluded that whatever Hartz condemned must be praiseworthy. After all, America's new nemesis across the seas exalted itself as the land of collectivism, of communalism in the service of a future condition described as a final common good. Intellectuals on the right were prone to reason that if this was our enemy, and if they were wrong, then their principles must be the polar opposites of ours. If they were the country of pristine collectivism, then we must be the country of individualism. This habit of thinking probably characterized self-described conservatives even more than self-described liberals during the post-war period.

This way of thinking about America became almost a national imperative, and was taught pervasively in universities during the period. It found expression, among other ways, in the sudden curricular prominence of *The Federalist Papers* in civics courses during the first decades of the Cold War. Though it has always been admired, this text came then to be regarded—as it never had been before—as a kind of Rosetta Stone for interpreting the Constitution. *Federalist 10* in particular became enormously popular with civics teachers, for it does not distinguish between federal and state jurisdictions, and it seems to repudiate the American tradition of publicly-cultivated virtue and piety. Though James Madison probably did not intend it this way, *Federalist 10* became the dominant vehicle for teaching that America was designed to be officially indifferent to moral and religious concerns, and that its Constitution was nothing more than a value-free mechanism for organizing the selfishness (i.e., the freedom) of private individuals. This way of thinking prevailed in law schools, where it was absorbed by aspiring judges—later to be enforced by them.

MATURE NEUTRALITY AS A RELIGIOUS ESTABLISHMENT

Even if we cannot nail down all the reasons, it is clear that approximately fifty years ago the U.S. Supreme Court began to enforce governmental religious neutrality as a constitutional mandate, and to hold every public undertaking, from the highest act of Congress to the lowest policy decision of the smallest local school board, to the same standard. What have we learned from five decades of mandated public secularism? We have learned that the Constitution's original (and still textually standing) arrangements were better than their replacements. Indeed we are now in a position to see the merits of the original rules more clearly than ever by observing the consequences of rejecting them.

We have discovered that a comprehensive policy of top-to-bottom religious neutrality has perverse effects unanticipated by its early proponents (though anticipated by some of its early critics, like Edward S. Corwin[38]). Religious neutrality turns out to be impossible to attain. Secular neutrality becomes, in practice, secularistic neutrality. Secular neutrality has many of the same features and problems of what we normally might call a religious establishment—but with a major difference. Unlike ordinary religious establishments, this one is covert and unacknowledged—indeed its very premises require it to be so and render it almost invisible in the character of establishment. By its very nature it is especially invisible to its most ardent advocates. The fact that this covertness is unintended absolves guilt but does not change the effect. A covert and unacknowledged religious establishment is more powerful and harder to resist than any previously known establishment. The effects of secular neutrality as a religious establishment are to be found most directly in cultural matters—education, family law, social policy; that is, in any dimension of public life that is bound up with the articulation and transmission of meaning.

American judges committed to this approach often mention the impressionability of young children as one of the natural facts that necessitate a secular neutrality approach, especially in education; consequently, for instance, classroom prayers mandated by local or state school boards are judged improper. Such judges act, they say, on behalf of impressionable children, whose liberty of conscience must be protected from the powerful pressure of politically-sanctioned religion. But such judges—and the legal theorists whose ideas support them—are strangely oblivious to the reverse implication of impressionability.[39] Children are indeed impressionable, but for that reason they are deeply susceptible to the politically sanctioned absence of God, to the state-sponsored refusal to recognize, in public or common life, God's relevance and His claims. What habits of mind does this induce in impressionable children who grow up to be adults? It induces either a discomfort with the topic of God as something unfamiliar, or else it induces a tendency among religious believers to regard their beliefs as true in only a private sense: "It's true for me, but not necessarily for you," as Americans are now pervasively inclined to say.[40] Despite the prevailing jurisprudential rationale for religious neutrality, the facts of impressionability suggest that, when it comes to education and culture, there is no default, neutral position that state authority can assume toward religion.

Secularist establishments are worse than overt religious establishments because they get their force—at least as practiced in recent decades in the United States—by denial and by indirection. They are almost impossible for most people to see, much less to resist, and their consequences are pervasive for culture. As Stephen Macedo acknowledges, the "mechanisms and practices" of liberal neutrality "have the effect of shaping our commitments and habits very deeply, without exactly announcing that purpose on their face." He celebrates this effect, however, rather than lamenting it. After all, he reminds us, "The operation of these institutional tendencies and biases is also gentle rather than oppressive, influencing the deeply held beliefs of vast numbers of people without coercion or force."[41] Yet if this influence operates invisibly and covertly, does it really operate without coercion? The invisible nature of the process—which Macedo admits—necessarily moots consent to the process; it also moots resistance to the process for all but the most self-conscious and intransigent dissenters. By contrast, remaining silent during an official classroom prayer in pre-1962 America was a straightforward and easily intelligible act of resistance (which deserved, and typically enjoyed, legal protection).

The culturally transformative power of America's public secularism was borne home to me recently in conversations with neighbors from overseas, visiting scholars from many countries living together in an international academic community in Princeton, New Jersey. One neighbor had been exposed to the American observance of Easter through the local public schools. Truly puzzled, she asked us what Easter was, since she was unfamiliar with any holidays centered around rabbits. When we explained that Easter commemorated the resurrection of Jesus, she understood immediately; she knew it by another name, and without rabbits, in her own language. We had to explain that for legal reasons American public schools are skittish about any mention of God in connection with holidays and special observances. Consequently, there is little or no transmission of communal memory about such things. Scrupulous about maintaining the constitutionally mandated posture of neutrality, public school teachers, even though they are permitted to do so, are uncomfortable talking about the religious content of Christmas, Easter, Passover, and Yom Kippur; consequently, such days lose their religious content in the minds of impressionable children. Or where teachers choose pluralism instead of silence, and give each religious holiday equal time and equal respect, children (who do not cease being impressionable under this policy) learn not indifference but equivalence: the public, and therefore respectable, attitude accords equal truth value to the claims of all. Under this scheme, children imbibe either the notion that all religions are ultimately pursuing the same vision, or else the notion that competing religious truth claims cannot be navigated by reason. Whatever the mechanism, the effect is that of a religious establishment: the state promotes a preferred religious message, whether of indifference, equivalence, or incommensurability. And children—and their parents—are induced to acquiesce to this establishment message because it is presented as the absence of establishment.

AFTER NEUTRALITY

The U.S. Supreme Court, official custodian of secular neutrality, has yet to acknowledge the paradoxical consequences of its nonestablishment doctrines. We can observe, however, a certain rethinking among the legal scholars and activists who have given intellectual aid and comfort to the policy of public secularism. There is, in fact, another sea-change occurring in American intellectual life, and not only among academics. The new idea is this: where religious neutrality was once praised because it impartially let people choose their own values, it is now praised because it changes the culture (that is to say, people's values). Religious neutrality is now lauded precisely because its effects are not neutral. Stephen Macedo's work, cited above, gives a relatively benign expression to this approach.

Others are less temperate than Macedo. Many now promote the policy of religious neutrality in education because, they say, we must ensure that "our schools don't raise bigots." In other words, official secularism helps wean students from retrograde religious and moral convictions that they bring with them from their families and churches—such as a belief that Christianity provides the only sure way to God, or a belief that homosexual acts are morally improper. Students can be induced to shed vulgar beliefs by being exposed to the official doctrine that no beliefs are true enough to deserve public sanction, or to the allied doctrine that all beliefs are equally valid. Public school curricular changes in California probably represent the leading edge of this impulse. For example, new legislation in California not only bars discrimination based on sexual orientation by public schools and by any private religious school receiving state funds, the new legislation also mandates revised public school curricula designed to "foster appreciation" for sexual diversity and to discourage disapproving attitudes toward homosexuality. It also provides for kindergarten through twelfth grade access to tolerance programs and curricular resources to combat bias concerning gender or sexual orientation. A California Department of Instruction task force has proposed implementing these laws by adding new requirements to the state's education code, including a directive that schools post "positive grade-level-appropriate visual images" portraying "all sexual orientations and gender identities," and that comparable written materials be integrated into every subject in the curriculum (including science, history, language arts, and mathematics).[42]

Presumably all orientations and identities must be given equal time to ensure that the influence of the state of California is neutral among them. Behind this rule is the recognition that religious beliefs are usually the foundation for a preference among such identities. Such curricular mandates are typically defended, however, not on the grounds of neutrality, but on the grounds of the socially desirable tolerance that it instills. Those who object are apt to receive a surprising retort. The point of education, they will likely be told, is to form students—their character and values: "Bigots can't be good citizens."

Government, it seems, is now to function—via the schools —as an official "nursing parent" to nurture proper beliefs among young citizens. The policy of official religious neutrality now comes full circle. Nonestablishment neutrality will appear, in retrospect, as a kind of interregnum, temporarily necessary to dissolve the old pieties until the new ones were ready to receive governmental patronage under the new dispensation.

This observation is easily misunderstood. The outcome I describe should be faulted, but not primarily for its hypocrisy. The problem is not that educational leaders could have kept the curriculum morally and religiously neutral but failed to do so; they could not have done so. The error is not that the new pieties, as I describe them, are receiving official patronage when no piety should receive official patronage; such an outcome would be impossible. Going back to straightforward neutrality will not solve these problems, only deepen them. We are facing new problems that could not have been fully understood at the threshold of official secularism after World War II. For only now can we see that adhering scrupulously to a policy of moral and religious neutrality inescapably entails its own negation.

The real question thus emerges clearly. The question is not whether some version of piety shall receive official endorsement, or whether none shall receive such endorsement. The question is rather *which* pieties shall receive governmental patronage, what *kind* of patronage, and at what *level* of government?

The original American answer to these questions is still available, and it does not require changing even one word of the constitutional text. The Constitution, as written, protects religious liberty without requiring religious neutrality. Under the benign influence of the free exercise provision of the First Amendment and of the Fourteenth Amendment rightly (and originally) understood, it protects all individuals from coercion in the exercise of their religion, including coercion from governmental bodies at any level. The Constitution does not—because it could not—protect individuals from being governmentally influenced by their communities in these matters. The Constitution addresses the substantive questions—which piety, what patronage, and what level of government—indirectly, through the Tenth Amendment, the establishment provision of the First Amendment, and the jurisdictional scheme of federalism.

The common good requires, at some level of public life, some kind of public endorsement of religious convictions that foster civic decency. Moreover, every political community (even a liberally neutral one) inescapably does give its patronage to some such convictions. Yet even those unimpressed with considerations of the common good, who value individual liberty more than civic decency, can affirm the original constitutional formula. The patchwork of noncoercive, geographically diverse religious establishments that it permits can powerfully protect individual religious liberty, by blocking the amalgamation of a centralized, national religious ideology, and by giving people jurisdictional options to choose among. Indeed, proponents of individual liberty should feel considerable anxiety about the status quo—that is, the comprehensive national religious ideology that has sprung up under cover of religious neutrality.

Americans are very much under the governmental influence of this ideology and the anti-traditional piety it cultivates. Of course citizens can never be free from governmental influence in matters of religion. But they can be free from coercion, and the kind of religious freedom that the Constitution protects—freedom from governmental coercion in religious belief and practice—is still intact in America. In this we should rejoice. Self-conscious and determined dissenters can and do refuse to embrace the religious outlook currently promoted by government. Their freedom to do so is protected. They can even freely educate their children in accord with their dissenting views, although they must do so at their own expense and they must continue to pay tax support to the school system which propagates the established religion. The dissenters—among them home schooling families and supporters of Christian schools—understandably complain about having to pay for an educational system dedicated to advancing a religious outlook fundamentally at odds with their own. But it is important to see that their complaint is about lack of fairness, not lack of freedom.

This allows for a surprising conclusion. According to the analysis offered here, the status quo—much as it deserves to be lamented—is, in a sense, constitutionally permissible. That is to say, under liberal neutrality in its mature form Americans experience religious liberty without religious neutrality, as they always have. In formal terms, it is the same kind of arrangement that prevailed in colonial times, at the founding era, during the nineteenth century, and in the early decades of the twentieth century before the Supreme Court eliminated school-sponsored prayer. The only difference is that the established religion is a different one.

Leaving aside the question of whether our new established religion is a good religion or a true one, the status quo can be faulted on at least two counts. First, the status quo came into being, and is maintained, by the claim that it was not merely constitutionally permissible but constitutionally required. That claim was (and is) false. That claim contravened the text of the Constitution, the structure established by the text, and the history behind the text. Second, the status quo came into being via unconstitutional means. The new religious establishment emerged not as the result of amendments to the state constitutions but as a result of centralized national judicial fiat. This procedure did violence to the provisions of the Constitution that give jurisdiction over laws respecting an establishment of religion to the states, not the central government. As Edward S. Corwin of Princeton argued at the beginning of this process in the 1950s, the Constitution does not give the Supreme Court the powers of a national school board.[43] Had the Court held back, it is possible that the states would eventually have come around on their own, and, given secular neutrality, the public prerogatives once enjoyed by Christianity.

Given the climate of opinion in the post-war period, I think that the Supreme Court's nonestablishment jurisprudence should be seen as a series of understandable and forgivable mistakes. But at the tail end of this process it is hard to find any compelling excuse for persisting in those mistakes.

The Constitution's original configuration of religious freedom without religious neutrality recommends itself not only because it is mandated by the text, but also because it is wise. Under the original configuration, the federal government need not be religiously neutral but could engage in noncoercive, nonfiscal rhetorical affirmation of a common piety. The states and localities could determine for themselves whether, how, and to what degree to actually establish religion, so long as individuals could freely exercise their dissenting religions. These features of the American Constitution do not answer every public policy question regarding religion but, unlike the convoluted neutralist jurisprudence devised in the past five decades, they provide a healthy and viable framework for resolving them.

FAITH-BASED FREEDOM

In the light of these considerations, we may conclude by reflecting on current faith-based controversies. Under original American constitutional principles, the basis of the Sixth Court of Appeals' ruling in the Ohio motto case is crystal clear. In choosing a Christian motto that even most non-Christian residents could affirm, Ohio was merely exercising its constitutionally protected prerogatives.

President Bush's faith-based initiative can also be assessed more clearly now. The Constitution, as we have noted, does not require the federal government to be religiously neutral, but allows it to offer symbolic affirmation of a favored religious viewpoint. How much more, then, does it allow the federal government to run grant competitions in which service providers of all types—both traditionally religious and religiously secular—are eligible for funding. If anything, the president's rule of open-ended, all-inclusive eligibility is an expression of the very principle of religious neutrality that has animated the nonestablishment jurisprudence of the past fifty years. Such a principle, as I have argued, is the functional equivalent of a nonneutral religious establishment, and would certainly not be constitutionally required of a program run by any of the fifty states. As applied to a program of the federal government, however, the rule of all-inclusive eligibility guarantees that any federal patronage of a favored religion will be rhetorical rather than fiscal. President Bush's combination of rhetorical support for religion with religiously neutral funding for social service agencies seems almost exactly to embody the appropriate constitutional posture for the federal government.

Apparently reluctant to face a legal challenge, however, the president has conceded more to the neutrality principle than is wise. As detailed so far, the faith-based initiative would require eligible religious organizations to segregate their religious activities from their nonreligious ones, receiving funding for the latter but not the former. Presidential advisor Stephen Goldsmith says, for instance, that government money must not be used to purchase Bibles. This creates a considerable incentive to abandon the religiously holistic approach that makes faith-based treatment programs so successful. To understand this perverse incentive, it is important to keep in mind not only the easy cases like literacy and job training programs, but also the hard cases that President Bush himself keeps mentioning—alcohol and drug addiction and prisoner rehabilitation. In such cases, it is impossible to segregate funds between religious and nonreligious activities. Are Bibles, for instance, separable from and incidental to the drug rehabilitation program run by Teen Challenge? Or are they an integral element, a source of the very success for which the president has praised that program?

President Bush's plan can pass the test of wisdom if it reserves the right to exclude antisocial groups from eligibility. In view of existing federal antidiscrimination law, this exclusion cannot be on the basis of religious affiliation. But there is no reason why the grant competitions envisioned cannot exclude organizations that practice or advocate illegal activities like coercion and lynching. President Bush's plan can also pass the test of wisdom if it does not insist on a division of funds between religious and nonreligious activities. After all, most of these programs are dealing with fragile and impressionable human beings. Are rehabilitation programs that pointedly refuse to identify the need for God actually neutral in their religious impact? Do they not rather have a marked influence on the world view of their clients? If so, must secular rehabilitation programs segregate their funds between their religiously formative activities and other activities? Such questions answer themselves.

If the evaluation criteria are not theological criteria, it should not make any difference if those criteria are met by mingling or by dividing the grant funds (which are fungible in any case). Either the client is or is not free from drug addiction when he leaves the program. Why should the federal government object if he believes that Jesus liberated him from his addiction—or that his own inner strength freed him, for that matter? After all, the president, in announcing the project, declared his own cardinal rule on this point: Faith-based charities "should be able to compete for funding . . . in a manner that does not cause them to sacrifice their mission."[44] It must be added that secular social service agencies have not felt pressure to sacrifice their missions because, up to now, their missions dovetailed with the governmentally preferred religion of neutral secularism. In fact, it was the quest for governmental approval, which, in many cases, dictated the orientation of their missions with respect to religion.

President Bush's original plan, adjusted as described here, can pass the test of wisdom and the test of constitutionality—so long as that test hinges on the words of the Constitution rather than on the fashionable theories of judges and law professors wedded to the secularist status quo. Anyone for a fight over the Constitution?

NOTES

1. Isaac Kramnick and R. Laurence Moore, *The Godless Constitution: The Case Against Religious Correctness* (New York: W.W. Norton, 1997).

2. *Torasco v. Watkins*, 367 U.S. 488 (1961).

3. James H. Hutson, *Religion and the Founding of the American Republic* (Washington: Library of Congress, 1998; dist. by University Press of New England).

4. Hutson, *Religion and the Founding of the American Republic*, 60–61.

5. Hutson, *Religion and the Founding of the American Republic*, chapter 2, Religion in Eighteenth-Century America.

6. Hutson, *Religion and the Founding of the American Republic*, 19; quoting Jon Butler, *Awash in a Sea of Faith: Christianizing the American People* (Cambridge, Mass.: Harvard University Press, 1990), 2.

7. As embodied in the Declaration and Resolves of the First Continental Congress, October 14, 1774; and in the Articles of Association, October 20, 1774.

8. Hutson, *Religion and the Founding of the American Republic*, 53. The theology of the national covenant involved Athe belief that the war with Britain was God's punishment for America's sins and that national confession and repentance would reconcile Him to the country and cause him to bare His mighty arm and smite the British.

9. Hutson, *Religion and the Founding of the American Republic*, 54.

10. Given their history of both fleeing and practicing religious persecution, Americans, of all people, knew what religious coercion was: the application (or threat) of physical or financial measures aimed at securing acquiescence by recourse to fear. In this way of thinking, persuasion is the antithesis of coercion.

11. Hutson, *Religion and the Founding of the American Republic*, chapter 5, "Religion and the State Governments," esp. 62–65; see also Thomas J. Curry, *The First Freedoms: Church and State in America to the Passage of the First Amendment* (New York: Oxford University Press, 1986); also Edwin S. Gaustad, *Faith of our Fathers* (San Francisco: Harper & Row, 1987); also John Witte Jr., *Religion and the American Constitutional Experiment: Essential Rights and Liberties* (Boulder, Co.: Westview Press, 2000); also Paul Eidelberg, *The Philosophy of the American Constitution* (New York: Free Press, 1965), esp. Appendix 2, Provisions in state constitutions respecting religion . . . ; also Barry Alan Shain, *The Myth of American Individualism: The Protestant Origins of American Political Thought* (Princeton: Princeton University Press, 1994), esp. chapt. 2.

12. Hutson, *Religion and the Founding of the American Republic*, 79–80.

13. Hutson, *Religion and the Founding of the American Republic*, 91.

14. Hutson, *Religion and the Founding of the American Republic*, 96.

15. *Wallace v. Jaffree*, 472 U.S. 38, 40 n.2, 1985.

16. For recent examples see Steven B. Epstein, "Rethinking the Constitutionality of Ceremonial Deism," *Columbia Law Review*, 96 (1996):2083; also Kurt T. Lash, Power and the Subject of Religion, *Ohio State Law Journal*, 59 (1998):1069; also S. I. Strong, "Christian Constitutions: Do They Protect Internationally Recognized Human Rights and Minimize the Potential for Violence Within a Society?" *Case Western Reserve Journal of International law*, 29 (1997):1. (Strong says that the answer is No.)

17. Madison, Thanksgiving Day Proclamation, November 16, 1814.

18. Hutson, *Religion and the Founding of the American Republic*, 96.

19. Akhil Reed Amar, "Some Notes on the Establishment Clause," *Roger Williams University Law Review* 2 (1996):1–14. Daniel Dreisbach argues that the principal objective of the constitutional framers was to defer to state and local jurisdictions on all matters pertaining to religion; Dreisbach, "Sowing Useful Truths and Principles," *Journal of Church and State*"39 (Summer 1997). See also Dreisbach, "The Constitution's Forgotten Religion Clause," *Journal of Church and State* 38 (Spring 1996).

20. Daniel L. Dreisbach, "Another Look at Jefferson's Wall of Separation: A Jurisdictional Interpretation of the 'Wall' Metaphor," no. 10 in the series *The Witherspoon Fellowship Lectures* (Washington: Family Research Council, 2000), 12.

21. *Barron v. Baltimore*, 32 U.S. (7 Peters) 243, 250 (1833).

22. Joseph Story, *Commentaries on the Constitution of the United States*, 3 Volumes. (Boston: Hilliard, Gray, and Co., 1833), 3: 730, 731, sec. 1873 (cited by Dreisbach at 7).

23. *Everson v. Board of Education*, 330 U.S. 1, 16, 18 (1947).

24. *Stone v. Graham* 449 U.S. 39 (1980)

25. Concerning nonsectarian prayer, *Engel v. Vitale*, 370 U.S. 421 (1962); concerning a moment of silence, *Wallace v. Jaffree*, 472 U.S. 38 (1985).

26. *Lee v. Weisman*, 505 U.S. 577 (1992).

27. *Santa Fe Independent School District v. Jane Doe*, 530 U.S. 290 (2000).

28. *Wallace v. Jaffree*, 472 U.S. 2479 (1985), *Lemon v. Kurtzman*, 403 U.S. 602 (1971).

29. *West Virginia Board of Education v. Barnette*, 319 U.S. 624 (1943).

30. For a recent example see *R.A.V. v. St. Paul*, 112 S.Ct. 2538 (1992), in which the Supreme Court unanimously invalidated a municipal ordinance that made hate speech a crime. For commentary see Edward J. Clearly, The Fight on Fighting Words. Beyond the Burning Cross: the First Amendment and the Landmark R.A.V. Case, *Boston University Law Review* 72 (1992), 953.

31. *Lamb's Chapel v. Center Moriches Union Free School District*, 508 U.S. 384 (1993); *Rosenberger v. Rector and Visitors of the University of Virginia*, 515 U.S. 817 (1993).

32. *Equal Access Act*, 20 U.S.C. 4071–74.

33. Notably Michael W. McConnell; see, for example, McConnell, "Believers as Equal Citizens," in *Obligations of Citizenship and Demands of Faith: Religious Accommodation in Pluralist Democracies*, ed. Nancy L. Rosenblum (Princeton: Princeton University Press, 2000), 90–110.

34. The relevant portion of the Fourteenth Amendment reads: "No State shall make or enforce any law which shall abridge the privileges or immunities of citizens of the

United States; nor shall any State deprive any person of life, liberty, or property, without due process of law; nor deny to any person within its jurisdiction the equal protection of the laws."

35. Amar, "Some Notes on the Establishment Clause," 13.

36. Dreisbach, "Another Look at Jefferson's Wall of Separattion," 22 n53.

37. Louis Hartz, *The Liberal Tradition in America: An Interpretation of American Political Thought Since the Revolution* (New York: Harcourt, Brace, 1955). Noteworthy in this connection is H.D. Forbes, "Hartz-Horowitz at Twenty: Nationalism, Toryism and Socialism in Canada and the United States," *Canadian Journal of Political Science* 20 (1987), 287–315.

38. Edward S. Corwin, "The Supreme Court as National School Board," in *A Constitution of Powers in a Secular State* (Charlottesville, Va.: Michie Co., 1951).

39. In *Engel v. Vitale* (370 U.S. 421, striking down New York's nonsectarian theistic prayer in 1962) the U.S. Supreme Court asserted: "When the power, prestige, and financial support of government is placed behind a particular religious belief, the indirect coercive pressure upon religious minorities to conform to the prevailing officially approved religion is plain" (370 U.S. at 430-31). The Court failed to foresee the obvious: when the power and prestige of government are deployed to make classrooms God-free zones, the indirect coercive pressure to conform to the officially approved attitude is *not* plain. Instead it is hidden. Unlike New York's official classroom prayer policy, the new policy is an even more indirect form of coercion. Its effects are almost impossible to resist precisely because they are concealed even, or perhaps especially, from those who support the policy. See Shelley Burt's discussion of the problem of impressionability in "Religious Parents, Secular Schools: A Liberal Defense of an Illiberal Education," *The Review of Politics* 56 (1994):51–70.

40. See Stephen Carter, *The Culture of Disbelief: How American Law and Politics Trivialize Religious Devotion* (New York: Basic Books, 1993). On the language habits of internalized relativism among the American middle classes, see Alan Wolfe, *One Nation After All: What Americans Really Think about God, Country, Family, Racism, Welfare, Immigration, Homosexuality, Work, The Right, The Left and Each Other* (New York: Viking Press, 1998).

41. Stephen Macedo, "Transformative Constitutionalism and the Case of Religion: Defending the Moderate Hegemony of Liberalism," *Political Theory* 26 (1998):69–70 (emphasis in original).

42. Barbara Curtis, "(Gay) School Days," *Focus on the Family Citizen*, June 28, 2001.

43. Corwin, "The Supreme Court as National School Board."

44. "Bush Pushes Faith-Based Plans," *Washington Post*, January 29, 2001.

III

JUDICIAL PRACTICE AND THE CULTURE WARS

8

Stare Decisis: Conservatism's One–Way Ratchet Problem

John C. Eastman

The doctrine of stare decisis, or the idea that prior decisions should stand as precedent, is a pretty conservative idea. Indeed, many historians date its origins back to the early thirteenth century, the result of Bracton keeping a notebook of judicial decisions.[1] William Blackstone notes in his *Commentaries on the Laws of England*, published just a decade before the American Revolution, that "it is an established rule to abide by former precedents, where the same points come again in litigation."[2]

The full Latin phrase has even more of a conservative feel about it: "Stare decisis et non quieta movere," or "to stand by matters that have been decided and not to disturb what is tranquil."[3] What could be more conservative than tranquility? In its vertical form,[4] which means the obligation of lower courts to follow the decisions of higher courts, the doctrine serves as a necessary underpinning of the entire federal court system envisioned by Article III of the Constitution. Article III, after all, provides for a Supreme Court and such inferior courts as Congress may establish.[5] Congress has established many lower courts;[6] without some form of stare decisis, the Supreme Court would simply be incapable of keeping the law uniform throughout the country, and the very idea of law itself would be seriously undermined.

Even in its horizontal form—the obligation or at least the propensity of one court to follow its own precedents—the doctrine serves to make the system of judicial review workable. Without it, every single issue would forever be open to debate. Such inefficiency would make the task of managing even a discretionary Supreme Court docket unmanageable and, more importantly, the law itself would take on a vastly unsettled character. Efficiency, consistency, manageability, the ability to rely on settled law—all of these byproducts of stare decisis—appeal to the conservative mind.

The point of this chapter, however, is to emphasize what may be an obvious point. After the advent of progressivism, the continued adherence to the doctrine of stare decisis by conservatives ends up being anything but conservative. The so-called progressives do not adhere to precedent as a matter of their principle, but rather view stare decisis as amounting only to the rule that "precedents ought always to be followed except when they should not."[7] Indeed, precedent is one of the things to be overcome, because in the progressive view, precedent stands in the way of the inevitable march of history and progress. It is therefore no accident that liberal or progressive courts account for most of the overruling cases in the Court's history (i.e. those cases that have explicitly overruled prior precedent). A recent empirical study by political scientist Christopher Banks identified 201 decisions between the Court's inception and 1991 in which the Supreme Court explicitly overruled prior precedent.[8] That's an average of one case per year, yet 118 of those decisions—nearly 60 percent—were produced by the post–1937 New Deal court and the Warren and Burger courts of the 1960s and 1970s. In its heyday, the Warren court was explicitly[9] overruling prior cases at the rate of five or six a year, and in 1967 alone, it overruled eight—eight times above the historical average.

A wonderful example of this is evident in a couple of cases Murray Dry discusses in his chapter earlier in this book.[10] *Hurley v. Irish-American Gay, Lesbian, and Bisexual Group of Boston, Inc.*[11] was decided by a unanimous court in 1995, Justice David Souter writing the opinion for the Court. In that case, the Court upheld the right of a privately organized parade to exclude groups who wished to convey a message about the morality and normalcy of homosexuality that the parade organizers did not wish to convey. The parade organizers had this right, according to the unanimous Court, despite the fact that the parade was not otherwise organized around any kind of coherent or even consistent message, and despite the fact that it had no purpose—express or otherwise—to foster a message contrary to that which the organization sought to convey, and even despite the fact that the parade organizers had not previously had a position opposing the group's message. It was enough, according to the Court, *in reliance on long-established precedent,* that the private organization did not wish to convey the group's message at the time.[12]

Five years later, James Dale's challenge to the Boy Scouts—to Troop 73 of the Boy Scouts, to be more precise (coincidentally the troop in which I began my own career as a cub scout back in Matawan, New Jersey in 1968)—raised precisely the same issues as were addressed and fully resolved in *Hurley*. The same issues, that is, if you accept the nearly self-evident proposition that allowing an open and active homosexual to don a Boy Scout uniform and serve as an adult leader in the organization sends an unmistakable message about the morality and normalcy of homosexuality that was 180 degrees at odds with the message the Boy Scouts organization itself wished to convey. With *Hurley* on the books, and with no intervening changes in the law or even in the people occupying the seats at the bench, *Boy Scouts of America v. Dale*[13] should have been an easy case. In fact, if vertical stare decisis had been followed, the New Jersey Supreme Court could not have issued the ruling that forced the Boy Scouts to take the case to the Supreme Court in the first place.[14] As the trial court correctly ruled at the first step of the vertical stare decisis ladder, there was no option under *Hurley* but to conclude that the Boy Scouts have a right to exclude James Dale because of the message his very presence would convey, a message with which the Boy Scouts organization disagreed.[15] The trial court recognized that under *Hurley* the fact that the Boy Scouts had not explicitly been opposed to homosexual conduct from the time of their founding in 1910 was not a reason to deny the organization protection under the First Amendment.[16] It was enough that they now wished not to support the message James Dale sought to convey.[17]

So *Boy Scouts v. Dale* should have been an easy case. And it should have been unanimous, just as *Hurley* had been. *Hurley* was not a close, 5-4 case; the opinion in the case was not written by Chief Justice Rehnquist or Justice Scalia, barely holding on to Justices O'Connor and Kennedy in the middle. It was written by Justice Souter, the most liberal member of the current Supreme Court. And it was unanimous.

Boy Scouts v. Dale was not unanimous, of course. *Hurley* was followed, but only by the barest 5-4 majority of the Court. In his dissenting opinion, Justice Stevens argued that the Boy Scouts did not really have a position on homosexuality—that the language in the Boy Scout oath about being "morally straight" meant something else.[18] And that, in any event, the inclusion of Dale in the organization would not really alter the Boy Scouts' message as he deemed it to be, even though the Boy Scouts say it would effect a radical change.[19]

But these feeble attempts to distinguish *Hurley* were not the real thrust of Justice Stevens' dissent. Rather, Justice Stevens provided us with an uncharacteristic window into the progressive view of these things. *Hurley* should not be followed, he said, nor the long-established First Amendment rights recognized and reaffirmed in that case, because public perception of homosexuality had changed in the five years since *Hurley*, and that was enough for the Court to alter the constitutional right underlying the Boy Scouts' claim, according to Justice Stevens.[20] It was an extraordinary admission of what the progressive movement means with respect to its understanding of the rule of law.

And Justice Souter, also in dissent, implicitly invited additional challenges to the *Boy Scouts* decision.[21] Justice Souter asserted that the Boy Scouts did not really have a position about homosexuality.[22] Because the case was decided on summary judgment at the trial court level, there was never a trial to determine what the Boy Scouts' position actually was. In future cases, therefore, we can anticipate factual challenges to the sincerity of the Boy Scouts' stated beliefs, and Justice Souter has invited everyone to ignore the existing precedent once those new trials are held.

Adherence to precedent by conservatives, therefore, operates as a one-way ratchet. Every time a majority of the Court consists of self-styled progressives or liberals, that majority overrules prior cases and develops a new body of precedent ratcheted toward their progressive view of the world. Oftentimes the overruling is not even explicit. In *Romer v. Evans*,[23] for example, Justice Kennedy, writing for the majority, struck down Colorado's Amendment 2 because he could not ascertain any identifiable legitimate governmental purpose underlying the statute that prohibited governments from enacting laws giving preferential treatment to homosexuals. No conceivable governmental purpose, in Justice Kennedy's view, despite the fact that on the books for only a decade was *Bowers v. Hardwick*,[24] which had upheld a Georgia law criminalizing the conduct that defines homosexuality. If the conduct itself can be criminalized because to do so sufficiently furthers a legitimate governmental purpose, surely a law taking the much smaller step of prohibiting preferential treatment to people that engage in that conduct meets the minimal rational basis test by which the Supreme Court assesses the constitutionality of legislation not involving suspect classifications or fundamental rights. Here is how Justice Kennedy distinguished *Bowers*: Silence. That's right; not one word about it. And it is not as though Justice Kennedy just overlooked the decision. Justice Scalia made sure of that in his dissent, criticizing the majority for not even mentioning *Bowers*, a case that, according to Justice Scalia, provided a resounding affirmative response to the question of whether there was any legitimate purpose underlying Colorado's amendment.[25]

When a more conservative majority occupies the bench, it is therefore faced with a dilemma: Overrule the more recent precedent and undermine the traditional doctrine of stare decisis, or adhere to stare decisis and live with the new precedent (at least until the next time the progressive ratchet swings into action).[26] All too often the latter course has been followed, but more about that later.

Of course, conservative jurists are encouraged to adopt this course by their more liberal brethren, particularly when an era of especially active progressive rulings is coming to a close. In what is perhaps one of the great ironies on this point, Justice Thurgood Marshall, one of the top six all-time overruling justices in our nation's history (and whose career prior to his appointment to the Supreme Court was devoted to overruling the ignominious decisions of the Jim Crow era), issued on the day of his retirement from the

Court in June 1991 a strong defense of stare decisis and a scathing criticism of the Court for its repudiation of the doctrine of stare decisis.

The majority in the case, *Payne v. Tennessee*,[27] overruled two prior cases and held that the admission of victim impact statements at the sentencing phase of a capital trial was not unconstitutional. According to Justice Marshall, this modest decision completely undermined the doctrine of stare decisis, a doctrine to which he now wanted to adhere in order to lock in two decades of Warren Court activism that had expanded the law in the progressive direction that he wanted. The Court's decision in *Payne* was, according to Justice Marshall, "a clear signal that scores of established constitutional liberties [were] now ripe for reconsideration, thereby inviting the very type of open defiance of our precedents that the majority rewards in this case."[28] Yet Justice Marshall failed to note that most of the so-called established constitutional liberties about which he spoke had not been established in the Bill of Rights in 1791 or even in the Fourteenth Amendment after the Civil War, but were instead "discovered"—created ex nihilo might be a more accurate description—by the Warren Court in the 1960s.

Now you might think that Justice Marshall's position is the more just one. After all, we are talking about rights here. Should it not be the case that once the Court has given us rights that we ought to be able to keep them? Quite apart from the faulty assumption regarding the nature of rights underlying Justice Marshall's position,[29] the question of rights enhancement is often in the eye of the beholder. As Justice Scalia has previously noted, the progressive move to allow alleged victims of child molestation to testify behind screens out of view of both the public and their alleged molester is less-protective of the defendant's constitutional right to confront witnesses, not more.[30] The case of *Payne v. Tennessee* itself, involving victim impact statements, can just as easily be characterized as an expansion of victims' rights as the retraction of defendants' rights that Justice Marshall decried. And Murray Dry's description of the *Boy Scouts* case provides an equally good example. He asserts that the case involved a conflict between the rights of homosexuals not to be discriminated against and the right of the Boy Scouts to make decisions about the composition of their private association,[31] so no matter which way the Court ruled, a case could be made that someone's rights were expanded.

In short, in order to accept Justice Marshall's view that the one-way ratchet I have described is a good thing because it is protective of rights, we have to know what we mean by rights—and on that score, perhaps more than any other, the progressive vision is at odds with the natural rights vision held by our founders and embodied in the Constitution.

Let me turn now to the granddaddy in the stare decisis fight, *Planned Parenthood of Southeastern Pennsylvania v. Casey*,[32] decided in 1992 after the Reagan revolution's impact on the federal judiciary reached its zenith. A few years before, the Court in *Webster v. Reproductive Health Services*[33] had strongly signaled not just a retreat from *Roe v. Wade*,[34] but that it was prepared to overrule that controversial case. Justice Clarence Thomas had joined the Court the previous October, replacing Justice Marshall, giving the Court the five votes necessary for the purpose. Justice Blackmun candidly acknowledged as much in his partial concurrence in *Casey*: "Three years ago, in *Webster* . . . four members of this Court appeared poised to 'cas[t] into darkness the hopes and visions of every woman in this country' who had come to believe that the Constitution guaranteed her the right to reproductive choice."[35] We all know what happened. Justices O'Connor and Kennedy—both Reagan appointees—joined with Justice Souter—President Bush's "stealth" nominee[36]—to retain the core of *Roe* because of the importance of stare decisis in retaining settled expectations and in protecting the institutional integrity of the Court. The stare decisis analysis applied by the three justices in their joint opinion was flawed even by stare decisis standards. More fundamentally, it was not consistently applied from one part of the trio's joint opinion to another.[37] It is often forgotten, but in that opinion, Justices O'Connor, Kennedy, and Souter overruled several post-*Roe* decisions that had afforded even greater protection to the right to an abortion expounded in *Roe*. Justices O'Connor, Kennedy, and Souter viewed these post-*Roe* decisions as inconsistent not with the language of *Roe* itself but with what they now divined to be the core central meaning of *Roe*, as modified by their opinion in *Casey*.[38] And they did this all in the name of stare decisis.

While the particular post-*Roe* decisions overruled in *Casey* were more protective of the abortion "right" than *Roe* itself, the principle underlying the plurality opinion's new view of stare decisis will enshrine the "central holding" of *Roe* in our law, at least until a more solidly progressive Court regains the votes to further expand the right articulated in *Roe*. Under the plurality's rationale, any incremental attempt to restrict *Roe*'s holding will be as impermissible as were the incremental attempts to expand its holding were. The trio thus exacerbated the one-way ratchet problem of stare decisis for conservatives, making it clear that adherence to stare decisis by them prevents not just the reversal of incorrect past decisions, but adherence to decisions rendered subsequent to the incorrect precedent that might narrow the ruling that was flawed in the first place.

Let me be clear. Both sides in the debate acknowledge that *Roe v. Wade* is a terribly reasoned and wrongly decided decision, even those who like the outcome.[39] So we are not talking about something that is designed to get the benefit of stare decisis as that doctrine was originally understood. The doctrine of stare decisis as originally understood was grounded in humility[40]—the idea that judges would not lightly reconsider or overturn the considered judgment of their predecessors without strong and good reason. Part of what is furthered by the doctrine is efficiency. If a court continues to revisit its prior decisions, the same issues will come up over and over, without ever being settled. But what we are faced with now is a claim of stare decisis that operates in an entirely different realm that it has before. Rather than deferring to the considered judgment made by a predecessor court about the constitutionality of a particular action or statute, the new stare decisis operates even where the predecessor court's holding is acknowledged to be wrong, and even when the predecessor court itself acknowledged that its ruling was rendered in spite of the Constitution, not in accord with it.[41] To continue to adhere to stare decisis in the face of such a transformation in how the doctrine is used simply to undermine the core rationale of the doctrine itself—namely, that stare decisis is grounded in a view of humility about one's own abilities.

I often make the analogy to a football game. In football, there is a rulebook and also a set of referees for each game. Suppose that in one game a ball thrown into the end zone is caught by a receiver with one foot out of bounds. The referee mistakenly signals a touchdown, despite a clear provision in the rulebook requiring that both feet be in bounds. What does a referee in the next game do when faced with another one-footed end-zone reception? Is the rule now that you only need one foot in the end zone? Of course not. We go back to the rulebook, especially when the referee acknowledges that he made a mistake or when he made the claim that he was not required to follow the rulebook in the first place.

The joint opinion in *Casey* rejects the rulebook in favor of the admittedly erroneous decision of a prior referee. The new understanding of stare decisis adopted in that opinion signals that subsequent courts must adhere to prior decisions, even when they are acknowledged to be wrong. And Justices O'Connor, Kennedy, and Souter come very close to making just that admission in *Planned Parenthood v. Casey*—I would argue that they actually make that admission, but at the very least they come very close to making the admission that *Roe* was wrongly decided, as a matter of constitutional law, history, and principle. For them, it did not matter whether *Roe* was wrongly decided. They reach that conclusion by drawing on a strand of stare decisis thought that originated in cases dealing with commercial and contractual relations. The Court has established a rule in such cases that it will not change prior precedent lightly because to do so would unsettle the expectations of the people entering into the contract. Application of the "settled expectations" rationale is particularly inapposite in the abortion context, however, where the relevant effects of the settled expectations have a very short half-life. Unlike a long-term contract or a lease, the settled expectations that were involved in *Casey* would last all of nine months. If the Court was truly concerned about settled expectations, it could simply have required that no new restriction on abortion take effect for a year. That way, no one would engage in activity without knowing the consequences of the new rule, and their settled expectations with regard to the consequences of their conduct prior to the enactment of the new rule would be given full effect.

The other argument the plurality in *Casey* made was that the institutional credibility of the Court would be undermined if the Court were to overturn *Roe* such a short time after it was decided. Here it is important to recall the last part of the definition of stare decisis discussed above—to ability to keep things tranquil. Now I understand that some may believe that the abortion debate has been relatively tranquil since 1973, but just the opposite is true. However much the Court thought in 1973 that by deciding a hotly contested political issue it would resolve the controversy once and for all so that we could all go back and lead our nice tranquil lives and not have to deal with it any more, subsequent events have proven the Court wrong. So the notion that the Court was preserving its institutional integrity by keeping this tranquil issue tranquil was just absurd. Indeed, by essentially admitting that the earlier decision was wrong, the plurality opinion has itself undermined the continuing institutional integrity of the Court, choosing by mere will to abide by a decision—not because of the Justices's humility about the correctness of the prior decision but despite its acknowledged wrongness. That turns the principles of stare decisis on their head.

Thus the conservative principle of stare decisis, in the hands of conservative justices—two of the three authors of the joint opinion in *Casey* are often called conservative—locks in place precedents enacted by more progressive Courts, precedents, which themselves ignored the principles of stare decisis, but refuses to move back toward a view of the law more consistent with the principles of the American founding when a more conservative majority is in control. Such a principle is guaranteed over time to further undermine the moral foundations of this country.

NOTES

I wish to thank Chapman law student Tim Sandefur for research assistance; Dr. Bradley C. S. Watson for organizing the "Courts and the Culture Wars," the conference sponsored by the Center for Economic and Policy Education at Saint Vincent College in Latrobe, Pennsylvania, at which a draft of this paper was presented; the participants at the conference—Judge Robert H. Bork, Fr. Francis Canavan, professor emeritus of political science at Fordham University, Dr. Charles E. Rice, professor of law at the University of Notre Dame Law School, Dr. Christopher P. Manfredi, professor of political science at McGill University, Dr. Anthony A. Peacock, assistant professor of political science at Utah State University, Dr. Jeremy Rabkin, associate professor of government at Cornell University, Dr. Murray Dry, Charles A. Dana professor of political science at Middlebury College, Dr. Graham Walker, associate professor of political science at Oklahoma Wesleyan University, Dr. Edward J. Erler, Professor of political science at California State University, San Bernardino, and Dr. Keith Whittington, associate professor of politics at Princeton University—all of whom provided useful feedback on this paper or general insight into the topics addressed, but of course bear no responsibility for any errors in my argument; and the Chapman University School of Law faculty research fund. I also wish to convey special thanks to Mrs. Rosey Doelling, for superb logistical support at the conference.

1. John Wallace, "Stare Decisis and the Rehnquist Court: The Collision of Activism, Passivism, and Politics in *Casey*," *Buffalo Law Review* 42 (Winter 1994):187, 189 and n.8 (citing Robert A. Sprecher, "The Development of the Doctrine of Stare Decisis and the Extent to Which It Should Be Applied," *A.B.A.J.* 31 (1945):501, 501–02 and n.9; Sir William Holdsworth, *A History of English Law* (1938):146–47; and A. K. R. Kiralfy, *Potter's Historical Introduction to English Law and Its Institutions* 276–78 (4th ed. 1958)).

2. William Blackstone, 1 *Commentaries on the Laws of England* 69 (University of Chicago Press, 1979) (1765); see also Wallace, *supra*, note 2, at 190 n.9.

3. *Dictionary of Phrases and Abbreviations* 187, trans. K. Guinach, 3rd ed., (1983) (quoted in John Wallace, "Stare Decisis and the Rehnquist Court: The Collision of Activism, Passivism, and Politics in *Casey*," supra n.2 42 (Winter 1994):187, 189 and n.7); see also *Black's Law Dictionary* 6th ed. (St. Paul, Minn.: West Publishing, 1990) 1406, ("to adhere to precedents, and not to unsettle things which are established"). For a humorous account of the doctrine, see Jonathan Swift, *Gulliver's Travels*, ("[Stare decisis] is a maxim among . . . lawyers, that whatever has been done before may legally be done again: and therefore they take special care to record all the decisions formerly made against common justice and the general reason of mankind") (quoted in Saul Brenner and Harold J. Spaeth, *Stare Indecisis: The Alteration of Precedent on the Supreme Court, 1946–1992*, (New York: Cambridge University Press, 1995), 1).

4. I borrow the useful descriptive phrases, "vertical stare decisis" and "horizontal stare decisis," from Brenner and Speath, *supra* note 4, at 1.

5. U.S. Constitution, Article III, 1 ("The judicial Power of the United States, shall be vested in one supreme Court, and in such inferior Courts as the Congress may from time to time ordain and establish").

6. See, e.g., 28 U.S.C. 151 (bankruptcy courts); 28 U.S.C. 251 (Court of International Trade); 28 U.S.C. 171 (Court of Federal Claims).

7. Deborah Hellman, "The Importance of Appearing Principled," *Arizona Law Review* 37 (1995):1108, 1110 (quoting Richard A. Wasserstrom, *The Judicial Decision* 46 (1961)).

8. Christopher P. Banks, "The Supreme Court and Precedent: An Analysis of Natural Courts and Reversal Trends," *Judicature* 75 (1992):262 (discussed in Brenner & Spaeth, *supra* note 4, at 16).

9. This does not take account of the many cases in which prior precedent was only implicitly or subtly overruled.

10. Murray Dry, "Tolerance and American Constitutionalism: The Case of Gay Rights," reprinted herein at 79–97.

11. *Id.* 515 U.S. 557 (1995).

12. *Hurley v. Irish-American Gay, Lesbian, and Bisexual Group of Boston, Inc.* at 569–70 (citing, e.g., *Turner Broadcasting System, Inc. v. FCC*, 512 U.S. 622, 636 (1994)).

13. 530 U.S. 640 (2000).

14. *Boy Scouts of America v. Dale*, 160 N.J. 562, 734 A.2d 1196 (N.J. 1999).

15. *Boy Scouts of America v. Dale*, No. MON-C-330-92 (Ch. Div. Nov. 3, 1995).

16. *Boy Scouts of America v. Dale*, No. MON-C-330-92 (Ch. Div. Nov. 3, 1995).

17. *Boy Scouts of America v. Dale*, No. MON-C-330-92 (Ch. Div. Nov. 3, 1995).

18. Justice Stevens offered as proof of this proposition the 1910-era founding documents of the Boy Scouts, which say nothing about homosexuality, from which he concluded that the Boy Scouts organization could not have had a view on the subject. 530 U.S. at 668–69 (Stevens, J., dissenting). The absurdity of Justice Stevens' logic is manifest. The reason the Boy Scouts did not mention homosexuality prior to 1978 is because homosexuality was before then considered "unmentionable." The Boy Scouts took an explicit position on homosexuality as soon as homosexuality became an open topic of conversation in the 1970s, when pro-homosexual advocates started to make claims of moral equivalence of the kind Ed Erler discusses elsewhere in this volume. See Edward J. Erler, "The California Supreme Court in the Culture Wars: A Case Study in Judicial Failure," *reprinted supra* at 139–150. For twenty years the Boy Scouts organization has hired very expensive lawyers to defend the organization's position, so the view that it really does not have a belief about homosexuality is just absurd. But even if the Boy Scouts had not held a view opposing homosexual conduct all that time, the First Amendment does not protect only long-established views; it also protects the right to hold views that one adopts only today. Indeed, one of the principles underlying the First Amendment is that, by virtue of our ability to reason and have free speech, we might actually persuade one another and bring about a change of views. So the whole premise of the argument proffered by Justice Stevens is flawed.

19. *Hurley v. Irish-American Gay, Lesbian, and Bisexual Group of Boston, Inc.* 530 U.S. at 675–78.

20. *Hurley v. Irish-American Gay, Lesbian, and Bisexual Group of Boston, Inc.* 530 U.S. at 699–700.

21. *Hurley v. Irish-American Gay, Lesbian, and Bisexual Group of Boston, Inc.* 530 U.S. at 700, 701 (J. Souter, dissenting).

22. *Hurley v. Irish-American Gay, Lesbian, and Bisexual Group of Boston, Inc.* 530 U.S. at 700, 701 (J. Souter dissenting).

23. *Romer v. Evans, Bowers v. Hardwick, Romer v. Evans*, 530 U.S. at 700, 701 (J. Souter dissenting).

24. 478 U.S. 186 (1986).

25. 517 U.S. at 636 (Scalia, J., dissenting).

26. *See, e.g., Camps Newfound/Owatonna v. Harrison, Maine*, 520 U.S. 564, 595, 608-09 (1997) (Scalia, J., dissenting).

27. *Turner v. Tennessee*, 501 U.S. 808 (1991).

28. *Turner v. Tennessee*, at 844, 845 (Marshall, J., dissenting).

29. The authors of the Bill of Rights went to great pains to use language that "recognized" rights rather than "created" rights. See e.g., U.S. Constitutional Amendment IV ("The right of the people to be secure in their persons, houses, papers, and effects, against unreasonable searches and seizures, shall not be violated"); see also U.S. Constitutional Amendment IX ("The enumeration in the Constitution, of certain rights, shall not be construed to deny or disparage others retained by the people"). In their

view, rights exist apart from and prior to government; they are not gifts from government. See Declaration of Independence Paragraph 2 (recognizing that all human beings "are endowed by their Creator with certain unalienable Rights" and that the purpose of government is "to secure these rights").

30. *Maryland v. Craig*, 497 U.S. 836, 860 (1990) (Scalia, J., dissenting); see *Coy v. Iowa*, 487 U.S. 1012 (1988).

31. Murray Dry, *supra* note 11.

32. *Planned Parenthood of Southeastern Pennsylvania v. Casey*. 505 U.S. 833 (1992).

33. *Webster v. Reproductive Health Services*, 492 U.S. 490 (1989).

34. *Roe v. Wade*, 410 U.S. 113 (1973).

35. *Planned Parenthood of Southeastern Pennsylvania v. Casey*, 505 U.S. at 922 (J. Blackmun, concurring in part, concurring in the judgment in part, and dissenting in part).

36. See, e.g., Liang Kan, "A Theory of Justice Souter," *Emory Law Journal* 45 (Fall 1996):1373,1375 (citing Ruth Marcus and Joe Pichirallo, "Seeking Out the Essential David Souter," *Washington Post*, September 9, 1990, at A1; Stephen Wermiel and David Shribman, "Bush's Choice: High Court Nominee Is Conservative But Isn't Seen as an Ideologue, *Wall Street Journal*, July 24, 1990, at A1; Margaret Carlson, "An 18th Century Man," *Time*, August 6, 1990, at 19).

37. See, e.g., John Wallace, "Stare Decisis and the Rehnquist Court: The Collision of Activism, Passivism and Politics in Casey," *Buffalo Law Review* 42 (Winter 1994):187, 189 ("the Court's decision in Casey is not only inconsistent in its own use of stare decisis, but is also inconsistent with traditional notions of stare decisis, and with *Roe*"); David K. Koehler, "Justice Souter's 'Keep-What-You-Want-and-Throw-Away-the-Rest' Interpretation of Stare Decisis," *Buffalo Law Review* 42 (Fall 1994):859, 892 ("Souter succeeded only in creating a 'jurisprudence of confusion,' and defaming the doctrine of stare decisis").

38. See, e.g., *Planned Parenthood of Southeastern Pennsylvania v. Casey*, 505 U.S. at 873 ("We reject the trimester framework, which we do not consider to be part of the essential holding of *Roe*").

39. See, e.g., Christopher P. Manfredi, "Courts, Culture, and Community," reprinted herein at 153–164 (describing Cass Sunstein's minimalism theory, by which Sunstein criticizes *Roe v. Wade* as without legal merit but nevertheless contends that *Roe* cannot be overruled); Cass R. Sunstein, *One Case at a Time: Judicial Minimalism and the Supreme Court* (Cambridge: Harvard University Press 1999).

40. See, e.g., David A. Strauss, "Common Law Constitutional Interpretation," *University of Chicago Law Review* 63 (Summer 1996):877, 913 (describing the Burkean view of stare decisis as one grounding in "humility and a sense of one's own limitations").

41. See, e.g., Michael Stokes Paulsen, "Captain James T. Kirk and the Enterprise of Constitutional Interpretation: Some Modest Proposals from the Twenty-Third Century," *Albany Law Review* 59 (1995):671, 679 ("Taken seriously, stare decisis means a deliberate practice of adhering to precedents that one knows to be incorrect interpretations of the Constitution, simply because that is what has been done before," or, in other words, "deliberately interpreting the Constitution in a way you know to be wrong").

9

The California Supreme Court in the Culture Wars: A Case Study in Judicial Failure

Edward J. Erler

For several decades California has been a principal battleground in the culture wars. Hollywood obviously comes to mind. But less obviously—and more importantly—is the battle that has been raging between California courts and the people of California. Fifteen years ago, the Chief Justice of the California Supreme, Rose Bird, and two of her activist colleagues were turned out of office in a hotly contested judicial confirmation election. The issue was California's death penalty statute, which the Court's majority refused to implement, inventing a variety of implausible legal and constitutional excuses for its dilatoriness.[1]

The California Supreme Court uses the doctrine of independent state grounds as one of the principal weapons in its activist arsenal. This doctrine allows state courts to interpret the same or similar language in state constitutions independently of the U.S. Supreme Court's interpretation of the federal Constitution. The one restriction is that the interpretation of the same or similar language cannot create lower standards of protection than is established by the federal Constitution, but it can create higher standards. Independent state ground is something of a misnomer because state courts are not entirely independent in the interpretation of state constitutions—rights can be interpreted only more expansively and state protections can never fall beneath the federal minimum. There can be little doubt that the doctrine of independent state grounds is a necessary and appropriate component of the American federal system; it is derived from the very nature of a system that delegates exclusive powers to the federal government and reserves powers to the states. Thus, with respect to the regulation of the health, welfare, and morals of the people in the states, state law, and state constitutions are final as long as there is no conflict with the federal Constitution.

Interest in independent state grounds on the part of judicial activists began in the 1970s when they began to believe that the Burger Court did not share the enthusiasm for judicial innovation that had been evidenced by the ideological liberalism of the Warren Court. The acknowledged leader in the revival of independent state grounds was the late Justice William Brennan. His advocacy even led him to disguise himself as a supporter of federalism: "Every believer in our concept of federalism, and I am a devout believer, must salute this development in our State courts."[2] What Brennan had in mind, of course, was not federalism or state constitutionalism, but the extension of the Warren Court "legal revolution" through the use of the "independent protective force of State law."[3] The incorporation of the provisions of the Bill of Rights through the Fourteenth Amendment's due process clause created, Brennan noted, "a Federal floor of protection" that "allow[s] diversity only above and beyond this Federal constitutional floor."[4] Whenever the U.S. Supreme Court refused to extend the federal floor into questionable areas, Justice Brennan was quick to advise states on how they might evade the Supreme Court's rulings. In a dissenting opinion in the 1975 case of *Michigan v. Mosely*, Brennan decried the majority's "erosion of Miranda standards as a matter of Federal constitutional law." Brennan concluded by inviting state courts to take up the constitutional cudgels that he thought had been abandoned by the Supreme Court: "Understandably, State courts and legislatures are, as matters of State law, increasingly according protections once provided as Federal rights but now increasingly depreciated by decisions of this Court."[5]

The California Supreme Court took up Brennan's call to expand the reach of ideological liberalism through state constitutionalism with a vengeance. Most of the Court's activism has been in the area of criminal procedures and the rights of criminal defendants. But the people of California have also been active in curtailing the Court's use of independent state grounds through the use of the constitutional amendment initiative. One initiative, passed in 1972, required the California Supreme Court to accept federal standards for cruel and unusual punishment in capital cases; another, the Victims' Bill of Rights, passed in 1980, mandated that the exclusion of evidence proceed on federal grounds rather than independent state grounds. Both of these initiatives were designed to curtail the Court's expansion of the rights of criminal defendants under the aegis of independent state grounds, and both of these restrictions on judicial authority were subsequently upheld by the California Supreme Court.

Emboldened by these successes, in 1990 the people of California passed another constitutional amendment initiative that contained extensive reforms of criminal procedures. The main purpose was to withdraw independent state ground powers from California courts in almost all areas touching upon the rights of criminal defendants, thus restoring federal standards to the

California Constitution. In the areas of search and seizure, the right to counsel and cruel and unusual punishment, the California Supreme Court had gone well beyond the requirements set by the United States Supreme Court. Inevitably, the issue came to a show down before the California Supreme Court. One curious feature of the California Constitution is that it allows amendments to proceed by initiative but revisions of the Constitution can be made only by constitutional revision commissions. Not surprisingly, the California Supreme Court declared the initiative unconstitutional because its curtailment of judicial power was, in the Court's opinion, so extensive as to amount to a revision of the Constitution rather than an amendment. As the Court noted in *Raven v. Deukmejian* in 1990, as a result of the initiative's restrictions "California courts in criminal cases would no longer have authority to interpret the state Constitution in a manner more protective of defendants' rights than extended by the federal Constitution, as construed by the U.S. Supreme Court." This, the Court noted, "would substantially alter the substance and integrity of the state constitution as a document of independent force and effect."

At the same time these constitutional issues were being fought out, another case was developing that would culminate in one of the most important battles in California's culture wars. That case would also use independent state grounds as its main constitutional weapon in the promotion of ideological liberalism. In 1987 the California legislature, then as now controlled by the Democratic Party, passed a parental consent law requiring that unemanicipated minor girls obtain parental permission or, alternatively, permission from a court, before receiving an abortion. This popular bill, which was carefully crafted to meet guidelines articulated by the U.S. Supreme Court, was signed by Republican Governor George Deukmejian. The law was enjoined immediately upon its passage, and eventually made its way to the California Supreme Court in 1996. In *American Academy of Pediatrics v. Lungren*, the California Supreme Court upheld the law by a 4-3 margin, with the majority opinion authored by the lone Democratic appointee on the Court, Justice Stanley Mosk. Both the trial court and the court of appeal had declared the parental consent law unconstitutional as a violation of the right to autonomy privacy guaranteed by the California Constitution. Justice Mosk acknowledged that the "right to procreative choice" was protected by the California Constitution and that the right existed as a matter of independent state grounds. The California Constitution contains an explicit guarantee of the right to privacy, whereas under the federal Constitution the right to privacy is only an inference from the "penumbras, formed by emanations" of various provisions of the Bill of Rights (to use Justice Douglas' phraseology from the Court's opinion in *Griswold v. Connecticut*). Furthermore, as Justice Mosk pointed out, the California Supreme Court had articulated a right to abortion four years before the U.S. Supreme Court acknowledged the right in *Roe v. Wade*. Both these factors argued in favor of the independent force of the right of procreative choice in the California Constitution.

Justice Mosk, however, refused to countenance the argument that minor girls possess autonomy privacy rights to the same extent as adults. "The grounds for distinguishing the rights of children from those of adults," Justice Mosk wrote, "are deeply rooted in our culture and society. They are based on normative assumptions about the family, including the mutual interests of children and their parents and the benefits to children of parental guidance and control." Indeed, restrictions on the autonomy of minors "are premised on a fundamental social tenet that children require protection against their own immaturity and vulnerability in making decisions that may have serious consequences for their health and well being." Furthermore, the parental consent law, Mosk argued, is justified as an aspect of the well-recognized right of parents "to direct his or her child's upbringing." Parental rights have long been recognized by both the California courts and the U.S. Supreme Court as a "compelling interest" before which the child's interest in privacy must yield. Under the California legislation the unemancipated minor girl is protected from arbitrary or capricious decisions of parents by the judicial bypass procedure where the minor girl can appeal to a court for permission. The court is bound by law to act in the interest of the child and if convinced that the minor's maturity is sufficient for informed consent can give permission for an abortion. The bypass procedure is required by U.S. Supreme Court decisions which have made it a necessary ingredient of the minor's right to privacy.

The trial court, in holding the legislation unconstitutional, had adduced from expert testimony that there was no evidence that "children over the age of thirteen or fourteen years lack the capacity for rational choice" or were in any way deficient in "the cognitive ability and maturity to make a fully-informed choice as to abortion." Justice Mosk rightly said that such evidence was, to say the least, "counterintuitive." It defies the universal experience of parents. As Mosk acerbically summed up the issue, the right of autonomy privacy for adults and minor girls cannot be coextensive because "the capacity to become pregnant and the capacity for exercising mature judgment concerning the wisdom of an abortion are not logically related."

The case produced three shrill dissents. Justice Joyce Kennard argued that "the best scientific evidence available" supported the notion that minor girls were fully competent to make informed choices. There was thus no ground for holding that the autonomy privacy rights of pregnant minors were any less extensive than that of adults. In fact, Kennard argued, the dilution of autonomy privacy rights for minor girls "may have an adverse psychological effect" since "the ability to make an autonomous decision about abortion is an important predictor of a minor's satisfaction with her decision." Autonomy privacy rights are matters of "profound importance" and "so fundamental and 'life-shaping,'"

Kennard asserted, "that age limits are not constitutionally acceptable as a means of conclusively determining that an adolescent below the prescribed age is not yet ready to assume sole responsibility for those decisions. The decision to continue or terminate a pregnancy is one such decision." Unemancipated minor girls, beginning at age thirteen or fourteen, therefore have a "reasonable expectation of privacy in the making of this decision."

Justice Kennard found Justice Mosk's assertion that such scientific evidence was counterintuitive rather troubling. After all, counterintuitive though it may be, it was the best available. Both Mosk and Kennard had excluded the propriety of making moral arguments because decisions about the morality or moral implications of abortion were beyond the capacity of the Court. Rather, it was a matter of statutory and constitutional construction. But whereas Justice Mosk was willing to recognize the "deeply rooted social norms" that distinguished between the privacy and liberty interests of children and adults, Kennard found those norms to be incompatible with the latest science. In the presence of science—however tentative or counterintuitive its conclusions may be—social norms, no matter how long standing or deeply rooted, must yield.

Justice Ronald George wrote the most radical dissent. His main concern was equal protection. His argument was that there was a fundamental violation of equal protection because the law discriminated between minor girls who chose not to abort and those who did. Parental permission was required only of those who elected abortion. The California Constitution's equal protection component, George argued, requires "the government, when it legislates in the intimate and sensitive realm of reproductive choice, to act evenhandedly with regard to this right of choice." But the legislature placed a greater burden on "a pregnant minor's access to medical care in the event she chooses to terminate her pregnancy than if she chooses not to terminate her pregnancy." The U.S. Supreme Court in its 1980 decision in *Harris v. McRae* had held that the Fourteenth Amendment's requirement of equal protection did not prevent the federal government from making a legislative judgment preferring childbirth over abortion. But George argued that the California's autonomy privacy rights did not depend on the federal Constitution but had independent force. The California Supreme Court had decided previously that such disparate and unequal treatment was forbidden by the California Constitution which imposes an obligation of "governmental neutrality" with respect to childbirth and abortion. The government thus has no constitutionally cognizable interest in choosing life over death when confronted by a claim of autonomy privacy.

Shortly after the decision in *American Academy of Pediatrics v. Lungren* was handed down, two members of the majority retired, including Chief Justice Malcolm Lucas. The Republican governor, Pete Wilson, nominated two replacements, Ming Chin and Janice Brown, and elevated Justice George to the Chief Justiceship. Almost immediately, the newly constituted court voted, in a rare procedure, to rehear the case. Less than a year and a half after the first decision the Court finally handed down its revised opinion striking down the parental consent law—without a single line of explanation or acknowledgement of the reversal. Indeed, there was only the barest hint that there had even been a previous decision. The only discernible difference was the ideological predilections of the newly minted majority. But is it possible that a change in the ideological predilections of the Court requires a change in constitutional doctrine? And, if so, is this consistent with constitutional government and the rule of law? The California Supreme Court has almost given new meaning to the cynical quip that the Constitution is merely what the judges say it is. If that is the case, then constitutions have no force as organic or fundamental law.

In the new decision, bearing the same name as the old one, Justice Mosk's majority opinion became a dissent, and Justice Kennard's dissent became a concurring opinion, and Justice George's dissent became the opinion of the Court. The most important feature of the Chief Justice's opinion for the purpose of drawing the battle lines in the culture war was his elucidation of autonomy privacy as the realm of moral autonomy. Autonomy privacy is the sphere in which individuals make decisions unencumbered by outside influences. This is the realm of privacy that the California Supreme Court says is a fundamental right that can be invaded only on the basis of the most compelling necessity. Within the sphere of autonomy privacy decisions can be made in accordance with a morality that is also autonomous. It is abundantly clear, however, that when the privacy provisions were added to the California Constitution in 1972 there was no thought that radical moral autonomy would be the core of the right to privacy. Indeed, the ballot pamphlets and other election materials indicate that the protection of informational privacy—the protection of personal information and records—was the principal thrust of the constitutional amendment. There was no mention or hint of anything like autonomy privacy; this was added by judicial construction. There was also no indication that the intent of the constitutional amendment was to protect the right to privacy to a greater degree than afforded under the federal Constitution—in fact, the legislative debate proceeded almost exclusively in terms of federal case law.

Chief Justice George spoke of autonomy privacy as the individual's right "to retain personal control over . . . fundamental autonomy interests." And perhaps the most fundamental autonomy privacy interest, according to the Chief Justice, is the right to choose whether or not to procreate. "The right of choice," the Chief Justice noted, "may implicate a woman's deepest philosophical, moral, and religious concerns, including her personal beliefs regarding the meaning of human existence, and the beginning of human life."

Many will recognize this statement as a paraphrase from Justice O'Connor's 1992 opinion in *Planned Parenthood v. Casey* in which she spoke of "choices central to personal dignity and autonomy." In what has become known to constitutional scholars as the "mystery clause," Justice O'Connor noted that "at the heart of liberty is the right to define one's own concept of existence, of meaning, of the universe, and of the mystery of human life." But can such liberty, based on radical moral autonomy, serve as the foundation of constitutional morality?

This precise question was raised by Justice Janice Brown in her penetrating dissent. Privacy autonomy for children, Justice Brown argued, conflicts with the long-standing right of parents to direct the upbringing of their children, a right recognized as "fundamental" in both the U.S. and California Constitutions. If the privacy rights of children are recognized to be coextensive with those of their parents, then no possible reconciliation of these competing rights is possible. Justice Brown, I believe, addressed the core of the issue when she remarked that the decision to accord autonomy privacy rights to minor children puts the Court in the position that allows it "to dismiss all societal values, and to become the final arbiters of traditional morality in a context in which their view of wisdom cannot be challenged." And with perhaps more irony than she intended or knew, Justice Brown noted that "[t]his case is an excellent example of the folly of courts in the role of philosopher kings. Here, the trial court 'found' there is no difference in the decisionmaking capacities of minors and adults. . . . There is only one problem. The 'finding' is contrary to what every adult in the country knows from experience . . . . Certainly, in matters of normative judgment, no court should be in the position to supplant a society's collective understanding, distilled through experience and express in legislative enactments, on the basis of evidence presented in a single case." It is the legislature, she concluded, that is charged with the principal task of expressing the collective experience and wisdom of society, not courts. Courts, of course, have an important check on the expression of legislative will; legislative will must conform to the constitution and be consistent with the protection of minority rights. But it is not for the court to substitute its will for that of the legislature. After all, courts exercise judgment, and should never find themselves in the position of exercising will. This is a basic tenet of the doctrine of separation of powers which is essential to constitutionalism and the rule of law.

We are left with this stark anomaly: a minor girl—perhaps as young as ten—has an unfettered right to an abortion as long as she can convince a for-profit abortion provider that she is mature enough to give informed consent. At the same time, however, California law forbids the same minor from getting a permanent tattoo without parental consent—or from using a tanning salon without permission, or body-piercing, or a drivers' license. Presumably these activities do not fall within the zone of autonomy privacy because—unlike procreational choice—they do not provoke questions about the mystery of being or the complexity of the universe.

Both the U.S. Supreme Court and the California Supreme Court have said that personal autonomy and autonomy privacy are somehow the core of constitutional liberty. Is this possible? Can autonomy ever be the source of liberty rightly understood as moral choice? Whatever else morality might mean, it certainly means making choices. But it means making choices with a view as to how those choices will affect others, whether family members or fellow citizens. Morality is by definition "other-regarding." Confronting the mystery of the universe or the mystery of life as an autonomous human being is simply to do so idiosyncratically. Any idiosyncratic answers will be unintelligible and uncommunicable. Under these circumstances it is impossible to distinguish between the greatest wisdom and the greatest folly. But are there any standards for morality? Isn't morality a matter of individual choice? We have been told often enough that morality is simply a matter of values and that there are no rational grounds to prefer one value to another. There are no standards to judge morality or value judgments, we are told, because value judgements do not rest on reason—value judgments are individual and idiosyncratic. All value judgments are therefore equal and equally deserving of respect. There is no better or worse—only differences.

Occasionally we are provoked to wonder whether these assumptions are adequate. We are still outraged by events such as the recent spate of school shootings. We are at a loss to explain or understand such outrages. But should we be? Teachers have taught their students that there is no such thing as morality, or at least no morality that has an objective ground or basis. We should clarify our values, we should make sure that the values to which we have committed ourselves are truly the ones we want, but there is no ground or standard by which we can say that any morality is right or wrong. Since there is no right or wrong morality, tolerance becomes the highest value. In a world where all values are equal and equally valuable, no judgment is possible; only tolerance of all values remains.

But teachers have also said that we should exercise our values in a way that does not harm others. Harming others is never good because it shows a lack of tolerance. And when students reply: is "not harming others" a morality, the teachers are forced to respond that it is not. Why then should this be a restriction on our autonomy, the students demand? If there is no morality how can you make an exception? And if this exception is only your personal autonomy choice, how does it apply to us? The students thus are more thoughtful and less timid than their teachers who, although they say there is no morality, act as if there were. Students want to be consistent: if there are no grounds for morality, then the prohibition against harming others cannot be valid. Students who act more consistently than their teachers cannot understand why their courage and honesty is not praised by their teachers who are prevented by their dishonesty and lack of courage from expressing their full moral autonomy. The teachers, of course, inconsistently believe that in a universe of moral relativism there can still be a moral absolute—respect for the moral autonomy of others. But the teachers don't see that there is no ground but their own idiosyncratic preferences for this moral injunction. The students thus understand their teachers better than they understand themselves. The teachers sow the seeds of nihilism but profess surprise and moral outrage when it bears fruit.

How did we come to this? Did the courts, *sua sponte*, foist this new morality—this autonomy privacy—upon an unsuspecting public under the guise of protecting rights and liberties? I fear greater forces were at work: the forces of modern philosophy that sought to undermine both reason and revelation as sources of morality. Some today—especially conservatives—say that the decline in morality was made inevitable by the nation's founding principles, because those principles were an expression of the modern thought that inevitably leads to moral relativism or—worse—nihilism. Once you have premised your politics on the principle that "all men are created equal," we are told, it is only a matter of time before the demand for equality in all things sweeps all before it. What once was a respectable principle of distributive justice based on equal opportunity has insensibly become a demand for equality of result. What was once moral freedom has inevitably become permissive egalitarianism. In short, when a nation is founded on the principle of equal rights, individual moral autonomy then will be the inevitable result. The emphasis on rights came at the expense of obligations—so we are told. We used to derive our obligations from traditional morality, which, in turn, was inspired by traditional religion. Both of these were undermined by the triumph of permissive egalitarianism. Thus, we are told by some observers, there is a straight line between the Declaration of Independence and the California Supreme Court's decision in *American Academy of Pediatrics v. Lungren*.

Is this explanation plausible? I think not. The Founders of America operated within a well-articulated moral universe informed by the "laws of nature and nature's God." That is, the principles that were to animate the political and moral life of the nation were to be drawn from the principles of human nature—principles that were confirmed by biblical teachings. The moral universe as understood by the Founders was not mysterious, but comprehended an articulated whole. In saying that "all men are created equal, [and] that they are endowed with by their Creator with certain unalienable Rights," the Declaration refers to both a Creator and a creation. Creation, of course, necessarily implies an intelligible universe, an ordered whole. While the whole may always remain elusive, since God works in mysterious ways, man can discover as much of God's plan as is vouchsafed to man's reason. This was the argument given by the Reverend Samuel West in 1776 in a sermon entitled "On the Right to Rebel against Governors"; it was an argument repeated almost ad infinitum by colonial ministers. "A revelation," Reverend West said, "pretending to be from God, that contradicts any part of natural law, ought immediately to be rejected as an imposture; for the Deity cannot make a law contrary to the law of nature without acting contrary to himself, —a thing in the strictest sense impossible, for that which implies contradiction is not an object of the divine power. Reason is the voice of God . . . [and] whatever right reason requires as necessary to be done is as much the will and law of God as though it were enjoined us by an immediate revelation from heaven, or commanded in the sacred Scriptures."[6] I believe that both the argument of the Reverend West and the argument of the Declaration of Independence agree with St. Thomas Aquinas' account of the relation of the natural law to eternal law. According to Aquinas, the natural law is the rational creature's participation in the eternal law, and the eternal law is the law by which God governs the universe. Man participates in the eternal law to the extent that the law is rational, and the results of man's reasoning might properly be called the natural law. The distinction between God, man, and the lower orders of being provided the source and ground of morality in the American Founding. Men do not have the perfect wisdom of God, nor are they simply the creatures of instinct as are the lower animals. This means that the rule of law—which attempts to ameliorate the imperfections of man's reason—is the proper order for man's social constitution. And the rule of law, properly so-called, is derived from the consent of those who are subject to the law. If the rule of law means anything, it means that those who are subject to the law must participate in the making of the law and those who make the law must be subject to the laws they make. This is the dictate of natural human equality and the principles of human nature. Those who argue that the "pursuit of happiness" in the Declaration has no limit because the pursuit of happiness inevitably will become pursuit of idiosyncratic autonomy privacy understand rights apart from the natural law. Jefferson spoke of the Declaration as an expression of "the American mind." The American mind was a collective unity—it could not be idiosyncratic. "Public happiness," not the idiosyncratic happiness that might emanate from the sphere of autonomy privacy was the object of the Declaration's moral injunctions that there are no rights without concomitant obligations.

It may be objected that the Declaration didn't spell out its moral basis. But the American mind—as Jefferson recognized—was virtually unanimous on the question of political morality; its sources were drawn from both reason and revelation, natural law and the Bible. The idea that the protection of individual rights was in tension with the existence of the common good—or with the moral obligations that derive from the common good—was never expressed by the Founders. None of the Founders viewed rights as idiosyncratic preferences divorced from duty or moral obligations. The idiosyncratic view of rights was the product of the late nineteenth century school of thought that we know as progressivism. The explicit goal of progressivism was to free the Constitution from it moorings in the Founding, most particularly from the static doctrines of the Declaration of Independence and it reliance on the permanent truths of the "laws of nature and nature's God." The notion of permanent truths and the laws of nature, the progressives argued, had been exposed as hopelessly outmoded by the progress of science, which had refuted the possibility of nature or natural right. The moral and political universe was not informed by the laws of nature as understood by the Founders, but the laws of evolution. Government is a living thing, the progressives declared; it is Darwinian in nature, and in the Darwinian universe there is no fixed moral horizon—there is only evolution and progressive change or adaptation. Progressivism itself was only one strain of modernity, but it shared with the other strains the depreciation of both reason and revelation as sources of moral and political authority. Progressivism was phenomenally successful in its debunking of the Founding and its reformist zeal appealed wholly to the passions. It sought to liberate the passions from the constraints of morality, whereas the Founders appealed to the "reason . . . of the public"[7] as the foundation of moral and political order. The appeal to reason, of course, will always be more difficult than the appeal to passion, especially when the appeal to passion has itself assumed a kind of moral authority as it has in the concept of moral autonomy.

The Declaration speaks of the people both in their moral capacity ("the good People") and their political capacity ("one people"). Indeed, Americans are "one people" by virtue of the fact that they are "the good people." The revival of the principles of the Declaration will, I believe, go hand in hand with the restoration of religion in both public and private life. Both the Declaration and mainstream religions have suffered under the onslaught of the forces of historicism and positivism. These forces of modernity have succeeded in undermining both reason and revelation as supports for moral and political life. The kind of value relativism promoted by notions of autonomy privacy has eroded the principles of the Declaration of Independence no less than "liberation theology" has weakened America's mainstream religions. Autonomy privacy is the antithesis of both reason and revelation. But the triumph of autonomy privacy is the triumph of modern philosophy, not the activist judiciary. It would be a mistake to think that the activist judiciary can be curbed by increasing the power of legislatures. The Framers envisioned a legitimate role—indeed an activist role—for the judiciary in the protection against majority faction. That is, the judiciary was to stand as a bulwark against those occasions when the majority attempted to extend its reach beyond constitutional limits. The role of the judiciary was to protect the organic law—the Constitution—against assaults by temporary majorities. But the organic law cannot be understood apart from the principles that animate it; and those principles were articulated in the natural right and natural law principles of the Declaration of Independence. It is the revival of those principles that must animate any reform, not any structural or institutional reform of the Constitution. Such reforms would be incomplete—and perhaps dangerous—without a thoroughgoing understanding of the principles of the Founding, the principles that must the starting point for any moral and political revival in our time. Jefferson wrote in the Bill for Establishing Religious Freedom, that "truth is great and will prevail if left to herself; that she is the proper and sufficient antagonist to error, and nothing to fear from the conflict unless by human interposition disarmed of her natural weapons, free argument, and debate." But today truth has been disarmed of her natural weapons by the pervasive assumption that there is no such thing as truth—there are only values and there can be no rational knowledge of values. Morality thus has no ground in reason. This unexamined assumption—which itself has taken on the character of a moral absolute—holds that all truth is relative, merely the product of autonomy privacy. Free argument and debate on matters of value and morality is irrelevant, because reason and debate can never be productive of truth. This is the principal weapon that ideological liberalism uses in the culture war today. That war will be lost unless we succeed in disarming the advocates of moral autonomy of their principal weapon.

NOTES

1. See Edward J. Erler and Ernest O. Vincent, "*The California Supreme Court and the Death Penalty*," *Benchmark* 2 (1986):143–53.
2. William J. Brennan, "*State Constitutions and the Protection of Individual Rights*," *Harvard Law Review* 90 (1977):489, 502.
3. Brennan, *State Constitutions and the Protection of Individual Rights*, 491.
4. William J. Brennan, "The Bill of Rights and the States: The Revival of State Constitutions as Guardians of Individual Rights," *New York University Law Review* 61 (1986):535, 550.
5. *Michigan v. Mosley*, 423 U.S. 96, 120, 121 (1975) (Brennan, J., dissenting).
6. Charles Hyneman and Donald S. Lutz, eds., *American Political Writings During the Founding Era, 1760–1805* (Indianapolis: Liberty Fund, 1983), vol. 1, 416.
7. Hamilton, Madison, Jay, *The Federalist Papers*, ed. Clinton Rossiter (New York: Mentor, 1961).

IV

COURTS, CULTURE, AND LIBERAL DEMOCRACY

10

Courts, Culture, and Community: Rescuing Constitutional Supremacy from Judicial Supremacy

Christopher P. Manfredi

In this chapter I discuss two longstanding and related skirmishes in what one might call the constitutional culture war. These skirmishes involve, respectively, the legitimate scope of judicial review and the constitutional right to abortion, two issues that became inextricably linked, of course, in *Roe v. Wade*.[1] Although the intensity of these skirmishes has varied over time, they are now a permanent part of the battle over the way in which courts shape both culture and community in the United States. Most recently, they can be found at the core of the U.S. Supreme Court's decision in *Stenberg v. Carhart*[2] and University of Chicago law professor Cass Sunstein's book *One Case at a Time: Judicial Minimalism on the Supreme Court*.[3] The Court's decision nullifying Nebraska's ban on partial-birth abortions and Sunstein's praise for judicial minimalism once again reinforce the importance of public debate about the role of American courts in the most serious moral and cultural issue in American democracy since slavery.

I approach this subject primarily, and cautiously, as an outsider, albeit one who has maintained a scholarly interest in American constitutionalism and judicial review.[4] However, I am a Canadian scholar who devotes most of my energy to the study of the Canadian Supreme Court, which may nevertheless provide a useful vantage point from which to observe the American scene. After all, in my professional career I have seen rights-based constitutional review grow from nonexistent in Canada to become a dominant political force. Until 1949 the Supreme Court of Canada was not supreme; until 1974 it had virtually no control over the composition of its docket; and until 1982 it did not have a constitutionally entrenched rights document to enforce. Today it is at the apex of a legal system in which the most successful interest group litigant over the past five years is called Equality for Gays and Lesbians

Everywhere. It is also a legal system where provincial human rights tribunals adjudicate the conflicting claims of lesbian community organizations and their preoperative male transsexual employees. From South Africa to Israel the Canadian Court's activism has become a model for the "global expansion of judicial power."[5] Nowhere are courts, culture, and community more closely linked than in contemporary Canada. I hope that my observations of these recent and rapid developments can add something to a discussion of courts and culture in the United States.

My discussion of this relationship proceeds in four stages. First, I tread over familiar ground by revisiting the impact that *Roe v. Wade* had on debates about judicial review and constitutional interpretation. Second, I examine Professor Sunstein's recent contribution to this debate. Third, I turn to the U.S. Supreme Court's most recent abortion decision, *Stenberg v. Carhart*, to examine the practical state of this debate in constitutional law. Finally, I return to the debate initiated by *Roe* in order to draw some conclusions about judicial and constitutional supremacy.

FROM *DRED SCOTT* TO *ROE V. WADE*

At the risk of exaggeration, one can be relatively confident in suggesting that for almost an entire century—from 1857 to 1954—no one looked to American courts or judicial review to accelerate so-called social progress. In *Dred Scott v. Sandford*,[6] the U.S. Supreme Court declared that "persons of the Negro race" could not be U.S. citizens and denied Congress's authority to prohibit the expansion of slavery into federal territory. Judicial review's impact on racial equality was similarly negative throughout the post–Civil War Reconstruction period. The Court exercised judicial review to undercut the Fourteenth Amendment's privileges and immunities clause; to deny Congress any power to enforce the Fourteenth Amendment by prohibiting private discrimination, and to constitutionalize state-enforced segregation. Having undermined efforts to advance civil rights, the Court turned to economic regulation in the twentieth century. Using the doctrine of substantive due process, the Court prohibited state and federal governments from setting maximum hours and minimum wages, and from regulating the working conditions of women and children. Finally, the Court resisted Franklin Roosevelt's New Deal initiatives.

For progressive-minded intellectuals, this record of performance made judicial review and the Court unattractive political institutions. The Court shed this antiprogressive image, however, with its decision in *Brown v. Board of Education*.[7] *Brown* represented a sharp departure from the past, and the Court's nullification of a morally repugnant practice granted new legitimacy to the judicialization of American political life. Although scholars like

Alexander Bickel and Raul Berger raised dissenting voices from time to time, *Brown* served for two decades as the touchstone of a strong positive consensus about the ability of courts, through judicial review, to improve American culture and community.

This consensus began to deteriorate in the wake of the Court's decision in *Roe v. Wade*, in which it extended the right to privacy articulated in *Griswold v. Connecticut*[8] to include abortion. In *Griswold*, the Court struck down a Connecticut statute prohibiting the use of contraceptives on the grounds that the law violated a general, constitutional right to privacy that the Court purported to discover in the penumbral emanations of several provisions of the Bill of Rights. In *Roe*, seven justices held that this right "is broad enough to encompass a woman's decision whether or not to terminate her pregnancy." The Court described this right as absolute during the first trimester of pregnancy, but allowed for some state regulation of abortion during the second and third trimesters to protect, respectively, maternal health and the potential life of unborn human beings.

The majority's inability to demonstrate that either the right to privacy or the right to abortion could be found in the express words, or even in the "manifest tenor" of the Constitution, was a critical blow to the constitutional legitimacy of modern judicial review. As Justices William Rehnquist and Byron White said in their dissenting opinions in *Roe* and its companion case, the abortion decision represented "an exercise of raw judicial power." *Roe* also resurrected the discredited the doctrine of substantive due process on which the Court had relied in its anti-regulatory decisions. For these reasons and others, the decision distressed even constitutional scholars sympathetic to the liberalization of state abortion laws. *Roe* thus reopened in rather dramatic fashion a normative debate about judicial power that appeared to have been settled as a result of *Brown*.

This debate generated an extensive body of constitutional theory in the 1980s.[9] Some, like John Hart Ely, tried to articulate a limited defense of judicial review that could save it from the excesses of *Roe*. Others, like Michael Perry and Arthur Selwyn Miller, sought to defend the broad use of judicial power epitomized by *Roe*. Finally, conservatives articulated a "jurisprudence of original intention" as a means of preventing the judicial usurpation of legislative power represented by *Roe*. The debate reached its political apex during the Senate's confirmation hearings to consider the nomination of Judge Robert H. Bork to the Supreme Court. Support for the right to privacy, and by implication the right to abortion, has since become a liberal litmus test for appointment to the Court. That this test has been successful, even if by deterring presidents from proposing certain nominations to the Court, is evident in *Roe*'s continued status as good precedent. Indeed, in June 2000 a majority of the Court affirmed that the "Constitution offers basic protection to the woman's right to choose."

Republican presidents, one should note, appointed three of the five justices composing this majority.

THE MINIMALIST VIRTUES

Roe v. Wade makes several appearances in Professor Cass Sunstein's effort to identify and defend a particular form of judicial decision making that he calls "judicial minimalism".[10] According to Sunstein, the practice of constitutional judicial review has generated at least four theoretically ambitious attempts to resolve the relationship among the Supreme Court, the Constitution, and legislatures.[11] These attempts include originalism, the rule of "clear mistakes," the advocacy of independent interpretive judgment by courts found in the work of Ronald Dworkin, and the democracy-reinforcement approach advocated by Ely. Sunstein rejects each of these attempts to varying degrees, preferring instead the minimalist practices of justices like Ruth Bader Ginsburg, David Souter, Sandra Day O'Connor, Stephen Breyer, John Paul Stevens, and Anthony Kennedy. These minimalist judges, Sunstein argues, "seek to avoid broad rules and abstract theories, and attempt to focus their attention only on what is necessary to resolve particular disputes".[12]

As a theory of constitutional interpretation, minimalism has two principal features.[13] The first is narrowness, which counsels judges to decide cases rather than to set broad rules. Minimalist judges "render decisions that are no broader than necessary to support the outcome." A second feature is shallowness, which counsels judges to avoid issues of basic principle. This characteristic of minimalism assumes the "possibility of concrete judgments on particular cases, unaccompanied by abstract accounts about what accounts for those judgments."[14]

Minimalism, in Sunstein's account, is a democracy-promoting form of constitutional judicial review because minimalist nullification of legislation both points to specific errors and leaves room for democratic deliberation about the appropriate way to correct those errors.[15] In fact, Sunstein identifies four distinct choices available to courts: maximalist validation, maximalist invalidation, minimalist validation, and minimalist invalidation. The least democratic of these choices is maximalist invalidation, because it "creates the greatest foreclosure of political deliberation."[16] By contrast, minimalist invalidation is the choice most consistent with deliberative democracy because it promotes both political accountability and reason-giving.[17]

Minimalism is particularly appropriate in the face of "issues of high factual or ethical complexity that are producing democratic disagreement and debate."[18] The basic objective in these cases is to minimize decision making and error costs. As Sunstein argues, minimalism "allows the democratic process a great deal of room in which to adapt to coming developments, to produce mutually advantageous compromises, and to add new information and perspectives to legal issues."[19] Herein lies his criticism of *Roe*, which Sunstein characterizes as a shallowly theorized, yet broad decision in which the Court decided "too many issues too quickly."[20] Indeed, *Roe* exemplifies the sort of maximalist invalidation of a statute the courts should generally, if not absolutely, avoid.[21] This is not to say that Sunstein thinks the Court should have deferred to the Texas legislature in *Roe*. A minimalist Court might still have struck down the nineteenth-century abortion statute at issue in *Roe*, but without establishing any constitutional right to abortion. For example, the Court could have declared the law unconstitutionally vague, or restricted its holding to cases involving rape (which was Jane Roe's [false] claim about the origin of her pregnancy).[22]

This point about minimalism and abortion can be illustrated by the Canadian Supreme Court's abortion decision. In 1988 the Canadian Court dealt with the contentious abortion issue for the second time in thirteen years. On the first occasion, the court made it clear that it had no mandate to participate in the "loud and continuous public debate on abortion."[23] The 1982 Charter of Rights and Freedoms made this level of deference impossible, however, and in 1988 the Court acknowledged an "added responsibility" to ensure "that the legislative initiatives pursued by our Parliament and legislatures conform to the democratic values" expressed in the Charter.[24] Although seven justices produced four separate judgments (with two justices voting to uphold the law), the key judgment by the chief justice declared that it was "neither necessary nor wise" to "explore the broadest implications" of liberty raised by the abortion issue. Nevertheless, he declared the federal abortion law unconstitutional on the basis of administrative deficiencies that created undue delays and uneven access to legal, therapeutic abortions. This judgment provided the federal Parliament with the option of reestablishing criminal regulation of abortion under a different administrative scheme.

Professor Sunstein's support for judicial minimalism is not unqualified, however. One qualification is that minimalism encompasses a substantive core that is capable of expansion. More precisely, the purpose of even minimalist constitutional law "is to support the internal morality of democracy," which includes political equality, participation, deliberation, and accountability.[25] Even judicial minimalism, he argues, must protect political dissent, the right to vote, religious liberty, the rule of law, and the human body against government invasion. It must also prohibit torture, murder, and physical abuse by the government, and protect against unauthorized imprisonment, physical invasion of property, police abuse of person or property, slavery, or subordination on the basis of race or sex.[26] Judicial minimalism, in other words, protects most of the substantive constitutional law laid down from *Brown* to *Roe*.

Indeed, Professor Sunstein's book is an extended attack against the originalist arguments that reasserted themselves as a reaction to the twenty years of judicial social engineering that occurred from 1954 to 1973. The most obvious indicator of this objective is that more than one-tenth of the book is dedicated to a critique of Justice Antonin Scalia's alleged adherence to maximalism on a generally minimalist Court. According to Sunstein, Scalia's maximalism emphasizes the dimension of width, and it consists in broad judgments anchored in "the meaning of the relevant legal text as it was understood at the time of enactment," whether that text is a statute or the Constitution.[27] Scalia's strong commitment to "rule-bound justice" and his "desire to ensure that discretion is exercised by democratically elected officials rather than by judges,"[28] Sunstein continues, aims at legal stability, democratic self-government, and judicial restraint.[29] Yet, Sunstein argues, with respect to two of these objectives—democracy and restraint—Scalia's originalism ultimately fails. Using language strikingly similar to that employed by Justice William Brennan fourteen years earlier to criticize U.S. Attorney-General Edwin Meese's "jurisprudence of original intention," Sunstein urges that Scalia's originalism "be rejected . . . as an unacceptable form of maximalism—judicial hubris masquerading as judicial modesty".[30]

With respect to abortion, Sunstein's arguments about both judicial minimalism and originalism allow him to pursue two seemingly contradictory objectives. On the one hand, he is able to criticize *Roe*, and therefore distance himself from perhaps the least defensible Supreme Court decision since *Dred Scott*. On the other hand, he is able to preserve *Roe* as good precedent by attributing the same defect—maximalism—to the very theory of interpretation that would justify its reversal. Indeed, the ineffectiveness of a minimalist Court when confronted with an improperly maximalist precedent is clearly evident in *Stenberg v. Carhart*, where the Court's minimalist core joined to nullify Nebraska's prohibition against partial-birth abortions.

STENBERG V. CARHART

At issue in *Stenberg* was a Nebraska statute that prohibited partial-birth abortions except where necessary to save the mother's life. The statute defined partial-birth abortions as a "procedure in which the person performing the abortion partially delivers vaginally a living unborn child before killing the unborn child and completing the delivery." The statute defined the concept of partial delivery as "deliberately and intentionally delivering into the vagina a living unborn child, or a substantial portion thereof, for the purpose of performing a procedure that the person performing such procedure knows will kill the unborn child and does kill the unborn child." A bare majority of the Court declared the statute unconstitutional on the grounds that it violated the undue burden test established in *Planned Parenthood of Southeastern Pennsylvania v. Casey*.[31] According to the majority opinion by Justice Breyer, the undue burden arose under the Nebraska statute because it imposed a complete ban on a particular abortion procedure (dilation and extraction, or D&X) that was safer and medically superior to other procedures employed during the relevant gestational period (after the sixteenth week of pregnancy). In the majority's view, this constituted a substantial obstacle to a woman's right to abortion, contrary to the doctrine announced in *Casey*.

The *Stenberg* majority included five members of the minimalist block identified by Sunstein in his 1999 book (Justices Breyer, O'Connor, Stevens, Souter, and Ginsburg). The majority opinion's minimalism is evident in its lack of concern for the normative issues surrounding partial-birth abortions. Instead, the opinion focuses on narrow factual and jurisprudential questions: Does the Nebraska statute implicitly ban the D&X procedure? If so, does this ban impose an undue burden contrary to *Casey*? By focusing on these two questions alone, the majority acted consistently with Sunstein's three minimalist virtues of shallowness, narrowness, and democracy-promotion. These virtues are also present in Justice O'Connor's concurring opinion, which acknowledges the national controversy surrounding abortion and then follows Sunstein's counsel to avoid that controversy by defining the question at issue in *Stenberg* as one of technique. Similarly, Justice Ginsburg's concurrence seeks to separate the constitutional analysis of Nebraska's statute from the emotional uproar generated by abortion cases. Even the dissenting member of the minimalist block, Justice Kennedy, exercised minimalist virtues by arguing that the majority had simply misapplied *Casey*. According to Kennedy, Nebraska's prohibition against the D&X procedure advanced legitimate state interests in promoting the life of the unborn without blocking access to abortion. In his view, Nebraska had a right to draw a moral distinction between the D&X procedure and the alternative, dilation and evacuation (D&E).

The difficulty with the application of minimalism in *Stenberg* is that it allows the majority to conceal, or at least attempt to conceal, the real import of its decision. The implicit promise of the majority opinion is that, if Nebraska could find a method of banning partial-birth abortions without imposing an undue burden on the basic constitutional right articulated in *Roe*, then the majority would—even if grudgingly—uphold the restriction. However, the logic of the decision is quite different. After *Stenberg*, states are faced with the following paradox: the only way to exercise their constitutionally valid interest in protecting fetal life is to ban certain abortion procedures, but by banning those procedures states necessarily impose an undue burden on the right proclaimed in *Roe*. In this sense, minimalism functions not as a check on judicial overreaching in a context of normative and empirical uncertainty, but as a guarantee that judicially created pseudo-rights will survive despite widespread recognition that they have no roots in the constitutional text.

Which is precisely the point of Justice Scalia's dissent in *Stenberg*. Although Scalia joined Kennedy's dissent, as well as a second dissent by Justice Thomas, he wrote separately to ensure that the nature of his objection to the majority opinion was clear. In his view, the majority erred not in misapplying *Casey*, but in persisting to believe that the Court, "armed with neither constitutional text nor accepted tradition," is capable of resolving the contention and controversy over abortion identified by Justice O'Connor. According to Scalia, only the people, acting through their state legislatures, can resolve this controversy. This is particularly true, he argues, with respect to *Casey*'s undue burden standard. The problem with this standard is that there is no legal principle according to which it can be defined. The presence of an undue burden, Scalia implies, is in the eye of the beholder, and there is no reason to favor the Court's judgment in this regard over the one reached by state legislatures. If, in the final analysis, the validity of Nebraska's statute rests on a simple value judgment, then there is no principled basis for overturning it.

Scalia's dissent illustrates one of the weaknesses of judicial minimalism as a theory of constitutional interpretation. Under most circumstances it forces judges into making precisely the type of value judgment that minimalism is supposed to avoid. This point can be best illustrated by returning to Professor Sunstein's discussion of the right to die, which is closely analogous to the abortion issue. Sunstein argues that minimalism is the appropriate approach in this instance, but then argues that "when conditions are or appear to be medically hopeless, the individual's interest in physician-assisted suicide should probably qualify as one on which the state may intrude only with special justification."[32] The problem here, of course, is that the medically hopeless standard is as legally vacuous as the undue burden standard. Thus, to require that any state prohibition against physician-assisted suicide, or specific techniques for performing it, contain a medical hopelessness exception is likely to encounter the same difficulty as Nebraska's ban on partial-birth abortions. In the final analysis, the Constitution simply does not provide answers to such difficult moral questions, as much as one might want it to.

ORIGINALISM'S LIMITATIONS

Originalism holds that "judges deciding constitutional issues should confine themselves to enforcing norms that are stated or clearly implicit in the written Constitution." This approach asserts that judicial nullification of legislation is legitimate only when a statute contradicts specific constitutional provisions or violates rights clearly inferable from the document's language.[33] For originalism the purpose of constitutional adjudication is to give effect to the normative judgments of the majority. This does not mean blind judicial deference to legislative will, since liberal constitutionalism encompasses two distinct types of majority rule. On the one hand, there is the simple majority rule reflected in the statutory enactments of legislatures; on the other hand, there is the extraordinary majority rule reflected in the text of a constitution and its amendments. Originalism does not reject judicial review, but asserts that the normative judgments of legislative majorities must be respected unless they clearly contradict the normative judgments of the extraordinary majorities responsible for establishing constitutional rules. From the originalist standpoint, the normative judgments of legislative or constitutional majorities are authoritative not so much because of their content, but because of the process by which they became law.

The principal criticism of originalism comes from various theories of judicial activism, which encourage judges to "enforce norms that cannot be discovered within the four corners" of the constitutional text and thus view constitutional adjudication as a creative task of identifying and applying novel rights. In their more moderate form, these theories permit judicial creativity in reviewing the formal process of democratic decision making, but not in evaluating the substantive policy choices that emanate from that process. More expansive versions of these theories advocate value-oriented judicial activism on the grounds that courts are the only "policymaking institution that regularly deals with fundamental political-moral problems other than by mechanical reference to established moral conventions."[34] The purpose of judicial review within these variations of nonoriginalist interpretational theories is to create a more sophisticated and progressive political morality by subjecting the conventional values embodied in statutes and constitutional text to external critical analysis. From this perspective, the purpose of constitutional review is to overcome the moral skepticism implicit in the attachment to positive law by giving effect to normative standards derived independently of majority judgment. These standards are necessary because the normative judgments of legislative and constitutional majorities are both flawed. The problem with legislative majorities is that they are subject to electoral myopia, insensitivity to and exclusion of minorities, and the elevation of policy over principle. With constitutional majorities, the problem is that their normative judgments are either indeterminate or simply irrelevant for deciding contemporary moral-legal disputes. In essence, nonoriginalist theories of judicial activism view constitutions not as sets of constraining rules, but as a "delegation of power to later generations to write their own fundamental law."[35]

On close analysis, this criticism of originalism is unpersuasive. Its failure stems from the assertion that liberal legal positivism produces moral stasis. The reality, however, is that liberal constitutions provide for the moral development of positive law by granting legislatures the power to create statutory rights and by providing amending processes through which moral progress may be written into constitutional law. The real complaint of non-originalists is that moral progress does not proceed far enough, quickly enough, or necessarily in the right direction. However, the process of improving constitutions or other legal instruments is necessarily slow, contentious, and incremental in heterogeneous liberal democracies governed by the principle of majority rule. Indeed, it is precisely this feature of liberal democracy that leads nonoriginalists to criticize both constitutional and legislative majorities as sources of moral progress, since the necessity of constructing either extraordinary or simple majorities forces moderation and compromise on alleged matters of principle. By contrast, the judicial arena appears to provide a place where "right [rather than merely expedient] answers . . . to fundamental political-moral problems" can be discovered.[36] It is problematic, however, to grant courts sole, or even primary, responsibility for changing positive constitutional law to reflect moral progress because reasonable people differ about the content of progress. The fact that positive constitutional law may in some instances reflect compromises over fundamental principles does not mean that it is devoid of moral content altogether.

Contrary to what nonoriginalist activist theories argue, the real weakness in originalism is that it reinforces the perception that the moral authority of a constitutional text derives less from the exercise of "reflection and choice" by majorities than in the "accident and force" of their numerical superiority.[37] In other words, originalism understates the extent to which the text's authority is a function of the normative principles it embodies as well as of the process that adopted it. Indeed, the respect for positive law required by liberal constitutionalism from its political institutions, including courts, is based on the understanding that "popular sovereignty divorced from a universal conception of human right is a complete absurdity." Indeed, a truly liberal government is dedicated to something more than "the mere process of arriving at decisions without coercion by any formula embodying the principle of majority rule."[38] Moreover, originalism does this without necessarily advancing its most important objective, which is to constrain judicial power. Originalist constitutional theory is a variation on the theme of judicial self-restraint, but self-restraint is precisely what liberal constitutionalism refuses to rely on as the main device for controlling political power. Consequently, to rely on a "jurisprudence of original intention" to control judicial power ironically contradicts the very intentions of liberal democracy's founders,[39] who put their faith not in the individual virtue of rulers, but in structural constraints on their rule.[40]

Originalism and the wide variety of nonoriginalist theories of judicial activism emerged in contemporary liberal theory as distinct ways of justifying judicial review in constitutional systems based on the principle of majority rule. On the one hand, originalism subordinates judicial review to majority rule by limiting its scope to enforcing the express will of constitutional majorities against the policy decisions of legislative majorities. In this sense, judicial review becomes an instrument of majority rule by giving effect either to legislation or to explicit constitutional rules. On the other hand, nonoriginalism elevates judicial review above majority rule by assigning it a unique function that is purportedly absent from the constitutional and legislative process. In this sense, judicial review becomes an instrument of abstract moral reasoning. Ironically, both of these justifications for judicial review suffer from a similar flaw: they do not take seriously the normative judgments embodied in majority rule. While this flaw is most obvious in nonoriginalism, which essentially denies the capacity of majorities to rule systematically in a principled way, it is also evident in originalism, which often seems to promote majority rule for its own sake rather than because of the principles it may seek to achieve.

If originalism is not the most powerful antidote for judicial social engineering, as it clearly has not been in the area of abortion, then what options remain? Perhaps the answer lies in recognizing the inherently political nature of decision making by national high courts. These courts make policy not as an accidental byproduct of performing their adjudicative function, but because their members believe that certain rules will be socially beneficial. Constitutionally entrenched rights documents increase judicial policymaking power because they expand the range of social and political issues subject to a court's jurisdiction. If this characterization is true, then the response to judicial activism must be political rather than legal. In the American context, the most common political strategy has been to use the judicial appointment process to change the Supreme Court's direction. This strategy has at least two flaws. First, it is unreliable—recall that Richard Nixon appointed Harry Blackmun (the author of *Roe*) because of his adherence to strict construction. Second, it leaves intact the idea that constitutional interpretation is a function performed exclusively by judges, and the task is to select the right personnel. But what if one rejects the notion that courts are the authoritative voice of constitutions, and therefore of the supreme law?

In order for communities to reclaim their cultures from the courts, they must reassert themselves as legitimate sources of constitutional meaning.[41] The U.S. Constitution provides at least one instrument with which to do this: the exceptions clause contained in Article III, Section 2. This clause gives Congress the authority to remove certain issues from the appellate jurisdiction of the federal courts, and it could be invoked in those areas where the people, through their elected representatives, have identified persistent errors of judicial interpretation of the Constitution. The clause is not a perfect instrument, however. It would leave the targeted issues within the jurisdiction of state courts, and because it is not statute specific it could operate more like a cleaver than a scalpel. The Canadian Charter contains an analogous, but potentially more effective instrument, in the form of a "notwithstanding mechanism." This provision allows the federal and provincial governments to declare that statutes shall operate "notwithstanding" most provisions of the Charter. In effect, the notwithstanding mechanism immunizes statutes from judicial review under the Charter for a period of five years.

In both cases, however, the use of these instruments depends on the exercise of considerable political will. If communities find it easier to surrender their constitutional development to courts than to participate actively in that development, then judicial supremacy will replace constitutional supremacy as the regime's central political and legal principle. The triumph of minimalism (which left intact a judicial interpretational error of the highest magnitude) over originalism (which would have restored the centrality of constitutional text in the abortion debate) in *Stenberg v. Carhart* illustrates the danger of succumbing not to the "political seduction of the law," but to the legal seduction of politics.

NOTES

1. *Roe v. Wade* 410 U.S. 113 (1973).
2. *Sterberg v. Carhart* (2000).
3. Cass Sunstein, *One Case at a Time* (Cambridge, Mass.: Harvard University Press, 1999).
4. The most recent example of this interest is my book, *The Supreme Court and Juvenile Justice* (Lawrence Ks.: University Press of Kansas, 1998).
5. C. Neil Tate and Torbjorn Vallinder, eds. *The Global Expansion of Judicial Power* (New York: New York University Press, 1995).
6. *Dred Scott v. Sanford* 60 U.S. 393 (1857).
7. *Brown v. Board of Education* 347 U.S. 483 (1954).
8. *Griswold v. Connecticut* 381 U.S. 479 (1965).
9. See John Hart Ely, *Democracy and Distrust: A Theory of Judicial Review* (Cambridge, MA: Harvard University Press, 1980); Michael J. Perry, *The Constitution, the Courts, and Human Rights* (New Haven: Yale University Press, 1982); Arthur Selwyn Miller, *Toward Increased Judicial Activism* (Westport, CT: Greenwood Press, 1982); Robert Bork, *The Tempting of America: The Political Seduction of the Law* (New York: Simon & Schuster, 1990).
10. Sustain, *One Case at a Time*, ix.
11. Sustain, *One Case at a Time*, 6–7.
12. Sustain, *One Case at a Time*, 9.
13. Sustain, *One Case at a Time*, 10–14.
14. Sustain, *One Case at a Time*, 13.
15. Sustain, *One Case at a Time*, 26–27.
16. Sustain, *One Case at a Time*, 30.
17. Sustain, *One Case at a Time*, 31.
18. Sustain, *One Case at a Time*, 46.
19. Sustain, *One Case at a Time*, 53.
20. Sustain, *One Case at a Time*, 17, 54.
21. Sustain, *One Case at a Time*, 30.
22. Sustain, *One Case at a Time*, 250–52.
23. *Morgentaler v. The Queen*, I.S.C.R. 616 (1976).

24. *Morgentaler et al. v. The Queen*, I.S.C.R. 30 (1988).
25. Sustain, *One Case at a Time*, 70.
26. Sustain, *One Case at a Time*, 64–67.
27. Sustain, *One Case at a Time*, 211.
28. Sustain, *One Case at a Time*, 241.
29. Sustain, *One Case at a Time*, 218.
30. Sustain, *One Case at a Time*, 262.
31. *Planned Parenthood of Southeastern Pennsylvania v. Casey* 505 U.S. 833 (1992).
32. Sustain, *One Case at a Time*, 115.
33. Bork, *The Tempting of America*, 143–160. For a more recent definition and defense of originalism, see Keith Whittington, *Constitutional Interpretation: Textual Meaning, Original Intent, and Judicial Review* (Lawrence, Ks.: University Press of Kansas, 1999).
34. Perry, *The Constitution, the Courts, and Human Rights*, 101–102.
35. Miller, *Toward Increased Judicial Activism*, 247.
36. Perry, *The Constitution, the Courts, and Human Rights*, 112–113.
37. This language is borrowed, of course, from The Federalist Papers. See Alexander Hamilton, James Madison, and John Jay, *The Federalist Papers*, ed. Clinton Rossiter (New York: New American Library, 1961), 1, 33.
38. Harry Jaffa, *Crisis of the House Divided: An Interpretation of the Issues in the Lincoln-Douglas Debates* (Chicago: University of Chicago Press, 1982), 348–49.
39. John Agresto, *The Supreme Court and Constitutional Democracy* (Ithaca, N.Y.: Cornell University Press, 1984), 112–16.
40. *The Federalist Papers*, 51, 322, 321; 10, 84.
41. See Mark V. Tushnet, *Taking the Constitution Away from the Courts* (Princeton, N.J.: Princeton University Press, 2000).

11

The Voting Rights Act and the Politics of Multiculturalism: The Challenge to Commercial Republicanism at Century's Turn

Anthony A. Peacock

In this chapter I examine the Voting Rights Act (VRA) of 1965[1] with a view to illustrating how in its present form it threatens to undermine the principles of American commercial republicanism. American republicanism was originally conceived—as it remains today—a distinctly commercial republicanism.[2] It was founded, among other things, on the recognition that factious conflicts, such as those anchored in the passions of sectarian or religious enthusiasm, were the most notorious sources of violent conflict that were to be avoided by anchoring commonality in the more congenial pursuits of acquisition and exchange. This, of course, is not to say that commerce or commercial relations do not lead to conflict or that American politics and the character of the American people are defined solely in economic terms. Rather, it simply acknowledges the limits of legitimate political activity in liberal constitutional regimes and the consequences of ignoring these limits for constitutional principle and civic harmony. John Locke, who demonstrated the virtues of religious freedom in *A Letter Concerning Toleration*, remarked in his *Second Treatise of Government*: "the great and *chief end* . . . of Men's uniting into Commonwealths, and putting themselves under Government, *is the Preservation of their Property*."[3] James Madison, who similarly defended religious liberty in *Memorial and Remonstrance*, observed in *Federalist 10*: the "first object of Government" is the "protection of different and unequal faculties" "from which the rights of property originate."[4] America's distinct form of constitutionalism would perfect the objects of the commercial republican regime by creating a constitutional order that would ensure domestic tranquility, promote the general welfare, and secure the blessings of liberty through government that was both limited and commercial in nature; through government that reduced politics to political economy and that proscribed public recognition or the promotion of arbitrary classifications, such as those based on race or religion.

The central theme of this chapter is that this view of American representative government is under assault. The sectarian conflict that characterized preliberal regimes and that was to be avoided by the liberal separation of church and state is today being resurrected by the politics of multiculturalism, a vision of America that defines racial and ethnic differences not merely as sources of identity and of mutual interest but as legally determinative categories that provide a legitimate foundation for claims to political rule.[5]

Over the last generation, the politics of multiculturalism has progressively captured the VRA, its animating vision now providing the foundation for the adjudication and administration of the act. The consequence of this has been the division of the electorate into racial and ethnic enclaves through the creation of safe minority electoral seats that have been deemed required by the VRA. The division of the electorate into racial and ethnic constituencies, particularly through the device of redistricting, and the racial and ethnic faction this could engender, was at the center of attention throughout the Supreme Court's voting rights jurisprudence of the 1990s. In its seminal 1993 decision, *Shaw v. Reno*, Justice O'Connor admonished that racial classifications with respect to voting were particularly dangerous. "Racial gerrymandering, even for remedial purposes, may balkanize us into competing racial factions; it threatens to carry us further from the goal of a political system in which race no longer matters—a goal that the Fourteenth and Fifteenth Amendments embody, and to which the Nation continues to aspire."[6]

O'Connor was no doubt correct that the Fourteenth and Fifteenth Amendments embodied the goal of a political system in which race no longer mattered and that this was what the vast majority of Americans continued to aspire to. Whether this was still the objective of the VRA by the 1990s was a different story. Under the act, race apparently very much mattered. The administration and adjudication of the VRA had increasingly promoted the creation of majority-minority districts (MMDs)[7] as the remedy of choice in voting rights controversies. The very group characteristics to be disregarded in civil rights law, race, and ethnicity, had become the precondition for compensatory justice under the act, as had happened with other civil rights initiatives. Equal opportunity had been exchanged for preferential treatment, a colorblind society for one that was racially balanced.[8]

In this chapter I argue that these developments occurred because the VRA has been captured by the politics of multiculturalism and that this undermines the objects of American commercial republicanism. How the VRA became captured by the politics of multiculturalism, transforming the meaning of equality and discrimination in the process, is recounted in the first part of the chapter. The first part examines the original objects of the VRA and the act's initial successes. I then review later transitions in the objectives of the act and the VRA's incorporation of the politics of multiculturalism as its animating vision. The next section outlines the reversal in the meaning of equality that was finally consummated with the 1990s rounds of redistricting engaged to comply with section 5 of the VRA. The final section of this part of the chapter surveys how the VRA has evolved in a manner consistent with other civil rights law.

In the second part of the chapter, four constitutional and institutional repercussions of the VRA's historical development are investigated: the incompatibility of the current VRA with the laws of equal protection; the growing centralization of the source of decision making respecting electoral practices and procedures the VRA has engendered; how race-based representation and the assumptions it makes corrode deliberative democracy in American government; and how the racial and ethnic divisions the VRA threatens undermine the principles of commercial republicanism in addition to the principle of colorblindness at the heart of the American constitutional order. This latter theme is the central theme of the chapter, speaking to what is perhaps the most significant threat the VRA currently poses to American republicanism.

The third part of the chapter briefly reviews critiques of the politics of multiculturalism, particularly as these apply to current voting rights policy. A conclusion follows that.

Before beginning, it is worth asking what the relevance of the VRA is to a book devoted to "Courts and the Culture Wars." A simple response is this: We live in a liberal democracy in which half of the liberal democratic equation is defined by what we understand by equality and the VRA has arguably done as much as any other federal legislation over the past generation to change the meaning of that term. And it has been the courts, in particular, through their construction of the act, that have contributed to that transformation. More than the administration of the VRA by the federal Department of Justice or the amendments to the act made by Congress, the federal judiciary has transformed the core of American republicanism, the representational process itself, by institutionalizing the politics of multiculturalism through the vehicle of the VRA. Promoting the creation of MMDs as the remedy of choice in voting rights litigation, federal courts have given their imprimatur to the classification of voters by race and ethnicity. As Abigail Thernstrom has remarked, although there was a time in American politics when the deliberate segregation of blacks and whites was called racism, "the belief that skin color matters profoundly, and that decisions involving political representation (and other matters) must be guided by the fact of racial difference, is now considered positively enlightened."[9] How we arrived at this sorry state of affairs and what it augurs for the future of the VRA is discussed below.

THE STRANGE BUT PREDICTABLE EVOLUTION OF THE VOTING RIGHTS ACT: FROM EQUAL OPPORTUNITY TO RACE-BASED SOCIAL TECHNOLOGY

The Original VRA and the Transformation of Southern Politics

The VRA was passed in 1965 with the object of eliminating those barriers to exercise of the black franchise that existed in the South. Litigation under earlier civil rights legislation aimed at increasing black voter registration had proven dilatory, costly, and of only nominal effect in the face of Southern intransigence toward the emancipation of the black vote.[10] The key to resolving these problems was, on the one hand, avoiding litigation and, on the other hand, preventing southern jurisdictions from circumventing federal protections of voting rights by replacing old means of disfranchisement with new ones.[11]

Sections 4 and 5 of the VRA were the principal provisions designed to achieve these objectives. Section 4 employed a formula that would cover those states in the South with the most egregious history of black disfranchisement. It also suspended, for a period of five years, all literacy tests and other devices used as a qualification for voting in "covered" jurisdictions. Section 5 required that states covered by Section 4 would have to have any changes in electoral practices or procedures "precleared" by the Department of Justice or the District Court for the District of Columbia. Since Section 4 and Section 5 represented a significant encroachment on state constitutional rights to control electoral practices, they were set to expire in 1970.

The VRA was very well conceived and effective. As almost every commentary on the act has noted, the VRA enjoyed enormous nascent success, reshaping both Southern politics and American politics more generally.[12] The original section 4 "trigger" provisions had succeeded in covering the seven most notorious voting rights offenders—Alabama, Georgia, Louisiana, Mississippi, North Carolina, South Carolina, and Virginia—under the VRA mantle.[13] Although a number of jurisdictions without a history of black disfranchisement were also covered, many of which successfully sued for exemption from the VRA, the act nevertheless had a swift impact on black voting and registration. It also had a significant impact on black officeholding.[14] Even those who today advocate the necessity of sustaining affirmative action in voting rights acknowledge that when considering the large increase in black voter registration that took place in the late 1960s, "the Voting Rights Act—and the civil rights movement of which it was an outgrowth—was an unquestioned success."[15]

Expanding Objectives and New Meanings: The Incorporation of the Politics of Multiculturalism

In the wake of such success, it might have been expected that the VRA's temporary provisions would have been allowed to lapse in 1970 when they were set to expire. That, however, did not happen. Instead, Congress extended the act's temporary provisions in 1970 for an additional five years. It would extend these same provisions an additional seven years in 1975 and in 1982, remarkably, for an additional twenty-five years.

Why was the VRA consistently extended as the act got progressively more successful? One reason was the persistent expansion in the objectives of the act. What began as legislation providing a right to ballot access evolved to provide a right to effective representation and eventually a right to proportional representation based on race. As Timothy O'Rourke has observed, with each successive change in objectives came a host of new problems that had to be addressed. Although the number of minority voters and minority officeholders continued to grow dramatically following passage of the VRA, with each extension of the act, Congress continually identified new obstacles to political equality that required growing federal supervision over state and local electoral practices. "Thus the longer the history of the act, the longer its projected future has become."[16]

O'Rourke notes that a second reason for the continued extension and expansion of the VRA has been the transformation in the manner of enforcement that has accompanied the changes in the act's objectives. The 1965 act provided precise operational terms that applied to a specific goal: providing the right to vote to blacks. By contrast, when the objective of the VRA became ensuring fair representation for minorities, Congress failed to give this new goal precise operational meaning. Instead, it extended the act and delegated the authority to decide the meaning of fair or effective representation to the Department of Justice and federal courts. As the locus of decision making changed, so the terms of enforcement would also change. "While the original act banned certain practices in specific areas, the evolving act permitted the Justice Department and the courts to define discrimination case by case. The act, which had begun as a precise ban on particular legal devices, developed into a more conditional limitation on almost any kind of electoral procedure, depending on the circumstances in individual situations."[17] The conditions for the persistent expansion in the meaning of discrimination under the VRA had now been set.

Between 1970 and 1982, the powers of the federal government under the VRA grew both geographically and substantively. The 1970 extension and amendments to the act eliminated literacy tests nationwide for five years and extended coverage of the act's temporary provisions to states outside of the South. The 1975 act permanently banned literacy tests nationwide and applied the act's protections to "language minorities," defined as "persons who are American Indian, Asian American, Alaskan Natives, or of Spanish heritage."[18] The 1982 amendments to the VRA incorporated a "results" test into Section 2 of the act, thus eliminating the requirement of proving discriminatory intent in Section 2 actions.

The inclusion of language minorities as protected classes to the 1975 VRA indicated how far the act had evolved into an instrument of the politics of multiculturalism less than ten years after passage of the original legislation. By defining the primary obstacles to the political advancement of groups such as Mexican Americans in racial terms, the VRA downplayed, if it did not entirely ignore, other demographic, political, and social factors that might have contributed to the condition of these groups.[19] The 1975 VRA extended protection to groups whose history had little in common with the history of disfranchisement experienced by southern blacks. Although some evidence had been presented to Congress that Hispanics in Texas had been deprived of political power through such dilutionary mechanisms as at-large elections and gerrymanders, these groups had not suffered outright deprivations of the right to cast a ballot as blacks had in the notorious Democratic white primaries; they had not been subjected to discriminatory literacy or interpretation tests by corrupt registrars; they had no similar experience of violence that blacks had endured during Reconstruction, the lynching spree of the late nineteenth and early twentieth centuries, or the civil rights movement of the 1950s and 1960s.[20]

There was, similarly, little evidence of electoral discrimination against the other newly protected groups, certainly no more than existed for many other language minorities unprotected by the VRA. It was facts such as these that prompted Civil Rights Commissioner Stephen Horn, in a surprising turn of events, to oppose the recommendations of other members of the Civil Rights Commission, urging Congress in 1982, when the VRA's temporary provisions were set to expire, "not to extend the minority language provisions of the Voting Rights Act."[21] As one observer of Mexican-American politics has noted, the VRA, as an elite initiative of national magnitude, has provided "the single strongest incentive for Mexican Americans and their leaders to define themselves as racial minority claimants."[22]

The 1975 VRA was testament to how skillfully civil rights advocates had created the appearance of continuity between the original intentions of the act and what the VRA had become by 1975.[23] Yet as much as the inclusion of language minorities to the 1975 VRA expanded the list of beneficiaries under the act and signified a change in the act's objectives, the 1982 Section 2 amendments were perhaps the most important change to the VRA in the history of the act. Unlike Sections 4 and 5, Section 2 of the VRA applied nationally. By incorporating a results test into Section 2, as the 1982 amendments did, minority plaintiffs would now be able to bring lawsuits against states and localities anywhere in the country and not have to prove intentional discriminatory conduct on the part of the authorities challenged. The Section 2 amendments had been proposed ostensibly to overcome the Supreme Court's holding in *City of Mobile v. Bolden*.[24] In *Bolden*, the Court had required proof of discriminatory intent in both constitutional controversies over voting rights as well as in Section 2 litigation. But as the Senate subcommittee considering the Section 2 amendments noted, the implications of the results test proposed were both far reaching and fundamental:

> The debate over whether or not to overturn the Supreme Court's decision in *Mobile v. Bolden*, and establish a results test for identifying voting discrimination in place of the present intent test, is probably the single most important constitutional issue that will be considered by the 97th Congress. Involved in this controversy are fundamental issues involving the nature of American representative democracy, federalism, the division of powers, and civil rights. By redefining the notion of "civil rights" and "discrimination" in the context of voting rights, the proposed "results" amendment would transform the objective of the Act from equal access to the ballot-box into equal results in the electoral process. A results test for discrimination can lead nowhere but to a standard of proportional representation by race.[25]

The Senate subcommittee's comments would prove prophetic, anticipating the evolution toward increasingly proportional representation by race under Section 2 that would take place following 1982. Yet the redefinition of discrimination under the VRA and the transition in the purpose of the act from equal ballot access to equal electoral results measured by proportional racial representation had begun long prior to the 1982 amendments to Section 2. The transformation in the meaning of equality and discrimination under the VRA had begun as early as 1969, with *Allen v. State Board of Elections*.[26]

In *Allen*, the Supreme Court determined that "The right to vote can be affected by a dilution of voting power as well as by an absolute prohibition on casting a ballot."[27] By defining the scope of the VRA to cover questions of vote dilution in addition to questions of ballot access, the Court in *Allen* had committed the judiciary to the same political thicket that it had committed itself to once it had determined that reapportionment issues were justiciable in *Baker v. Carr* (1962).[28] The reapportionment cases had granted a constitutional right to effective representation. So too now did the VRA. Unlike the reapportionment cases, however, controversies involving the VRA would present courts and administrators the additional problem that what was now being sought to be made effective was not mere numerical representation but racial representation. If minorities had a right to an undiluted vote, as the Court in *Allen* suggested, courts, administrators, and jurisdictions attempting to comply with the VRA, would have to provide for effective minority representation without engaging in suspect classifications. As the purposes of the VRA moved closer and closer toward a requirement of proportional representation for minorities, this obstacle would prove to be increasingly difficult to avoid. Ironically, the VRA had been set on a collision course with the Equal Protection Clause out of which the right to effective representation originally arose. It would be only a matter of time before the incompatibility of the act with the laws of equal protection would invite constitutional challenges to such practices engaged under the auspices of the act as redistricting.

Although it would take almost twenty-five years following *Allen* before the Court in *Shaw v. Reno* would formally recognize the potential conflict between the race-conscious districting undertaken to comply with the VRA and the Equal Protection Clause, constitutional challenges to race-based redistricting had begun as early as the 1970s. Prior to *Shaw* the Court had not only allowed for the explicit use of race in voting rights controversies but had made it a precondition for compliance with the act. In *Beer v. United States* (1976),[29] the Court had ruled that the VRA prohibited the implementation of a reapportionment plan that "would lead to a retrogression in the position of racial minorities with respect to their effective exercise of the electoral franchise."[30] If states failed to meet the retrogression test, they would have to create the requisite number of MMDs to comply with the preclearance provisions of the act. This is what was at issue one year later, in *United Jewish Organizations v. Carey*. There the Court interpreted the *Beer* rule to imply "that the Constitution does not prevent a State subject to the Voting Rights Act from deliberately creating or preserving black majorities in particular districts in order to ensure that its reapportionment plan complies with Section 5."[31] The deliberate use of both race and racial quotas in the creation of MMDs was a permissible exception to the constitutional prohibition on racial classifications.[32]

Like the 1975 inclusion of language minorities, *United Jewish Organization* provided further evidence of the extent to which, by the late 1970s, the VRA had been interpreted to identify race with political interest. Hasidic Jews had sued the state for intentionally splitting their Hasidim into two assembly and two senate seats in order to meet the demands of the Department of Justice. The Justice Department had required as a condition of preclearance that the state create a sufficient number of MMDs with a 65 percent quota of nonwhite voting age population. Previous redistricting had left the Hasidic community undivided within a single assembly and single senate district. The United Jewish Organizations of Williamsburgh sued the state on two grounds. First, the state's new redistricting scheme diluted each plaintiff's vote, contrary to the Fourteenth Amendment. Second, by assigning the plaintiffs to their electoral districts solely on the basis of race the state violated the Fifteenth Amendment.

The Supreme Court denied both of the petitioners' claims. The plurality ruled that when considered with other whites in the county, the Hasidic Jews were not underrepresented relative to nonwhites; "even if voting in the county occurred strictly according to race, whites would not be underrepresented relative to their share of the population."[33] Moreover, to the extent there was any discrimination against the petitioners, it was benign since New York's redistricting "plan represented no racial slur or stigma with respect to whites or any other race."[34] The New York redistricting scheme simply sought "to achieve a fair allocation of political power between white and non-white voters in Kings County."[35]

As critics of *United Jewish Organization* pointed out, the difficulty with the plurality's interpretation was that by assigning the Hasidic community's political interests on the basis of race, it gave undue salience to the very political consideration—race—that the VRA and the Constitution were arguably intended to overcome. Writing in dissent, Chief Justice Burger observed that by granting designated minorities their deserved representation through the vehicle of racial gerrymandering, the use of race in the electoral process was given the imprimatur of the state.[36] Signaling a "retreat from the ideal of the American 'melting pot'" that was "curiously out of step with recent political history,"[37] the use of mathematical quotas for the establishment of MMDs would have the additional propensity of sustaining "the existence of ghettos by promoting the notion that political clout is to be gained or maintained by marshaling particular racial, ethnic, or religious groups in enclaves."[38]

The Department of Justice's preclearance demands in *United Jewish Organization* amounted to a county-wide requirement approximating proportional representation based on race.[39] In *Thornburg v. Gingles*, the Court would extend this rule of proportional representation to jurisdictions nationwide, construing the amended Section 2 to confer a right to roughly proportional representation for minority groups that were sizeable, compact, and cohesive.[40] A year after *Gingles*, the Department of Justice would adopt a regulation that required the attorney general to refuse preclearance to jurisdictions whose proposed electoral changes were free from discriminatory purpose and retrogressive effect but that nevertheless constituted "a clear violation of amended Section 2."[41] Section 5 analyses, in other words, were to be guided by prospective Section 2 actions and, by implication, the standard of proportional representation established in *Gingles*.

Equality Reversed: Multicultural Politics and Racial Maximization in Electoral Redistricting

The final transformation in the meaning of equality under the VRA occurred during the 1990s round of redistricting when the Department of Justice demanded as a condition of preclearance that states covered by the act maximize minority representation. Although this requirement of racial maximization took place in a number of southern jurisdictions, it was especially in the Georgia litigation that the courts wrote most emphatically about the impropriety of the Justice Department's activities.

In *Miller v. Johnson* (1995), for instance, Justice Kennedy spoke disparagingly of how the Department of Justice had required the state of Georgia to implement a "max-black" plan conceived and advocated by the American Civil Liberties Union (ACLU).[42] The trial court in *Miller* had similarly described the overriding influence of the ACLU on the voting rights decisions of the attorney general as an "embarrassment."[43] The relationship between the ACLU and the Department of Justice had become so intimate that the second objection letter prepared by the Justice Department for the state of Georgia was sent first to the ACLU and only later to the office of the state attorney general.[44] Excoriating Justice for its construction of Section 5, Justice Kennedy, writing for the Supreme Court in *Miller*, concluded that "the Justice Department's implicit command that States engage in presumptively unconstitutional race-based districting brings the Voting Rights Act, once upheld as a proper exercise of Congress' authority under Section 2 of the Fifteenth Amendment . . . into tension with the Fourteenth Amendment."[45]

Yet Justice Kennedy could hardly have been surprised at this development. The objectives of the VRA had been consistently moving in the direction of increasing racial representation for well over two decades. The explicit use of race in the creation of MMDs had been the remedy of choice in voting rights disputes since the 1970s. Justice Thomas pointed out in *Bush v. Vera* that the creation of an MMD had to mean more than mere *awareness* of race—what the Court was prepared to tolerate in redistricting plans in *Shaw v. Reno*.[46] It had to mean "the express use of racial classifications." An MMD is created not merely in spite of, but precisely because of, racial demographics.[47] That the VRA by the 1990s required the presumptively unconstitutional race-based districting that brought the act into tension with the Fourteenth Amendment was in keeping with what the act had become by that time—an instrument of race-based social technology captured by clientele groups, a process that began shortly after passage of the VRA,[48] that was arguably the principal reason for the 1982 amendments to Section 2,[49] and that took the VRA to unparalleled new extremes by the 1990s. By that time the VRA was not merely in tension with the laws of equal protection. It had become the antithesis of their colorblind objective.

The VRA and the New Objects of Modern Civil Rights

The pattern of the VRA's evolution was consistent with the evolution of other civil rights legislation throughout the decades following the 1960s. In the same way "disparate impact" had become the measure of discrimination in Title VII law, proportional minority hiring the measure of equal treatment under Title VI, and gender quotas the measure of gender equality in education and athletics under Title IX of the Education Act , proportional electoral officeholding on the basis of race became the measure of equal opportunity in voting rights law.[50]

Hugh Davis Graham has observed that the civil rights revolution of the 1960s provided the impetus for the transition from the economic regulatory state of the Progressive and New Deal periods to the social regulatory state of the Great Society.[51] The expansive, time-tested model of national administration which saw economic regulatory agencies such as the Federal Reserve Board (1913), the Federal Trade Commission (1914), the Federal Communications Commission (1934), and the National Labor Relations Board (1935) emerge from the Progressive and New Deal eras, would produce such social regulatory agencies as the Equal Employment Opportunity Commission (1964), the Environmental Protection Agency (1970), and the Occupational Safety and Health Administration (1970). After 1965, when the implementation of civil rights shifted from an intentional tort and equal treatment model to a no-fault and equal results model, the VRA would become part of this new matrix of social regulation.[52] Throughout this period of transition toward greater administrative control of social process, federal courts were instrumental in creating the conditions and precedents through which civil rights enforcement agencies could consolidate their rulemaking authority.[53] As Herman Belz has observed of the era, "If the political impulse to redefine equality came from the civil rights bureaucracy and the civil rights lobby, the legal rulings that confirmed race-conscious affirmative action in public policy were the product of judicial government."[54]

In the case of voting rights, Sections 4 and 5 of the VRA were exemplary of the growing federal control of traditionally local prerogatives, implementing new electoral programs through the use of statistical data and results-driven measures of discriminatory conduct.[55] Even judicial elections came to be covered by the VRA, a particularly troubling development since "the essence of judging ought to be to follow the preexisting rules of the law, not to alter legal doctrines 'equitably' in order to redress grievances of particular segments of the population."[56] Ironically, what began as a statute intended to root out the institutionalized racism of Southern politics itself came to institutionalize race as the measure of equal opportunity under the VRA.

The historical course traveled by the VRA was as predictable as it was strange, reflecting not only the dominant political forces of the day but the ethos of the Warren and Burger courts and to a lesser extent the Rehnquist Court. The federal judiciary has been one of the principal vehicles through which the American Left has transacted its culture war against the Constitution, American traditions and history, and the longstanding principles of the American liberal democratic order. The VRA has been critical to the Left's success in this cultural conflict, convincing even Republicans themselves that criticism of the race-based social engineering engaged under the act is a bad thing and may undermine benefits to the party's fortunes. Recent Republican administrations, in particular, have been as guilty as Democratic advocates of affirmative action in voting rights. Embracing the creation of MMDs as a condition of preclearance under the VRA, Republicans have benefitted from packing overwhelmingly Democratic minorities into such districts, thus "bleaching" the surrounding districts and making them more auspicious for Republican candidates.[57]

Although there was a significant period during the 1990s when it appeared as though the Supreme Court would rein in race-conscious affirmative action in voting rights, its decision in *Easley v. Cromartie*[58] signaled a retreat from this development. Proof of unconstitutional racial gerrymandering has now been set so high as to be extremely difficult—if not impossible—to attain. By the first year of the new millennium, the Supreme Court had returned to its earlier ambivalence toward racial classifications in VRA law, creating yet again an exception to the principles of equal protection. The politics of multiculturalism had captured the administration and adjudication of the VRA by the early 1990s. After a brief respite, it has once again captured a majority of justices on the nation's highest court.

CONSTITUTIONAL AND INSTITUTIONAL IMPLICATIONS

The evolution of the VRA and its incorporation of the politics of multiculturalism as its animating vision has had significant constitutional and institutional repercussions. Four of these developments are examined below.

Undermining the Constitutional Meaning of Equality

As the last part of this chapter illustrated, the VRA has evolved in such a way as to render it incompatible with the Equal Protection Clause. And it is incompatible in a fundamental way. The two equality rights initiatives are predicated upon antithetical conceptions of equality. The VRA is predicated upon an affirmative action, equal results or race-conscious conception of equality. The Equal Protection Clause is predicated upon an equal opportunity, individualist or race-neutral understanding of equality. As the Court has emphasized time and again, the provisions of the Fourteenth Amendment are personal rights guaranteed to the individual and not to groups.[59] To the extent the VRA grants rights to groups, not individuals, and allows relief for vote dilution claims only to designated classes of individuals defined by race and ethnicity, it stands opposed to the spirit and letter of the Fourteenth Amendment.

Centralizing Control of Electoral Practices and Procedures

The institutional problems raised by the prerogatives granted to the federal judiciary and Department of Justice under the VRA are many but perhaps the most intractable is that relating to the problem of relevance or of what criteria will count in representational theory. What is deemed fair or effective representation under either the VRA or the Constitution will mean different things to different people depending on what democratic theory is preferred by the advocate or decision maker.[60] Just as the "one person, one vote" decisions accentuated the difficulties involved in attempting to impose numerical equality on federal and state governments when the Constitution contemplates other considerations that may require nonequipopulous districts, the introduction of race as an overriding consideration in the calculus of representation under the VRA highlights both the unprincipled nature of such representation as well as its similarly arbitrary character. In Madison's well-known formulation, the framers of the Constitution were concerned with providing a "republican remedy to the diseases most incident to republican government."[61] This meant not only respecting the principle of consent and concerns for equal justice, but providing stable and energetic government that was deliberative, autonomy to the states and to citizens who were to be active and self-governing, the promotion of commerce and those civic virtues the pursuit of industry facilitated, and above all "the protection of different and unequal faculties of acquiring property," what Madison described as "the first object of government."[62]

The multiplicity of objects the Constitution was to fulfill, fulfill primarily through the vehicle of representation and within a distinctively federal system, meant that beyond the basic republican blueprint provided in the Constitution, the difficult question the framers had to resolve was not so much what democratic theory should prevail at the federal or state level but rather who should get to choose that theory, a particularly delicate question given the suspicion harbored toward the federal government during the founding period as well as the novel experiment with an extended sphere—the multiplicity of interests, opinions, and jurisdictions this would incorporate. In *Federalist 59* Alexander Hamilton observed that "It will not be alleged that an election law could have been framed and inserted in the Constitution which would have been applicable to every probable change in the situation of the country; and it will therefore not be denied that a discretionary power ought to exist somewhere."[63] State governments would obviously control state elections. Article I, Section 4 made clear where discretionary power lay with respect to the election of senators and congressmen: The time, place, and manner of holding congressional elections would be determined, first, by state legislatures and only secondarily, and in "extraordinary circumstances,"[64] by Congress. There was no provision for the courts or executive determining these issues and for good reason. They were political questions—of the most fundamental variety—that could not be resolved in a judicial or administrative forum. Requiring the exercise of a flexible statesmanship that could accommodate the peculiar, transitory circumstances that might affect federal and state elections and that would not get lost in legalistic abstractions divorced from the messy contingencies of everyday political life,[65] the resolution of issues concerning the regulation of elections was best left, ultimately, in the hands of those directly involved. "Suppose an article had been introduced into the Constitution empowering the United States to regulate the elections for the particular States," Hamilton queried, "would any man have hesitated to condemn it, both as an unwarrantable transposition of power and as a premeditated engine for the destruction of State governments?"[66]

Yet this transposition of power is precisely what has happened under the VRA. Vote dilution cases through the 1990s had seen federal courts pass judgment on numerous aspects of state electoral practices, from what methods were appropriate for choosing local school boards, to what property could be annexed by cities, to the right distribution of state senate and assembly seats, even demanding proportional representation of judges on state courts. Chief Justice Warren may have been correct in *South Carolina v. Katzenbach* (1966) that the exceptional conditions of the time warranted the constitutional encroachments on state prerogatives the VRA imposed[67] but it is doubtful these conditions persisted into the 1990s. Even if they did, could it be argued that the remedies proposed under the act were a recipe for comity between the races? On the other hand, if redistributing political power to designated classes of minorities was now the object of the VRA, were there not better means to achieve this object than through the inefficient, awkward, and highly selective means employed by the act?[68]

Racial Representation and the Corroding of Deliberative Democracy

Racial group representation threatens American deliberative democracy not only because it places undue salience on race but because it overemphasizes the importance of group representation in Congress and in state and local government. Theories of representation dominant in voting rights commentary and adjudication tend to restrict the role of representation to the representing or mirroring of constituent interests in legislative bodies as well as to the fulfilling of an ombudsman's role. Advocates of racial redistricting and alternative electoral systems, such as proportional representation and cumulative voting, are consumed by a single idea: equality and, specifically, the promotion of some sort of group-based or group-interest equality to the exclusion of the other objects of American republicanism such as moderate, effective government and the promotion of the public interest through deliberation. The problem for American republican government is not whether it can attain greater democracy. It is whether it can restrain the democracy it has.[69] American democracy is a deliberative democracy and the focus of redistricting and reapportionment litigation on limited or specific group interests is symptomatic of assumptions dominant not only in modern jurisprudence and public administration but in the law schools and the social science academies.

No idea has been more responsible for the decline in the scholarly study of the deliberative functions and capacities of American government "than the view that politics reduces to the struggle of group interests."[70] But it is arguably the very impossibility of accommodating these interests in any absolute sense that makes representative democracy, and the deliberative forum it facilitates, imperative. The framers of the Constitution understood this. As Joseph Bessette has noted: "Those who created the American constitutional system believed that on most issues, most of the time, deliberative majorities would not exist independently outside of government, but rather would be formed through the operation of the governmental institutions, as the representatives of the people reasoned about public policy for their constituents."[71]American government consists of more than mere bargaining or logrolling or the aggregating of partial interests into national policies.[72] The assumption of racial representation, however, presumes the opposite: That by enhancing the number of minority-preferred candidates in America's legislative halls, minority interests will somehow be better represented through a process of aggregating those interests into public policy. How, precisely, this is to occur has never been adequately explained. Nor has there been any compelling evidence that it has actually taken place.

There may be evidence—particularly in the wake of the congressional elections of the 1990s—that racial redistricting helps to elect minority candidates. But it is equally evident that this occurs at the expense of the fortunes of the party to which these candidates belong. The disregard of political parties by the Supreme Court in assessments of effective representation has been roundly criticized both by the judiciary[73] and in academic scholarship.[74] Without considering the role of parties, along with a host of other factors, assessing the effectiveness of minority representation or of MMDs is difficult if not impossible.

How then are minorities best represented? As Justice John Harlan queried over thirty years ago in *Allen*, are blacks better represented when they have more control over fewer legislative seats or when they have greater influence over numerous legislative seats?[75] In addition, there would appear to be little evidence pointing to race being a very strong proxy for those characteristics contributing to deliberative government, just as there would appear to be little evidence indicating race is a very strong proxy for those attributes contributing to intellectual diversity in education.[76] It may then be erroneous to assume that increasing racial representation will necessarily contribute more to America's deliberative form of government or to deliberative diversity. In fact, such thinking might smack of the very racial stereotyping the Constitution was intended to avoid.

Advocates of racial representation have failed to answer important questions and we should be reluctant to institutionalize their platforms in light of the affront to the principles of constitutional equality and American republicanism their advocacy presents.

The Multicultural Challenge to Commercial Republicanism

In this final section I highlight that the VRA, as it has been administered and adjudicated through the 1990s rounds of redistricting, offends not only the principle of colorblindness at the heart of American constitutionalism but the principles of commercial republicanism. What I mean by this can best be illustrated by contrasting the assumptions underlying the politics of multiculturalism with those assumptions, particularly concerning human nature, that underlie the liberal constitutional theory from which American commercial republicanism springs.

The politics of multiculturalism emerged in the late twentieth century as a response to traditional conceptions of equality and individualism that originated in the classical liberal doctrine of natural rights, the animating philosophy of the Declaration of Independence and the Constitution. Although it is difficult to speak generally about such a diffuse movement as the politics of multiculturalism, the categories of political analysis typically used by its proponents, as James Ceaser has demonstrated, derive from certain discrete ideological concepts.[77] In the United States, the central idea underlying multicultural politics is the identification of race with culture.

Although multicultural theorists are opposed to classic racialist thought that held that there was a biological hierarchy to the races, they have not adopted liberalism as the means of opposing this racialism. One reason for this is that liberalism is connected to the modern project of reason and Enlightenment that presumes a common truth and justice. It thus arranges cultures in a hierarchical order, allowing for the determination of better and worse, higher and lower, forms of culture. Another reason is that liberalism subordinates racial or cultural identity to the identity of the individual attached to a common political community. Liberal cultural theory might be distinguished from modern multicultural theory precisely because it separates race and culture, attributing the distinctions between cultural groups to different patterns of socialization rather than to innate biological characteristics. Whereas European multiculturalism tends to identify culture with national, linguistic, or ethnic groups (Serbs, Croats, Basques, Germans, etc.), American multiculturalism has inclined to identify culture in biological terms. A typical list of American cultures consists of African Americans, Asian Americans, Native Americans, and in some cases women. Ironically, the multicultural identification of race with culture has translated into a renewed emphasis on race in law reform—something we have already seen in the case of the VRA. As much as racial distinctions may have been banished following World War II, they have returned in force as fundamental categories of legal distinction, this thanks in large measure to the politics of multiculturalism. As Ceaser notes,

> [Race] has returned . . . not as an obstacle to be removed or even as an important but secondary characteristic, but as the primary feature of social identity

and the deepest source of authenticity. Race classifications have been reinstated as an ordinary part of the legal framework, and race is widely viewed as the most important element of social identity. If we are cultural beings and if race is a defining element of cultural identity, we cannot escape its importance. Race not only matters but is fundamental."[78]

The importance of race in voting rights law, recounted in the last part of this chapter, signaled a reversal in the original objectives of the VRA. By inviting individuals to define themselves by prerational traits such as race and ethnicity, the politics of multiculturalism has helped to convert the emphasis in nonconstitutional equality rights initiatives from the classical liberal emphasis on individual rights, which tolerates inequality between groups, to the multicultural emphasis on groups and group rights. Multiculturalism works to equalize group representation through the granting of special dispensations to legally recognized classes of individuals on the basis of race. But in doing it not only offends the principle of colorblindness in constitutional law, it offends those principles of commercial republicanism that were intended to inform the Constitution. By creating potentially divisive pathologies, as the Court in *Shaw* recognized, the multiculturalist assumptions underlying racial redistricting invite the very passionate factions commercial republicanism was intended to overcome.

The VRA has been exemplary of the institutionalization of race in public policy, emerging as part of a broader civil rights strategy in which the meaning of equality and discrimination have been changed and in which social scientific and legal academic opinion have been wedded to voting rights advocacy, forming a powerful coalition. As with other civil rights initiatives, the administration and adjudication of the VRA have wedded knowledge to power, academic expertise to administrative efficiency and judicial authority.[79] The implementation of the act has also subordinated markets to race, commercial republicanism to identity politics.

The Constitution was intended to transform the nature of factional struggle in American politics through the creation of an extended commercial union that would, in the language of Hobbes, crush the children of pride and the spirit of vanity. It was also intended to extinguish politics understood as widespread and perennial contests over political and constitutional principles.[80] Although the ostensible object of race-based representation may be to enhance deliberative and legitimate government, by introducing race into the calculus of effective representation it has undermined those very principles that were thought to be settled by the Constitution, the resolution of which was presumed by the idea of representative government itself.[81]

The race-based theory of representation that underlies the VRA poses many problems to liberal democratic government. One of the principal problems it poses is its failure to demonstrate the existence of any fundamental interests that are not already protected against majoritarian rule by individual rights.[82] The very institutional changes introduced by the VRA have arguably threatened individual rights by exaggerating certain considerations in representative government—particularly considerations of race—to the disregard or exclusion of other considerations.

This was the substance of Justice Clarence Thomas' concurring opinion in *Holder v. Hall* (1994),[83] the most provocative and comprehensive indictment of voting rights jurisprudence dating back twenty-five years. In *Holder*, Thomas excoriated the Supreme Court for acting like Platonic guardians in its adjudication of vote dilution disputes.[84] Not only had vote dilution conflicts proven to be intractable, the judiciary's preference for MMDs had unjustifiably imposed a single theory of representation on jurisdictions throughout the country and could not have been better calculated to exacerbate racial tensions, segregating the races into political homelands.[85] Examining the potential for racial strife voting rights practices had caused, Justice Thomas identified racial with religious faction, enlisting Justice William O. Douglas' admonition in *Wright v. Rockefeller*: "When racial or religious lines are drawn by the State . . . antagonisms that relate to race or to religion rather than to political issues are generated; communities seek not the best representative but the best racial or religious partisan."[86] In *Shaw*, Justice O'Connor had referred to this same passage from *Wright*, drawing many of the same conclusions.[87]

The identification of racial with religious partisanship and the distinction of racial and religious antagonisms from true political issues speaks to two central themes in commercial republican theory: The primacy of passion over interest in politics and the irrelevance of race and religion as legitimate categories of legal distinction in republican government. These issues were familiar to many of America's founders. In *Federalist 10*, for instance, James Madison distinguished factions "united and actuated by some common impulse of passion" from factions united and actuated by interest.[88] Like many liberal thinkers before him, Madison understood that the most tempestuous and explosive factions were those animated by passion. It had been the particular downfall of governments whose object was the salvation of souls that they incited the volcanic passions of rage that attached to differing religious opinions.[89] The Supreme Court's concern in *Shaw* and its subsequent voting rights cases was that race might present many of these same incendiary pathologies. This was also the concern of Justice Douglas in the *Wright* decision.

Justice Douglas' opinion underscored that the American republic remains in its essential features a commercial republic, a republic in which the common currency of political transaction is primarily economic, not racial or religious. The Constitution was indeed intended to provide "a republican remedy to the diseases most incident to republican government." But that republicanism was to be commercial in nature. The republican order promoted and maintained by the Constitution was predicated upon the idea that politics was least factious when reduced to political economy; that there were certain issues, such as those involving racial and religious identity or classifications, that it was no business of government to recognize or to promote. Only when questions of revealed religious truth and the innate biological inferiority or superiority of races were excluded from politics and the deliberations of political majorities could the conditions for the rule of law essential to liberal constitutionalism prevail.[90] Freedom in the modern commercial republic was not primarily political freedom. It was the freedom to pursue "the more or less free range of nonpolitical activities."[91] Framed on the basis of the modern discovery that politics is inferior to the private and independent world of individuals and associations that move within civil society,[92] the commercial republic was based not only on high considerations of principle—the natural equality of all and freedom of conscience, for instance—but on considerations of expediency.

The difficult question for commercial republican theory was not so much how to receive interests into the legislature but, rather, how to combine them effectively for the public interest.[93] How, and around what specific interests, would political bonds be formed? Classical liberal political science, developed by Hobbes and later refined by the likes of Locke, Montesquieu, and Hume, originated in a political anthropology that understood individuals to be divided naturally by their passions but capable of being united artificially by their interests.[94] Property (for Locke) and commerce (for Montesquieu and Hume) were essential to this project of unification, the preconditions for stable and energetic government. They were also the precondition for civilization, as a number of constitutional framers apparently agreed. "A landed interest, a manufacturing interest, a mercantile interest, a moneyed interest, with many lesser interests, grow up of necessity in civilized nations" Madison informed us in *Federalist 10*.[95]

The commercial republic was not limited to simply providing for stable and energetic government or the relief of man's estate. It had the more sublime object of cultivating and perfecting civilization. It was arrayed against the two great residues of premodernity opposed to civilization: scholasticism and the biblical tradition. The Christian commonwealth, whose citizens sought salvation through faith and that placed a premium on conversion, was not a regime of brotherly love or Christian charity but was distinguished, as Hobbes observed, by chaos and civil war.[96] Premodern or preliberal regimes may have had classical or Christian virtue as their ostensible object, but the principal problem of politics, as the best minds at the constitutional convention recognized, was the ambition for dominion, an ambition that all too frequently paraded under the pretext of virtue.[97] As Hayek and others would later recognize, the progress and civilization of free societies was due not merely to their accumulation of wealth and capital but to their better utilization of knowledge,[98] a knowledge that would undermine religious authority and all forms of tradition. But the effects of wealth and capital on human character as well as on deliberative government, combined with the distinct nature of political conflict that commercial regimes engendered, paved the way to the institutional modifications that would define American liberal constitutionalism, including its forms of representation.

On the classical liberal model, political conflict originating in emotion or passion was typically excited by frivolous, insubstantial causes. By contrast, political conflict originating in interest derived primarily from relations of property.[99] Madison, who recognized that "the most common and durable source of factions has been the various and unequal distribution of property," also acknowledged (in the same paragraph) that the kindling of "unfriendly passions" was linked to the "most violent conflicts." The regulation of "various and interfering interests" originating in relations of property might form "the principal task of modern Legislation, and involve the spirit of party and faction in the necessary and ordinary operations of Government."[100] But the most destructive and explosive factions were anchored in passion—in pride, in hatred, and in vanity. As historians and political theorists have informed us, the new science of politics that would provide the blueprint for the Constitution, and that the Constitution would improve upon yet again, emerged against a backdrop of violent and tyrannical religious wars that marked the nadir of European politics throughout the seventeenth and eighteenth centuries. Commercial republicanism would provide a constitutional order founded on the recognition that factious conflicts, such as those based on passionate attachments to revealed religion, could be smoothed over, if not eliminated altogether, by anchoring political bonds in relations of property with a view to promoting security and well-being.

The central theme of this chapter is that with the emergence of the politics of multiculturalism as a challenge to the original, constitutional understandings of equality and representation, the American constitutional order now stands exposed to a form of sectarian conflict similar in nature to that of pre-liberal regimes. This was what the Court meant in *Shaw* when Justice O'Connor warned that "Racial gerrymandering, even for remedial purposes, may balkanize us into competing racial factions." It is also what Justice Douglas warned of in *Wright*. It is what Justice Berger cautioned against in *United Jewish Organization*.

In the case of voting rights, the differential treatment of racial and ethnic groups demanded by advocates of racial representation has been defended on grounds it is necessary to promote fair and effective representation, to provide compensation for past wrongs, and to produce more deliberative and legitimate government—the idea being that people of different racial and ethnic backgrounds will bring different experiences and perspectives to the legislative forum, thus broadening deliberation while enhancing democratic legitimacy. As well meaning as such advocacy is, for the same reason that multiculturalism and policies of diversity fail in education and employment, treating individuals differently because of their biological and sociological characteristics, so too it fails in the world of electoral politics. To suggest that race and ethnicity are defining elements that determine individual judgment or provide the definitive experiences that will or should affect legislative deliberation exaggerates the significance of such experiences at best and at worst is both illiberal and dangerous.

Moreover, if using race as a proxy for individual experiences, outlooks, and ideas is illegal in the context of employment law and jury selection,[101] why should it be legal in voting rights law? As Eugene Volokh has observed, for over thirty years antidiscrimination law has attempted to discourage people from engaging not merely in irrational discrimination but rational discrimination.[102] State and federal law has attempted to emphasize that it is wrong to use race and sex as proxies for individual attributes not merely when invidious distinctions are involved but even when—and perhaps above all when—statistically plausible distinctions are involved.

Finally, to the extent racial and ethnic groups are claimed to have common interests that deserve to be represented in the legislative forum through the manipulation of electoral outcomes, further problems of procedural fairness and distributive justice in electoral law are also implicated in VRA disputes.

THE MYTH OF THE POLITICS OF MULTICULTURALISM

Multiculturalism undermines the principles of American constitutionalism and its distinct form of republicanism. It is not surprising then that scholars and political commentators have expressed alarm at the broad acceptance of the multiculturalist vision. In a *Times Literary Supplement* essay, for instance, Irving Kristol observed that the underlying theory of multiculturalism, that America's national culture has been replaced by a litany of subcultures, has been accepted not only by liberals but by many conservatives. The liberal left has clearly won this round of the culture war. But it has been a rhetorical victory only. As the political principles in America have remained constant over time, people—including most ethnic groups and immigrants—still live by them—and this despite whatever the chattering classes might have to say. The idea that America consists of a variety of subcultures "is a case of mistaking media-imposed and government-sponsored 'virtual reality' for the real thing. Those subcultures do not exist. They are a myth created and nourished by the left, which tries to 'actualize' it in university and school curricula—but it remains a bookish myth whose roots are in academia, not in any social reality."[103]

Also critical of the language of multiculturalism, Kristol noted that terms such as Hispanic and Asian were, at bottom, meaningless linguistic and geographic symbols that referred to a wide array of groups with little in common and that frequently detested one another.[104] Other scholars have concurred with this assessment. Ceaser, for instance, pointed out that attributing cultural designations to groups such as Asian Americans reflected not only the extent to which culture has been identified with race by multicultural theory but the ensuing propensity of this view to generalize racial characteristics across a host of distinct groupings. To lump such different and sometimes adversarial cultures as Japanese Americans, Chinese Americans, Korean Americans, Vietnamese Americans, and Cambodian Americans into a single cultural category—Asian American—illustrates the extent to which race trumps other considerations, such as national origin and language, in current cultural thinking and law reform. What makes groups such as these "all members of one culture in America today is the racialist preconception of multicultural theory; it is culture by intellectual ukase and bureaucratic decree."[105] In *Race and Culture*, Thomas Sowell has similarly pointed out the extent to which race can dominate as a way of collectivizing people, serving not only as a biological concept but as a means of defining social reality.[106] That the VRA has adopted such categories as Asian American and persons of Spanish heritage as protected classes under the act, however well intentioned, indicates the degree to which the animating vision of the legislation has come to collectivize people by race and ethnicity, the very sort of classifications the original VRA was intended to overcome. Moreover, by establishing group-specific rights and allocating representation on the basis of racial group identity, the current VRA is anti-thetical both to the idea of individual rights as well as to the principle that there should be no fixed electoral outcomes or group entitlements to representation—especially entitlements based on race—in American politics.

Ultimately, we must ask what interests today are being served by the VRA. Is it the interests of African-Americans and individuals of Spanish descent or is it the interests of the politicians who claim to act on behalf of these minority classes? Of Republicans in Congress? In *Easley v. Cromartie*, Justice Breyer remarked that the Supreme Court's 1990s voting rights cases had emphasized that districting decisions ordinarily fell within the legislative sphere of competence and that "courts must 'exercise *extraordinary caution* in adjudicating claims that a State has drawn district lines on the basis of race.'"[107] By setting the threshold for proof of unconstitutional racial redistricting as high as the Court did in *Easley*, however, the Court did not so much defer to state legislatures as give free rein to the Justice Department to impose yet further race-based cartographical excesses on states subject to the VRA. *Easley* invited the same sort of racial maximization policies those jurisdictions covered by the VRA were compelled to promote in the 1990s.

What makes this worse is that today there is little political opposition to such brazen attempts at racially classifying citizens by government. In the spring of 2001 the Democrats announced that they would continue to support racial redistricting. Tom Davis, the National Republican Committee Chairman, similarly announced that the Republicans had lawyers ready to sue any state that proposed to reduce the percentage of minority voters in even a single district.[108] The consensus among Democrats and Republicans would appear to be that the maximization of racial redistricting is a perfectly acceptable—perhaps even salutary—governmental objective. As a recent editorial observed, Section 5 of the VRA continues to subject sixteen states, in whole or in part, to Justice Department supervision, a figure amounting to more than a third of the total U.S. territory and approximately 25 percent of the American population. "Can it be, in the year 2001, that Monterey, California, and Brooklyn, New York, cannot be trusted to administer nonracist voting booths? The law, very explicitly, says yes."[109]

Given the Supreme Court's renewed imprimatur of racial redistricting in *Easley* and the eagerness with which Democrats and Republicans appear ready to continue racial maximization policies in redistricting, we should not expect these presumptions in law to cease anytime soon.

CONCLUSION

The concern over fair and effective representation that has consumed so much attention in law and academic commentary since the reapportionment decisions of the 1960s is a reflection less of the need for electoral reform as the burgeoning growth of the American state. In the case of the VRA, a widespread assumption underlying the advocacy of racial redistricting is that minorities need government sponsored relief from their socially and economically disadvantaged position in American society. Whether or not, however, the VRA is of a piece with the false promise of modern liberalism that the problems of black America and other minority groups can be resolved through a further transformation of America's political institutions and a greater reliance on government, it is clear that as the state continues to regulate more and more aspects of civil society—of individual freedom, the market, property rights, consumer relations, political speech, private associational behavior, and so on—we can expect disputes over fair representation to continue. Too much is at stake for them not to. But we should understand these for what they are: A grab for political power. There is little likelihood the role of government in the lives of Americans will dissipate anytime soon. It is fair nevertheless to ask what legitimate role race can play in any future debate over electoral reform.

As the protracted and expensive litigation of the 1990s highlighted, the VRA arguably now does more damage than good, aggravating racial relations, undermining the constitutional separation of powers and principles of federalism, costing jurisdictions millions of dollars accommodating potential claims and litigating actual ones, disrupting and distorting legitimate electoral practices adopted for no discriminatory purpose, and enervating the principle of equality at the center of American liberal constitutionalism. It may be true that we do not yet live in a multicultural nation, a nation divided into a litany of distinct, antagonistic subcultures, but it should be evident that if we continue with policies such as the VRA the virtual reality Kristol described may become real.

Ironically, the VRA, an initiative originally conceived to protect the constitutional meaning of equality and the legitimacy of representation, has now evolved to threaten both equality and representation in the American constitutional order. As administered and adjudicated through the 1990s, the VRA should not be viewed as one choice among many about how to deal with voting rights given a fixed constitutional regime. Rather, it represents a choice between regime types themselves. In the culture wars at century's turn, the VRA represents the wrong approach to American republicanism and the wrong vision of where Americans should be heading.

NOTES

1. 42 USC 1973 [1994].

2. I use the term *commercial republicanism* here to capture those features of American republicanism that more current terms such as *liberalism, progressivism,* or *capitalism* fail to capture. See generally, Hiram Caton, *The Politics of Progress: The Origins and Development of the Commercial Republic, 1600–1835* (Gainesville, Fl.: University of Florida Press, 1988), esp. 1–14.

3. *The Second Treatise of Government,* in *Two Treatises of Government,* ed. Peter Laslett (New York: Cambridge University Press, 1988), 265, 350–51. With the exception of the chapter "Of Property," Locke both here and elsewhere defined "property" as "Life, Liberty, and Estate." Locke, "Of Property," 323. See Robert A. Goldwin, "John Locke," in *The History of Political Philosophy,* ed. Leo Strauss and Joseph Cropsey, third edition. (Chicago: University of Chicago Press, 1987), 476, 495–96.

4. Alexander Hamilton, James Madison, and John Jay, *The Federalist,* ed. Jacob E. Cooke (Middletown, Ct.: Wesleyan University Press, 1961), 58.

5. See Eric Metcalfe, "Illiberal Citizenship? A Critique of Will Kymlicka's Liberal Theory of Minority Rights," *Queen's Law Journal* 22: 1996, 167, 189.

6. 113 S. Ct. 2816, 2832 (1993), opinion of the Court.

7. MMDs are districts in which roughly 65 percent of the voting age population is comprised of a legally recognized minority.

8. See Thomas Sowell, *Civil Rights: Rhetoric or Reality?* (New York: Quill, 1984), chapters 1, 2, and 6; and Herman Belz, *Equality Transformed: A Quarter-Century of*

Affirmative Action (New Brunswick, N.J.: Transaction Publishers, 1992), esp. introduction and chapter 1.

9. Abigail Thernstrom, "*Shaw v. Reno*: Notes from a Political Thicket," *Public Interest Law Review* (1994):35, 37.

10. Between 1957 and 1960, for instance, the Justice Department filed only four lawsuits under the 1957 Civil Rights Act. As Barry Hawk and John Kirby observed in 1965, "Not a single Negro who had not been previously registered was enabled to register to vote by federal action during the three year period." Barry E. Hawk and John J. Kirby Jr. "Note: Federal Protection of Negro Voting Rights," *Virginia Law Review* 51 (1965): 1051, 1060. Things did not much improve despite changes to the civil rights acts of 1960 and 1964. See Abigail M. Thernstrom, *Whose Votes Count? Affirmative Action and Minority Voting Rights* (Cambridge, Mass.: Harvard University Press, 1987), 11–15. See also, *South Carolina v. Katzenbach*, 383 U.S. 301, 313–14 (1966), pointing out how time consuming and ineffective civil rights law suits were as a means of enhancing black voter registration in the South prior to the VRA.

11. Thernstrom, *Whose Votes Count?*, 16.

12. See Timothy G. O'Rourke, "The 1982 Amendments and the Voting Rights Paradox," in *Controversies in Minority Voting*, ed. Bernard Grofman and Chandler Davidson (Washington, D.C.: Brookings Institution, 1992) 85. The 1981 House Report on the *Voting Rights Act Extension* observed that "The Voting Rights Act of 1965 has been hailed as the most important civil rights bill enacted by Congress. Unquestionably, it has been the most effective tool for protecting the right to vote." House of Representatives, *Voting Rights Act Extension* H. Rept. 97–227, 97 Congress, 1 Session, 1981, 3.

13. See United States Commission on Civil Rights, *The Voting Rights Act . . . The First Months* (Washington, D.C.: November, 1965), 23.

14. The U.S. Civil Rights Commission reported in May 1968 that registration of the black voting age population was over 50 percent in every southern state. This had been the case in only three states prior to passage of the Voter Registration Act: Florida, Tennessee, and Texas. Black registration figures between 1965 and 1968 had risen in Mississippi from 6.7 to 59.8 percent; in Alabama from 19.3 to 51.6 percent; in Louisiana from 31.6 to 58.9 percent; in Georgia from 27.4 to 52.6 percent; in South Carolina from 37.3 to 51.2 percent; and in Virginia from 38.3 to 55.6 percent. U.S. Commission on Civil Rights, *Political Participation: A Study of the Participation by Negroes in the Electoral and Political Process in 10 Southern States since Passage of the Voting Rights Act of 1965* (Washington, D.C.: May, 1968), 1213.

Black office holding had also increased. Following the 1966 elections there were 159 local black officeholders and legislators throughout the eleven southern states. Following the 1967 elections, that number exceeded 200, more than double the number serving when the VRA was passed in 1965. U.S. Commission on Civil Rights, *Political Participation*, 15. The Civil Rights Commission further reported in 1975 that the total number of blacks elected to office in the seven southern states covered by the VRA had increased to 963 by April, 1974. U.S. Commission on Civil Rights, *The Voting Rights Act: Ten Years After* (Washington, D.C.: January, 1975), 49. Although in 1972 there still existed gaps between black registered voters and white registered voters that exceeded 20 percent in Alabama and Louisiana, overall the difference between blacks and whites in the seven southern states declined by over 30 percent between 1965 and 1972, dropping from 44.1 percent in 1965 to 11.2 percent by 1972. U.S. Commission on Civil Rights, *The Voting Rights Act*, 4243.

15. Bernard Grofman, Lisa Handley, and Richard G. Niemi, *Minority Representation and the Quest for Voting Equality* (New York: Cambridge University Press, 1992), 23.

16. O'Rourke, "The 1982 Amendments and the Voting Rights Paradox," 87.

17. O'Rourke, "The 1982 Amendments and the Voting Rights Paradox," 89.

18. 42 USC 1973 [1994], Section 14 (c) (3).

19. See Peter Skerry, *Mexican Americans: The Ambivalent Minority* (Cambridge, Mass.: Harvard University Press, 1993), 332.

20. See Thernstrom, *Whose Votes Count?*, 49–62, and J. Morgan Kousser, *Colorblind Injustice: Minority Voting Rights and the Undoing of the Second Reconstruction* (Chapel Hill: University of North Carolina Press, 1999), 23.

21. "Statement of Commissioner Stephen Horn on the Minority Language Provisions of the Voting Rights Act," in United States Civil Rights Commission, *The Voting Rights Act: Unfulfilled Goals* (Washington, D.C.: September, 1981), 94. Horn objected that "to continue to aid with specialized electoral services those who are in a few but not most minority language groups is itself discriminatory." It discourages such groups from self-help or the help of "community-based ethnic groups," perpetuating "the illusion that for every language group in the Nation a government agent must be employed or some form of government assistance must be made available to aid all members who understand English less well than their native language." To provide aid to one or merely a handful of the possible 387 languages the national census had coded by 1980 was, in Horn's description, "absurd." Horn concluded: "Before this Nation goes the way of Quebec or engages in the bitter language-based quarrels of some of the fragmented states of India, I recommend that we call a halt to what many of us have long recognized as a misguided experiment. (94)"

22. Skerry, *Mexican Americans*, 330–31.

23. Thernstrom, *Whose Votes Count?*, 62.

24. *City of Mobile v. Bolden*, 446 U.S. 55.

25. Report of the Subcommittee on the Constitution to the Committee on the Judiciary of the Voting Rights Act, S. Sub. Rept., V94/7, 97 Cong., 2 sess., 1982, 79.

26. 393 U.S. 544.

27. *Allen v. State Board of Election*, 393 U.S. at 569.

28. *Baker v. Carr*, 369 U.S. 186.

29. *Shaw v. Reno*, 425 U.S. 130.

30. *Shaw v. Reno* 425 U.S. 130, 141. Cited at *United Jewish Organizations v. Carey*, 430 U.S. 144, 159 (1977).

31. *United Jewish Organizations v. Carey*, 430 U.S. at 161 (1977).

32. *United Jewish Organizations v. Carey*, 162.

33. *United Jewish Organizations v. Carey*, 166.

34. *United Jewish Organizations v. Carey*, 165.

35. *United Jewish Organizations v. Carey*, 167.

36. *United Jewish Organizations v. Carey*, 186.

37. *United Jewish Organizations v. Carey*, 187.

38. *United Jewish Organizations v. Carey*, 186.

39. *United Jewish Organizations v. Carey*, 169, Brennan, J., concurring opinion.

40. *Thornburg v. Gingles*, 106 S.Ct. 2752, 2787, J. O'Connor, concurring opinion.

41. See C.F.R. § 51.55(b)(2) (1994), originally adopted by the Department of Justice in 1987. In *Reno v. Bossier Parish School Board*, 117 S. Ct. 1491 (1997), the Supreme Court ruled that this regulation was invalid. See Daniel H. Lowenstein, "Race and Representation in the Supreme Court," in *Voting Rights and Redistricting in the United States*, ed. Mark E. Rush (Westport, Ct.: Greenwood Press, 1998), 49, 62–63.

42. *Miller v. Johnson*, 115 S.Ct. 2475, 2491–93, opinion of the Court.

43. *Johnson v. Miller*, 864 F. Supp. 1354, 1368 (S.D. Ga. 1994).

44. *Johnson v. Miller*, 1354, 1368

45. 115 S. Ct. at 2493.

46. See *Shaw v. Reno*, 113 S. Ct. at 2826:

[R]edistricting differs from other kinds of state decisionmaking in that the legislature always is *aware* of race when it draws district lines, just as it is aware of age, economic status, religious and political persuasion, and a variety of other demographic factors. That sort of race consciousness does not lead inevitably to impermissible race discrimination. (Emphasis in original.)

47. 517 U.S. 952, 1001 (1996), concurring opinion.

48. See Hugh Davis Graham, *The Civil Rights Era: Origins and Development of National Policy, 1960–1972* (New York: Oxford University Press, 1990), esp. 362–65; and Gregory A. Caldeira, "Litigation, Lobbying, and the Voting Rights Bar," in *Controversies in Minority Voting*, 230.

49. See, for instance, Michael Pertschuk, *Giant Killers* (New York: W.W. Norton Co., 1986), ch. 6; and Thernstrom, *Whose Votes Count?*, chs. 5–6.

50. See, generally, Hugh Davis Graham"Voting Rights and the American Regulatory State," in *Controversies in Minority Voting*, 177; Belz, *Equality Transformed*; and Michael W. Lynch, "Title IX's Pyrrhic Victory," *Reason*, April, 2001, 29.

51. "Voting Rights and the American Regulatory State," 182.

52. "Voting Rights and the American Regulatory State," 179.

53. "Voting Rights and the American Regulatory State," 185–86.

54. Belz, *Equality Transformed*, 43.

55. Graham, "Voting Rights and the American Regulatory State," 189.

56. Stephen B. Presser, *Recapturing the Constitution: Race, Religion, and Abortion Reconsidered* (Washington, D.C.: Regnery Publishing, Inc., 1994), 204.

57. See Charles Bullock, "The South and the 1996 Elections," in *PS: Political Science and Politics* 29 (September 1996): 450.

58. 532 U.S. 234. (2001).

59. See, for example, *Shelley v. Kraemer*, 334 U.S. 1, 22 (1948), *University of California Regents v. Bakke*, 438 U.S. 265, 289 (1978), and *Richmond v. J. A. Croson Co.*, 488 U.S. 469, 493 (1989).

60. Bruce E. Cain has asked: "Since people can be thought of as bundles of many potentially politically relevant attributes, why should some of these attributes get political or legal recognition but not others? An electoral outcome might be unfair to a middle-aged male Latino in his identity as Latino, but perfectly fair in his identities as a male or a middle-aged person. Which is the relevant criterion by which we assess fairness and why?" "Voting Rights and Democratic Theory: Toward a Color-Blind Society?" in *Controversies in Minority Voting*, 261, 264. See

also, Mark E. Rush, "The Hidden Costs of Electoral Reform," in *Fair and Effective Representation? Debating Electoral Reform and Minority Rights*, Mark E. Rush and Richard L. Engstrom, intro. Bruce E. Cain (Lanham, Md.: Rowman & Littlefield, 2001), 69, 69–73 and 81.

61. *Federalist 10*, 65.

62. *Federalist 10*, 58.

63. *Federalist 59*, 398.

64. *Federalist 59*, 399.

65. See Daniel J. Mahoney, "Forward to the Liberty Fund Edition," in Bertrand de Jouvenel, *The Pure Theory of Politics* (Indianapolis: Liberty Fund, 1963), xiii.

66. *Federalist 59*, 399–400. See also the discussion of the Guarantee Clause in *Federalist 43*, 291–92.

67. *South Carolina v. Katzenbach*, 383 U.S. 301, 334 (1966), opinion of the Court.

68. See Richard A. Epstein, *Forbidden Grounds: The Case Against Employment Discrimination Laws* (Cambridge, Mass.: Harvard University Press, 1992), 12.

69. See Gordon S. Wood, "Tocqueville's Lesson," *The New York Review*, May 17, 2001, 46, 49.

70. Joseph M. Bessette, *The Mild Voice of Reason: Deliberative Democracy and American National Government* (Chicago: University of Chicago Press, 1994), 56.

71. Bessette, *The Mild Voice of Reason*, 212.

72. Bessette, *The Mild Voice of Reason*, 56–66.

73. See, for instance, *Wesberry v. Sanders*, 376 U.S. 1, 25 (1964), J. Harlan, dissenting.

74. See David K. Ryden, *Representation in Crisis: The Constitution, Interest Groups, and Political Parties* (Albany: State University of New York Press, 1996).

75. See *Allen v. State Board of Elections*, 393 U.S. at 586, dissenting opinion, and *Holder v. Hall*, 114 S.Ct. 2581, 2595, (1994) J. Thomas, concurring.

76. Eugene Volokh, "Diversity, Race as Proxy, and Religion as Proxy," 43 *UCLA Law Review* 2059, 2065–66 (1996). See also, Thomas E. Wood and Malcolm J. Sherman, *Race and Higher Education: Why Justice Powell's Diversity Rationale for Racial Preferences in Higher Education Must Be Rejected* (Report in PDF format by the National Association of Scholars, May 2001), www.nas.org/rhe.html.

77. James W. Ceaser, *Reconstructing America: The Symbol of America in Modern Thought* (New Haven: Yale University Press, 1997), 128. The summary of the politics of multiculturalism presented in this paragraph and the next draws from *Reconstructing America*, 124–35.

78. Ceaser, *Reconstructing America*, 126.

79. See, for instance, Bernard Grofman, "Expert Witness Testimony and the Evolution of Voting Rights Case Law," in *Controversies in Minority Voting*, 197.

80. See Thomas L. Pangle, *Montesquieu's Philosophy of Liberalism: A Commentary on The Spirit of the Laws* (Chicago: University of Chicago Press, 1973), 127.

81. See Ward E.Y. Elliott, *The Rise of Guardian Democracy: The Supreme Court's Role in Voting Rights Disputes, 1845–1969* (Cambridge, MA: Harvard University Press, 1974), 83.

82. Metcalfe, "Illiberal Citizenship," 194.

83. *Holder v. Hall*, 114 S. Ct. 2581 (1994).

84. *Holder v. Hall*, 2602.

85. *Holder v. Hall*, 2598–99.

86. Dissenting opinion, quoted at Holder v. Hall 2599.

87. See *Shaw v. Reno*, 113 S.Ct. at 2827–28.

88. *Federalist 10*, 57.

89. See David F. Epstein, *The Political Theory of The Federalist* (Chicago: University of Chicago Press, 1984), 80.

90. See Charles R. Kesler, "A New Birth of Freedom," *Claremont Review* (Fall 2000): S8, S9.

91. Hannah Arendt, *On Revolution* (New York: Penguin Books, 1973), 30. This is how Arendt defines *political* freedom. Obviously, I am using her phrase out of context.

92. See "Editor's Introduction," in Alexis de Tocqueville, *Democracy in America*, trans., ed., introduction. Harvey C. Mansfield and Delba Winthrop (Chicago: University of Chicago Press, 2000), xxv.

93. Epstein, *The Political Theory of The Federalist*, 159.

94. See Caton, *The Politics of Progress*, 470.

95. *Federalist 10*, 59, emphasis added.

96. See Caton, *The Politics of Progress*, 12.

97. See Eduardo A. Velásquez, "On Modernity's Low but not so Solid Foundations," *The Review of Politics*: 61 (No. 1) 164, 168.

98. Friedrich A. Hayek, *The Constitution of Liberty* (Chicago, Ill.: University of Chicago Press, 1960), 42–43.

99. See Caton, *The Politics of Progress*, 472.

100. *Federalist 10*, 59.

101. Volokh, "Diversity, Race as Proxy, and Religion as Proxy," 2060–62.

102. Volokh, "Diversity, Race as Proxy, and Religion as Proxy," 2062. "We condemn the use of race as a proxy not just when it is irrational or bigoted, but even when it is rational and unbigoted. We believe people ought to be judged by their personal traits, not by the sex or racial group to which they happen to belong, even when the group membership does provide reliable clues to the members' attitudes and experiences," 2076.

103. Irving Kristol, "Faith à la carte," *Times Literary Supplement*, May 26, 2000, 14.

104. Kristol, "Faih à la carte," 14.

105. Ceaser, *Reconstructing America*, 127.

106. Thomas Sowell, *Race and Culture* (New York: Basic Books, 1994), xiii-xiv.

107. *Easley v. Cromartie*, 532 U.S. at 242, opinion of the Court, emphasis in the original, quoting *Miller v. Johnson*, 515 U.S. 900, V.916 (1995).

108. David Tell, "Jim Crow Digs In," *The Weekly Standard*, March 19, 2001, 9, 10.

109. Tell, "Jim Crow Digs In," 9, 10.

Index

References to footnotes are indicated by an n.

About the Contributors

Robert H. Bork is senior fellow at the American Enterprise Institute for Public Policy Research. He served on the U.S. Court of Appeals for the District of Columbia Circuit from 1982–1988. Judge Bork is the author of two *New York Times* bestsellers, *Slouching Towards Gomorrah: Modern Liberalism and American Decline* and *The Tempting of America: The Political Seduction of the Law*. He also authored *The Antitrust Paradox* and has written numerous magazine, newspaper, and law review articles.

Francis Canavan, S.J., is professor emeritus of political science at Fordham University. Fr. Canavan has written numerous books including *The Pluralist Game: Pluralism, Liberalism, and the Moral Conscience*, *The Political Economy of Edmund Burke*, and *Freedom of Expression: Purpose as Limit*. His articles have appeared in *American Journal of Jurisprudence*, *Journal of Higher Education*, *National Review*, *Political Science Reviewer*, and *Review of Politics*.

Murray Dry is the Charles A. Dana professor of political science at Middlebury College. He has written widely on topics in American constitutional law and political philosophy. He has written book chapters on the founding of America and essays, articles, and book reviews on the separation of powers of federalism, and freedom of speech in the *Political Science Reviewer*, *The Supreme Court Review*, *Review of Politics*, *Constitutional Commentary*, and the *Journal of Supreme Court History*.

John C. Eastman is a professor of constitutional law at the Chapman University School of Law. He is also Director of the Claremont Institute's Center for

Constitutional Jurisprudence. Dr. Eastman's forthcoming work, "The Declaration of Independence as Viewed from the States," will appear in Scott Gerb, ed. *Declaration of Independence: Origins and Impact* (Washington, D.C.: Congressional Quarterly, 2002). He has published articles in several leading scholarly journals, including the *American Journal of Legal History*, *The University of Chicago Law Review*, and the *Harvard Journal of Law and Public Policy*.

Edward J. Erler is professor of political science at California State University. He has published two books—*The American Polity: Essays on the Theory and Practice of Constitutional Government* and *Equality, Natural Rights and the Rule of Law: The View from the American Founding*. Dr. Erler has contributed to numerous journals and newspapers including *Interpretation: A Journal of Political Philosophy*, *The Los Angeles Daily Journal*, and *Perspectives on Political Science*. In 1996, he served on the California Constitutional Revision Committee.

Christopher P. Manfredi is professor of political science at McGill University. He is also Chair of the Department of Political Science. Dr. Manfredi has written two books: *Judicial Power and the Charter: Canada and the Paradox of Liberal Constitutionalism* and *The Supreme Court and Juvenile Justice*. His articles have appeared in *American Journal of Comparative Law*, *Law and Society Review*, and *The Review of Politics*.

Anthony A. Peacock is assistant professor of political science at Utah State University. He is the editor of two books, including *Affirmative Action and Representation: Shaw v. Reno and the Future of Voting Rights* and *Rethinking the Constitution: Perspectives on Canadian Constitutional Reform, Interpretation, and Theory*. Dr. Peacock has also written numerous articles, book chapters, and book reviews.

Jeremy Rabkin is associate professor of government at Cornell University. He is also an adjunct scholar at the American Enterprise Institute. His most recent book is entitled *Why Sovereignty Matters*. Dr. Rabkin's views on international and constitutional issues have appeared in numerous academic journals and in *The Wall Street Journal*, *The Weekly Standard*, *The New Republic*, and *The National Review*.

Charles E. Rice is professor of law at the University of Notre Dame Law School. He has written numerous books including *Freedom of Association, Authority and Rebellion*, *The Vanishing Right to Live*, *50 Questions on the Natural Law*, and most recently, *The Winning Side: Questions on Living the Culture of Life*. Dr. Rice is a past consultant to the U.S. Commission on Civil Rights and to various Congressional committees on constitutional issues.

Graham Walker is professor of political science and vice president for academic affairs and dean at Oklahoma Wesleyan University. He is also a visiting scholar at the American Enterprise Institute in Washington, D.C. Dr. Walker is the author of *Moral Foundations of Constitutional Thought* and *The Ethics of F. A. Hayek*. His articles have appeared in *Nomos*, *Polity*, *Cardozo Journal of International and Comparative Law*, *Los Angeles Times*, and *Intercollegiate Review*.

Keith E. Whittington is associate professor of politics at Princeton University. He is the author of *Constitutional Interpretation: Textual Meaning, Original Intent, and Judicial Review* and *Constitutional Construction: Divided Powers and Constitutional Meaning*. His articles have appeared in *Law and Social Inquiry*, *Hastings Constitutional Law Quarterly*, and *Perspectives on Political Science*.

About the Editor

Bradley C. S. Watson is associate professor of political science and fellow in politics and culture at the Center for Economic and Policy Education, Saint Vincent College. He directs several of the center's educational initiatives, including its biennial Culture and Policy Conference on which this volume is based. His books include *Civil Rights and the Paradox of Liberal Democracy* (Lexington, 1999). He has written in a wide variety of professional and general interest forums, including *Armed Forces and Society*, *The Claremont Review of Books*, *Encarta Encyclopedia*, *Modern Age*, and *Perspectives on Political Science*. He is a contributor to *Rethinking the Constitution* (Oxford, 1996). He is an adjunct fellow of the Claremont Institute for the Study of Statesmanship and Political Philosophy, and the John M. Ashbrook Center for Public Affairs at Ashland University. He is also an adjunct professor in the Military Graduate Program of Norwich University in Vermont.

www.ingramcontent.com/pod-product-compliance
Lightning Source LLC
Chambersburg PA
CBHW071257180926
51613CB00001B/61
9780739104149